Building a Collaborative Advantage

Building a Collaborative Advantage

Network Governance and Homelessness Policy-Making in Canada

Carey Doberstein

UBCPress · Vancouver · Toronto

25 24 23 22 21 20 19 18 17 16   5 4 3 2 1

Printed in Canada on FSC-certified ancient-forest-free paper (100% post-consumer recycled) that is processed chlorine- and acid-free.

Library and Archives Canada Cataloguing in Publication

ISBN 9780774833257 (pbk.); ISBN 9780774833264 (pdf);
ISBN 9780774833271 (epub); ISBN 9780774833288 (mobi)

Cataloguing-in-publication data for this book is available from Library and Archives Canada.

Canada

UBC Press gratefully acknowledges the financial support for our publishing program of the Government of Canada (through the Canada Book Fund), the Canada Council for the Arts, and the British Columbia Arts Council.

This book has been published with the help of a grant from the Canadian Federation for the Humanities and Social Sciences, through the Awards to Scholarly Publications Program, using funds provided by the Social Sciences and Humanities Research Council of Canada.

Printed and bound in Canada by Friesens
Set in Segoe and Warnock Pro by Apex CoVantage, LLC
Proofreader: Alison Strobel
Indexer: Celia Braves
Cover designer: Martyn Schmoll

UBC Press
The University of British Columbia
2029 West Mall
Vancouver, BC V6T 1Z2
www.ubcpress.ca

Contents

Preface

My earliest conceptualization of the issue of homelessness was a typically sheltered, middle-class, and abstract one: I felt a vague sense of pity, yet also a clear sense that it was inconceivable this could ever happen to me. Moving from a small town to Vancouver to attend university made homelessness less of an abstraction, since I was so completely surrounded by it. Like all urban citizens, as I went about my daily routines, I would come across panhandlers, hordes of people crowded around drop-in centres, and street sleepers in alcoves or alleys. And like many, I held dismissive and essentialized attitudes towards the homeless and how they had arrived there, coupled with a fear of their actions and disgust with their presentation. Yet these sights and interactions, unnerving in my first months of living in Vancouver, eventually became part of the tapestry of urban life – or what some would call a disturbing normalization of homelessness in Canadian urban life.

For many years, the normalization of homelessness was the lens through which I understood the issue – until very abnormal trends became visible to me when I moved out of the University of British Columbia nest to Yaletown, a previously derelict industrial area in downtown Vancouver that was undergoing gentrification. The spectacular sights of the city, mountains, and ocean from my new downtown high-rise apartment could not distract from what transfixed me at the street level: cardboard assembled for shelter in alleys, shopping carts as mobile homes, and hardened women and men working the streets before noon, most with visible signs of extensive drug use. Now that I was confronted by homelessness on a daily basis, it began to dawn on me how abnormal this scene was. There is nothing normal about children being raised in homeless shelters. There is nothing normal about lineups extending several blocks when a charitable organization offers a free lunch. And in a civilized society, there is nothing normal about allowing un-treated mental illness to destabilize every element of a person's life. Even if it neatly absolves me from political action, the prevailing theory of homeless-ness as personal destruction by lazy and self-indulgent single adult males simply did not match what I saw on the streets. Yet, for the most part, I approached the issue with benign neglect, not engaging in political action that would reflect my reconceptualization of homelessness.

It turned out that the scenes on the streets below troubled my fellow high-rise dwellers as well, though they were troubled in very different ways than I was about our new neighbourhood with "rough edges." Many expected their new urban life to marry the convenience and allure of downtown living with the suburban ethic of homogeneity and predictability. In short order, the re-engineering attempts began in an effort to make the neighbourhood con-sistent with the aesthetics of new urban life. My private discomfort with the seemingly legitimate and widespread "hobophobia" reached a fever pitch in the mailroom of my new apartment building:

PETITION

From Concerned Residents of 501 Pacific St

We the undersigned strongly oppose the expansion of the Covenant House youth shelter facility on the basis that it will upset the fabric of the neighbourhood by attracting more homeless and junkies, increas-ing threats to the safety and security of young children, women and the elderly in the neighbourhood.

_____
_____
_____
_____
_____
_____

Three petitions in a matter of months were circulated by "concerned residents" in this apartment building in an attempt to close down a shelter for abused women, prevent the expansion of a youth homelessness shelter, and ensure more police presence to sweep the streets clean of sex workers and the indigent. The cold economics of "declining property values" and phantom claims of "threats to personal safety" were the basis of the appeals, with decidedly little concern for where women and youth fleeing violent and abusive situations would go if these political actions were successful. Provoked out of passivity, I wrote a caustic letter for display in the mail-room, reminding residents that *we* were the ones new to the neighbourhood – not the sex workers, the homeless, and other marginalized people – and that surely compassion and productive political action to help stabilize lives was a much more reasonable approach than simply sweeping the neigh-bourhood clean. Needless to say, my indelicate attempt to calm the young urban professionals of Yaletown and channel their fears into compassion was unsuccessful, although I am happy to report that they were ultimately unsuccessful in all three of their petitions to the City. "Concerned residents" of many other neighbourhoods, however, have no doubt been successful in similar attempts.

These patterns of response extended beyond my spooked neighbours to the next area ripe for gentrification in downtown Vancouver: Gastown, which is adjacent to and overlaps with the notorious Downtown Eastside. A "concerned resident" named Mike Comrie was granted space in the edi-torial pages of the *National Post* on April 20, 2012, to lament over how, after moving into the poorest postal code in Canada, the surroundings were not idyllic enough for his young professional family. In his piece, titled "Raising Kids amid the Hookers, Junkies and Drunks of Vancouver's Worst Neighbourhood," Comrie used language characteristic of common dismissive attitudes towards the homeless and marginalized:

> We had found a condo that we could actually afford ... gambling that the neighbourhood would improve significantly by the time our building was completed. It didn't ... although the area would improve, eventually. But first, we would spend a few years raising our children in what could gener-ously be described as a disturbing new community.
>
> ... Junkies steal, they prostitute themselves, they leave needles and feces in the streets. The Downtown Eastside may be home to my city's least for-tunate, but it is also, in many cases, home to my city's least sanitary, least responsible, and least polite ...
>
> ... My wife and I had to quickly learn ... how to take it in stride when alarmingly filthy individuals, clearly intoxicated and probably insane, want-ed to exchange baby talk with our little ones ...
>
> It took a while, but we bet on gentrification, and – knock on wood – it's happening.

Such callous attitudes towards a vulnerable segment of society would be less troubling if they were not so widespread and legitimized in common discourses and media. Not only were these experiences in Vancouver replicated with eerie precision in my Toronto apartment building during my doctoral studies, but other observers, such as Mariana Valverde, in her book *Everyday Law on the Street: City Governance in an Age of Diversity* (2012), have documented these dynamics in Canadian cities, revealing a certain detached acceptance and ignorance of the plight of a permanent underclass in Canada.

Widespread and persistent homelessness in Canada is indisputably the result of policy decisions at several levels of government. Among those in the homelessness policy community, the Paul Martin budgets beginning in 1993 are seen as the most devastating setbacks to housing affordability and the broader social safety net in Canada, with the federal government withdrawing almost completely from affordable housing provision (and with subsequent provincial downloading to cash-strapped municipalities). The impact was dramatic: according to a 2007 article by Michael Shapcott called "Ten Things You Should Know about Housing and Homelessness," in 1982, all levels of government combined funded over twenty thousand units of social housing annually, while in 1995, only one thousand new social housing units were constructed by all levels of government in Canada. Yet only five years earlier, in 1990, the Official Opposition critic for Housing and Urban Affairs, Joe Fontana, wrote in a Task Force on Housing report co-authored with Liberal MP Paul Martin and called *Finding Room: Housing Solutions for the Future*, that Canada "is presently confronted with a major housing crisis ... and immediate action is necessary to correct the problem": hence, the shock and disbelief in the homelessness policy community when that very same opposition critic – Paul Martin – came to power as finance minister, in 1993, and did the opposite of what his own Task Force Report had recommended. By 2000, Canadian cities had experienced a massive spike in homelessness.

Patterns of abuse, mental illness, and personal tragedy will always dot Canadian society, but the question is whether the policy framework in place helps to stabilize the lives of those who are faced with incredible challenges, many of which are involuntarily thrust upon them. In his 2008 book, *Homelessness: The Making and Unmaking of a Crisis*, Jack Layton, an early political leader on the issue of homelessness in Canadian cities, articulated his conviction that "just as homelessness can be created, so too can it be ended" (p. xxv). In the absence of a strong federal government role in the provision of affordable housing across Canada – which is still undoubtedly the most important need – Layton claimed that one of the most important lessons he learned in his life in politics "is that energy and ideas spring from the community – what social scientists sometimes call 'civil society' ... not from mandarins in Ottawa" (p. xxviii).

This is quite a statement for someone who wanted to become prime minister! Like others in the homelessness policy community, Layton placed a high premium on the community as an agent of change and creator of policy ideas that should be brought into the policy process to challenge technocrats and elected officials "to help raise awareness and [advance] creative strategies and solutions" (p. 301).

Politicians may respond to the interests of "concerned residents," and bureaucrats to arcane institutional incentives, leaving civil society actors – those on the ground working with the homeless population – as key agents driving innovative policy and programs in this domain. *But is this true?* If civil society actors – in this case, shelter and drop-in centre providers, affordable housing providers and activists, mental health and addiction professionals – are included in substantive policy planning and decision making, what is the effect on homelessness policy? The answer to this question, which is the primary concern of this book, has consequences not only for homelessness policy development in Canada but also for modern governance and public administration issues across a number of sectors and areas.

Acknowledgments

This book could not have been written without the support and assistance from numerous individuals and organizations. I would like to express my sincere gratitude to all who have assisted me on this long journey.

I thank David Wolfe, Phil Triadafilopoulos, and Neil Bradford, all of whom played an instrumental role in the development of this project during my doctoral studies in the Political Science Department at the University of Toronto. David's approach to academic research – that is, remaining closely connected to real world problems of governance and public administration – is a model for all of us in the field and an ethic that I intend to replicate in my academic career. Phil demanded precision with arguments and clarity of purpose, all without dictating to me his preferred path, thus allowing me to carve out my own. Neil's extraordinary mind and previous scholarly work laid the groundwork for much of the conceptual development in this research.

Others at the University of Toronto to whom I owe thanks for their role in the advancement of this work include Graham White, Ed Schatz, Peter Loewen, David Rayside, Linda White, Grace Skogstad, Jonathan Craft, and David Hulchanksi. During my University of Toronto days, I developed cherished friendships with some very important colleagues and learned a great deal from them: Jerry Sabin, Gabe Eidelman, Heather Millar, Kyle Kirkup, Paul Thomas, Mike Morden, Alex Pelletier, and Nicola Hepburn. Outside of the University of Toronto, Katherine A. Graham, Stephen Gaetz, Naomi

Nichols, Alison Smith, Evert Lindquist, and Donald Green have been critical resources for specific challenges that I faced in the development of this work.

Since arriving at the University of British Columbia's Okanagan campus, I have been truly privileged to work with brilliant and generous colleagues. I have benefited greatly from the interdisciplinary focus of my political science, philosophy, and economics colleagues and the unique angles from which they have viewed my work. I have been very fortunate to work with a skilled research assistant, Jasmine Reimer, who went well beyond the call of duty in all her work for me. I wish to acknowledge and express my gratitude for research support from the Social Sciences and Humanities Research Council, the Ontario Graduate Scholarship program, the UBC Provost Start-up Research Fund, the UBC Irving K. Barber School of Arts and Sciences Start-Up Research Fund, and the UBC Hampton Grant for New Researchers.

I need to acknowledge all of the interview respondents as well as the leadership of the governance networks under investigation in this book for allowing me to be an observer over extended periods. It can be unsettling to allow a researcher to poke around the farm, so to speak, and these leaders displayed an extraordinary commitment to transparency. Truly, the contributions of this book could not have been realized without their cooperation and commitment to the advancement of research. Though gratitude is reserved for all of them, one in particular deserves special attention: Kingsley Okyere of the Greater Vancouver Regional Steering Committee on Homelessness showed a deep commitment very early on to this project, though tragically, he passed away before its completion. I am also grateful to Olivia Chow for agreeing to release to me Jack Layton's private records as a Toronto city councillor, which was a critical set of unvarnished data for the Toronto-based research.

Emily Andrew at UBC Press, an early champion of this work, skilfully shepherded me through to the completion of my first book. I am so grateful for her support, expert hand, and wonderful sense of humour. Emily, as well as Lesley Erickson, production editor, and the rest of the UBC Press team are held in the highest regard in our profession for a very good reason: they are professional and responsive, and they demand high-quality contributions. We all benefit from those commitments.

Finally, everything I have achieved has fundamentally derived from the support of my family. Jesse Godwin is not only a partner whose own professional achievements are a source of inspiration, but also one who has read and critiqued – devastatingly, but also wonderfully, frankly – every word I have published. Patricia and Colin Godwin have likewise offered immense support, including housing me during my fieldwork in Vancouver and providing support in virtually all other aspects of my life. My brother, Darcy, has been my number one fan and cheerleader during my academic career thus far, but he is a much greater source of inspiration than he will ever appreciate. And most importantly, I am grateful to my parents, to whom I dedicate this work and my achievements to date. When I left the small hamlet of Merritt, BC, in 2001 for my first days at university, they encouraged me to consider becoming a doctor – they should have been more specific, but I know they are proud.

Abbreviations

ACHSIP (or TO-emerg)	Advisory Committee on Homeless and Socially Isolated Persons, Toronto
AHSC	Aboriginal Homelessness Steering Committee, Vancouver
CAA	coordinated access and assessment
CAL-main	Calgary Action Committee on Homelessness and Housing
CCEH	Calgary Committee to End Homelessness
CGP	collaborative granting process
CHF and CAL-CHF	Calgary Homeless Foundation
CMHC	Canada Mortgage and Housing Corporation
CRG (or TO-main)	Community Reference Group, Toronto
DTES	Downtown Eastside
EWR	Extreme Weather Response
GVSS	Greater Vancouver Shelter Strategy
HAW	Homelessness Action Week
HPS	Homelessness Partnering Strategy
HRSDC	Human Resources and Social Development Canada
MTHC	Metro Toronto Housing Corporation
NHI	National Homelessness Initiative
RSCH (or VAN-main)	Greater Vancouver Regional Steering Committee on Homelessness

SHARC	Streets to Homes Assessment and Referral Centre
SNA	Street Needs Assessment, Toronto
TAEH	Toronto Alliance to End Homelessness
TCHC	Toronto Community Housing Corporation
TDRC	Toronto Disaster Relief Committee
TO-Ab (or UAHRC)	Urban Aboriginal Homelessness Review Committee, Toronto
TO-emerg (or ACHSIP)	Advisory Committee on Homeless and Socially Isolated Persons, Toronto
TO-main (or CRG)	Community Reference Group, Toronto
UAHRC (or TO-Ab)	Urban Aboriginal Homelessness Review Committee, Toronto
VAN-main (or RSCH)	Greater Vancouver Regional Steering Committee on Homelessness
VAN-Ab	Aboriginal Homelessness Steering Committee, Vancouver
VAN-emerg	Greater Vancouver Shelter Strategy

Building a Collaborative Advantage

1

The Homelessness Puzzle in Canada

As one of the most economically prosperous nations on earth, Canada is a country with an enviable human rights record, including some of the social and economic rights (health care, education, old age security). But our public and private institutions are organized in such a manner that one of the now "normal" outcomes is that a growing number of people are excluded from having an adequate and secure place to live. For some this is a temporary situation, for some an occasional situation, for others it is a long term reality.

... Without a physical place to call "home" in the social, psychological and emotional sense, the hour-to-hour struggle for physical survival replaces all other possible activities. Without an address it is virtually impossible to access some essential social services and it is very difficult to get a job.

People with no place to live, those who have no physical and psychological place of their own to call home, are the most completely excluded group of people in society. On becoming homeless, people enter a different world from the rest of society. Survival is the main goal. It is a nightmare world completely apart from the normal day-to-day pattern of living.

– Toronto Disaster Relief Committee (1998)

We have a problem in Canada. It is largely a hidden problem, but it is one that reveals a fundamental disconnect from the long-held, professed values that define Canadian citizenship and identity. In an incredibly rich country, and amid the great wealth of many, there are thousands of Canadians – 235,000 unique individuals each year and 35,000 on any given night, according to one recent estimate – for whom "normal" life now involves not having an adequate and secure place to live (Gaetz, Gulliver, & Richter, 2014). In Toronto, more than 5,000 live on the street or in homeless shelters on a given night; in Metro Vancouver, more than 2,500; and in Calgary, more than 3,500 – and these data are widely considered to underestimate the scale of the problem (City of Toronto Street Needs Assessment [SNA], 2013; Greater Vancouver Regional Steering Committee on Homelessness [RSCH], 2014a; Calgary Homeless Foundation [CHF], 2014). Among the street homeless population, nearly 40 percent in Vancouver have lived on the street for more than a year, while in Toronto that figure is 65 percent (Greater Vancouver RSCH, 2014a; City of Toronto SNA, 2013).[1]

Homelessness is not merely an academic problem of unequal resource distribution in this country. Homelessness kills Canadians. During the worst period of homelessness in Toronto, one homeless person died *every week*, on average, from 1996 to 2006. This is not a speculative conclusion of radical activists. Jack Layton, then a Toronto city councillor and homelessness advocate, in his book *Homelessness: How to End the National Crisis* (2008), documents how juries, in countless coroners' inquests into the deaths of homeless individuals in Toronto, established that "homelessness" was the ultimate cause of death (Layton, 2008, p. 34) and that proximate causes included freezing to death and persistent and untreated health conditions exacerbated by the pathologies of street life. Former Ontario premier Mike Harris famously asked, "Isn't it sad that these people just seem to want to be homeless?" – an attempt to frame the issue as a matter of individual choice rather than as a structural or systemic societal failing. Yet real stories of homeless people tell a different and more complicated story about the pathways in and out of homelessness, few of which are the result of laziness or an inexplicable desire to live in miserable conditions.

There is a striking overrepresentation of Aboriginal people within the homeless population in Canadian cities: in Vancouver, Calgary, and Toronto, they represent 31 percent, 21 percent, and 16 percent of the homeless, respectively, despite constituting between 1 and 3 percent of these cities' total populations (Greater Vancouver RSCH, 2014a; City of Toronto SNA, 2013; CHF, 2014). This disparity reveals that structural issues are key drivers of homelessness in Canada. Likewise, by some estimates, youth constitute 20 to 30 percent of the homeless population in Canadian cities, and despite prevailing myths of their self-indulgent desire for early freedom, homeless youth "often run away from something awful, not toward something hopeful"; they are often fleeing abusive, drug-dependent, mentally ill, or homophobic families (Ryan & Kelley, 2012, 7). The Covenant House Institute tracked youth that had accessed its services across North America and found patterns that challenge the common depiction of directionless youth: 40 percent had been in foster care; more than 25 percent had been hospitalized for depression, anxiety, or other mental health issues; 30 percent had experienced physical abuse; and 40 percent of the young women had been sexually abused as children (Ryan & Kelley, 2012, p. 4). In addition, shelters in some cities report that LGBT youth account for up to 40 percent of their inhabitants; many of these youth have been kicked out or subjected to shame by homophobic parents. Thus, people often become homeless through no fault of their own, even if some poor individual choices have been made along the way.[2]

Unfortunately, some children have always grown up in challenging households under difficult personal circumstances, so this alone does not explain the rapid growth in homelessness in Canada and elsewhere since the 1990s. Before that time, society's most marginalized individuals could count on a comprehensive policy framework to help them stabilize their lives – a safety net that allowed those fleeing terrible home situations to be able to afford independent housing, access social assistance, and receive counselling or institutionalized services if suffering from mental illness. Jack Layton insisted that "homelessness is not some mysterious affliction visited upon us by unseen forces. It is the tragic, but inevitable, outcome of a series of policy decisions" made at several levels of government (Layton, 2008, p. xxv).

Among large Canadian cities, Toronto, Vancouver, and Calgary are where homelessness and a lack of affordable housing are most acute (Laird, 2007), and governments have responded to the issue with various approaches over the years, thus offering the opportunity for a comparative analysis of governance and public policy. Comparing homeless populations across cities, even within the same country, is not without risk, given the complex reasons for homelessness in specific locations. These reasons include economic restructuring of the labour force, mental health and addiction, real estate market trends, and even the local climate – not to mention differences in governance patterns and political priorities. Furthermore, because of different criteria, measurements, and methodologies, directly comparable data with respect to shelter use and the enumeration of those experiencing homelessness across cities are often scarce. That said, it is nonetheless important to get a sense of some of the fundamental features of homelessness in Vancouver, Calgary, and Toronto. On the most important measures of homelessness – growth of street homelessness and average length of homelessness – Vancouver and Calgary display more positive trends than Toronto, as depicted in Table 1.1.

Since 2008, the number of individuals sleeping on the street (referred to as "street homeless") on any given night in Metro Vancouver and Calgary has decreased by 39 percent and 62 percent, respectively, whereas in Toronto it has increased by 24 percent. Homelessness among Aboriginal people declined in Metro Vancouver between 2008 and 2014, yet it continued to grow in Toronto and Calgary over the same period. And in Toronto, 65 percent of the individuals who were homeless in 2013 had been so for over one year, whereas in Metro Vancouver this proportion was considerably

TABLE 1.1

Homelessness data from Vancouver, Calgary, and Toronto

	Metro Vancouver (pop. 2.31M)	City of Calgary (pop. 1.2M)	City of Toronto (pop. 2.61M)
Homelessness count (street and shelters)	2,623	3,533	5,086
Homelessness per capita	0.1%	0.3%	0.2%
Growth in street homelessness (six-year trend)	−39.0%	-62.0%	+24.0%
Growth in Aboriginal homelessness (six-year trend)	−15.0%	+17.0%	+6.0%
Families in shelter system as percentage of total	5.0%	12.0%	20.0%
Percentage of street homeless being homeless for one year or more	40.0%	n/a	65.0%

Sources and Notes: Greater Vancouver RSCH (2008, 2011, 2014a, trend from 2008 to 2014); Calgary Homeless Foundation (2014; trend from 2008 to 2014); City of Toronto SNA (2013; note that trend data is four years in this case, from 2009 to 2013, due to data availability). The point-in-time data is from the most recent homeless counts in Metro Vancouver (2014), Calgary (2014), and Toronto (2013).

lower, at 40 percent, suggesting that the barriers to exiting homelessness remain high in Toronto. Again, given the complex drivers of homelessness, too much weight should not be placed in any single data point; nonetheless, it is valuable to track trends among the important indicators of an effective response to homelessness.

Leading researchers on homelessness in Canada such as Stephen Gaetz of York University and Michael Shapcott of the Wellesley Institute tend to link two key dimensions of policy – policy innovation and system coordination – with an effective response to homelessness (Gaetz, 2010; Shapcott, 2007a; see also Carter, 2001). These are key factors to track to explain the differences in homelessness trends from city to city. Policy innovation involves using approaches that break from the conventional response of "managing" homelessness (e.g., giving out clean socks), and system coordination means making the various systems related to homelessness (e.g., affordable housing, social assistance, mental health services, criminal justice, and so on) coherent, integrated, and, perhaps most importantly, non-competetive (Gaetz, 2010). Many observers recognize that policy innovation and system coordination have been characteristics of Metro Vancouver's and Calgary's approaches in recent years but have been less apparent in Toronto.

There are some important differences in how the three cities have addressed the problem of homelessness from a policy perspective, and their approaches have varied in effectiveness with respect to stabilizing and improving the lives of homeless persons, as seen in Table 1.1. This variation in homelessness outcomes cannot be explained by a dramatic difference in the amount of money spent on housing and homelessness in each city: counting all levels of government, annual expenditures in recent years were remarkably similar – in Metro Vancouver, $278M; in Calgary, $320M; and in Toronto, $297M (BC Housing, annual reports, 2012; Scott, 2012; City of Toronto, 2012, 2013).

In terms of innovation and coordination, homelessness policy and programs in Vancouver and Calgary have generally outperformed those in Toronto. For example, over the past two decades, Vancouver has pioneered low-barrier shelters and harm-reduction strategies and has implemented significant system coordination with the development of Homelessness Action Week, Extreme Weather Response protocols, and the Greater Vancouver RSCH (Regional Steering Committee on Homelessness) Investors Table for the coordination of public- and private-sector investment in homelessness. Calgary is notable for its creation of the Calgary Homeless Foundation (CHF), a quasi-government entity with a business-like orientation that was given the mandate by the City of Calgary to end homelessness by 2018. Its innovative approach involves using real-time data on homeless individuals to link them to housing and services and coordinated, single-window access for housing and support services. Toronto is also active in the homelessness policy domain and has an extensive shelter and social-housing system; however, except for the innovative Streets to Homes program, which targets the chronically homeless, the city has displayed fewer and less substantive examples of policy innovation and system coordination over the past twenty years. Promising efforts in Toronto towards inclusive Aboriginal policy planning, as well as an annual Report Card on Homelessness, were notable but short-lived. These specific policy and program differences among the three cities are a preview of the much more extensive comparative policy analysis that follows in the chapters ahead.

The Puzzle and the Argument

The above sketch of the data and policy dimensions of homelessness in Vancouver, Calgary, and Toronto sets up the key puzzle under investigation in this book: Why do Vancouver and Calgary have more innovative and co-ordinated homelessness policy and programs than Toronto, even though these cities all share similar homelessness challenges? Although the three cities have many similar demographic, economic, and institutional features, a key difference among them, which I argue accounts for these substantive policy differences, lies in the properties and dynamics of their homelessness governance networks.

Governance networks are composed of government and civil society actors in institutionalized and sustained relationships of policy planning and decision making, and these networks may serve as sites of deliberative problem solving and exchange among diverse policy actors. A comparative analysis of Vancouver, Calgary, and Toronto with respect to homelessness therefore presents an opportunity to systematically test the claims of Jack Layton and many others about the impact of civil society actors in the policy process.

These three cities differ dramatically in how government and civil society actors organize themselves in governance networks to solve public problems. Governance networks can vary considerably in structure and mandate, but many are equipped with policy-generating capacity, public dollars to allocate to housing and support services, and autonomous decision-making authority, all delegated by the state. In Metro Vancouver and

Calgary, the homelessness governance networks, though distinct in many ways, are highly institutionalized and inclusive; they are effectively a new form of governance characteristic of deliberative problem-solving. Toronto, however, takes a much more traditional political-bureaucratic governance approach; homelessness governance networks in that city remain weakly institutionalized and non-inclusive, with decision making largely closed to civil society actors.

In a broad sense, examining homelessness policy development over the long run shows that elected leadership at the municipal level matters considerably less than observers suggest. That is, Vancouver is not outperforming Toronto simply because Mayor Gregor Robertson has so explicitly identified his legacy with the homelessness issue (though it does help), and Toronto is not held back primarily because of the Rob Ford years (though they did hurt). Likewise, in the case of Calgary, substantial progress is being made despite the lack of sustained engagement and interest in the issue from the mayor, Naheed Nenshi, and the city council.

This book shows how governance networks in Metro Vancouver and Calgary represent an avenue to break out from the status quo. In those cities, new actors have engaged in joint planning and decision making, introducing new ideas and approaches that were previously deemed too risky by public servants and their elected masters and that are largely responsible for the variation in policy and outcomes. Fifteen years after the Federation of Canadian Municipalities declared a state of emergency with respect to homelessness, this book provides a rare comparative analysis of homelessness policy. Most homelessness research in Canada and elsewhere is conducted by researchers in social work (Hulchanski, 1995, 2000), education (Gaetz, 2010; Paradis, 2009), geography (Carter, 1997), and public health (Dachner & Tarasuk, 2002; Hwang, 2001); homelessness is rarely viewed through the lens of governance and politics. Other than Jack Layton's studies (2000; revised and updated in 2008), only a few significant studies have considered the governance issues associated with homelessness, and they were produced by major state-commissioned task forces, such as the landmark Mayor's Homelessness Action Task Force in Toronto (Golden, 1999) and the Standing Senate Committee on Social Affairs, Science, and Technology (Subcommittee on Cities), which issued the report *In from the Margins: A Call to Action on Poverty, Housing and Homelessness* (Eggleton, 2009). While these reports are critical pieces in the extended literature, they are sprawling tomes of description and advocacy, largely detached from theory and systematic comparative analysis of public policy.

Governance Networks in Canadian Cities

No major city in Canada has been spared from the homelessness crisis
that emerged in the late 1990s. So why study only Vancouver, Calgary, and
Toronto? Why not Montreal, Winnipeg, and Halifax, for example? There
are good reasons, from a comparative governance and policy analysis perspective, to choose the former set over the latter. Despite its comparable size
to Vancouver, Montreal's first homelessness count was conducted in 2015,
making it difficult to track policy outcomes in that city over time. Winnipeg,
too, conducted its first homelessness census in 2015, and Halifax, though
it began homelessness counts in 2003, experiences homelessness on a
much smaller scale, as does Winnipeg. In addition, these cities do not have
the acute housing affordability challenges that high-growth cities such as
Vancouver, Calgary, and Toronto are currently facing, and they are not con-
fronting homelessness on the same scale.[3] Although these three cities have
the same status and authority as municipalities within Canada's constitutional framework, they diverge in terms of the specific dimensions of their
homelessness policy and the design and structure of their homelessness
governance networks.

Because homelessness is a complex issue that draws in multi-sectoral
and intergovernmental policy players, each of the cities under investigation has more than one homelessness governance network. Each city
has three, and each of these networks has a near perfect equivalent in
each city in terms of functionality and purpose; the omission of any
would fail to capture the complexity of homelessness policy-making in
each city. The governance networks examined in Vancouver, Calgary,
and Toronto represent a comprehensive portrait of network governance
activity in each city but also allow for pair-wise comparisons of equivalent networks across the cities. The three types of governance networks
examined in this book are as follows: (1) a mainstream network, generally inclusive of all relevant actors in the sector; (2) an Aboriginal-
specific network, established because of the strikingly disproportionate
share of Aboriginal people among the homeless population and the desire to produce culturally appropriate policy and programs; and (3) an
emergency-needs, typically shelter-focused, network. In some cases,
these governance networks work closely with one another, and in other
cases, they conflict. Examining the dynamics among the networks adds
an important layer to the analysis, particularly in terms of understanding system coordination.

Vancouver

The Greater Vancouver Regional Steering Committee on Homelessness

The Greater Vancouver Regional Steering Committee on Homelessness (which I will call VAN-main) is a governance network that was initially created under the auspices of the Government of Canada's National Homelessness Initiative (NHI), announced in December 1999 and later renamed the Homelessness Partnering Strategy.[4] The NHI mandated the formation of community advisory boards consisting of civil society and government members; each advisory board was to create a community plan to address homelessness and to allocate federal funding (Greater Vancouver RSCH, 2003). The membership of VAN-main, the community advisory board for Vancouver, is diverse and inclusive of the policy community and comprises nearly forty active members. The expansive and diverse membership includes local, regional, provincial, and federal government administrators; health authorities; charitable groups and foundations; Aboriginal groups; and service providers. No elected officials are actively involved in the governance network. Since 2010, VAN-main has been formally attached to the Metro Vancouver regional government, based on the recognition that homelessness exists in the broader metropolitan area (not just the City of Vancouver) and that a regional, coordinated approach is required to make effective policy interventions (Greater Vancouver RSCH, 2007).

The Aboriginal Homelessness Steering Committee

The Aboriginal Homelessness Steering Committee (VAN-Ab), like VAN-main, was created in 2000 in conjunction with the federal NHI program, which required the creation of governance networks of Aboriginal civil society actors mandated with developing and implementing a local strategy for Aboriginal homelessness. An Aboriginal-specific governance network is particularly relevant in the homelessness domain, since Aboriginal people constitute a disproportionate share of the homeless population across Canada (Ward, 2008). Furthermore, many argue (and the Government of Canada acknowledged as much with this piece of the NHI) that the most effective means to reduce and prevent homelessness among Aboriginal people is through Aboriginal best practices and culturally appropriate policy and programs. The membership of VAN-Ab consists of shelter providers, housing organizations, youth advocates, and other service providers that primarily serve the homeless Aboriginal population in the all municipalities in Metro Vancouver. One significant difference from VAN-main is that VAN-Ab does not include government (bureaucratic) members; in fact, all members of VAN-Ab are from Aboriginal communities. VAN-Ab is also much smaller in membership than VAN-main, with twenty active members; this is commensurate with the much smaller policy mandate and envelope of money it has to allocate.

The Greater Vancouver Shelter Strategy

In 1998, in response to unmet needs for shelter in the winter months, homeless shelter providers formed a regional network, called the Greater Vancouver Shelter Strategy (VAN-emerg), to develop and implement a continuum of accessible shelter services (Greater Vancouver Shelter Strategy [GVSS], minutes, 2003, 2004). The principal task in the early years of VAN-emerg was to increase communication and coordination among shelter providers to ensure that services were accessible to the target population during inclement weather. Unlike VAN-main and VAN-Ab, the creation of VAN-emerg was community-driven rather than being the result of a government mandate, although provincial government departments have provided in-kind secretarial support and local governments have provided research and coordination funds to assist in the operations of the network. In contrast to both VAN-main and VAN-Ab, VAN-emerg is less of a policy-focused network and more of a coordination network (GVSS, 2010).

Over the years, VAN-emerg has expanded its mandate and role in the region. The need to strategize and coordinate during cold and wet weather remains a priority, but the mandate of the network now extends to the more general planning and coordination of shelter services (year-round), systematic service tracking, and the promotion of sharing resources and expertise among shelter providers (GVSS, terms of reference, 2011). Membership consists of nearly thirty organizations actively involved in meeting emergency shelter needs – whether providing, funding, or otherwise associating with shelter services – as well as local and provincial government bureaucrats.

Toronto

The Community Reference Group

In Toronto, the Community Reference Group (TO-main) is analogous to VAN-main in that it was created in response to the federal NHI program. It serves as the community advisory board, as mandated by the NHI, with the task of devising a community plan to identify and articulate key priorities for the investment of funds, but unlike other community advisory boards, it plays no role in the allocation of homelessness funding. The City of Toronto formally administers the program and assumes legal and financial liability for the policy development and expenditures identified by TO-main (Community Reference Group [CRG], terms of reference, 2003). The City of Toronto is distinct from Vancouver in that it had been heavily involved in homelessness funding ever since this task devolved from the provincial government in the 1990s; the City therefore already had the capacity to administer the new federal program, which Metro Vancouver did not when VAN-main was created. This early difference would prove to be immensely consequential: whereas VAN-main was created in a relative policy vacuum, TO-main was inserted into a crowded policy field, and as a result, TO-main, from its beginnings, has had a comparatively narrow mandate and role in policy-making. Membership in TO-main comprises a diverse cross-section of fifteen community, local government, and private sector actors. In contrast to VAN-main, TO-main meets only once or twice per year and has a low public profile, even though both networks derived from the same federal government mandate. TO-main, therefore, has not become the primary community-driven voice for homelessness in Toronto like VAN-main has in Vancouver; it remains a narrowly defined community advisory board for the purposes of the federal homelessness program (CRG, 2002).

The Urban Aboriginal Homelessness Review Committee

The Urban Aboriginal Homelessness Review Committee (TO-Ab), like VAN-Ab, was created in response to the federal NHI program. Like its equivalent in Vancouver, VAN-Ab was mandated by the Government of Canada as a prerequisite for accessing funds and is responsible for setting policy priorities, reviewing homelessness program proposals, and allocating funds within the Toronto Aboriginal social service community. The membership of TO-Ab consists of representatives from seven Aboriginal organizations, each of which covers a demographic or service segment of the Aboriginal homeless community (Urban Aboriginal Homelessness Review Committee [UAHRC], terms of reference, 2010). TO-Ab meets once every two months and, like VAN-Ab, has one full-time staff to support its work, as well as a local federal government official, as needed. In addition to its role in the setting of strategic policy priorities for urban Aboriginal homelessness in Toronto and funding specific projects consistent with those priorities, TO-Ab functions as a site for networking, communication, and information sharing with respect to issues of mutual interest. Unlike its equivalent in

Vancouver, TO-Ab does not have a connection, either formal or informal, to TO-main at the City of Toronto.

The Advisory Committee on Homeless and Socially Isolated Persons
The Advisory Committee on Homeless and Socially Isolated Persons (TO-emerg) was created in 1996 to provide advice to City decision makers, to identify emerging issues facing homeless and marginalized persons in Toronto, and to promote long-term solutions to homelessness (Advisory Committee on Homeless and Socially Isolated Persons [ACHSIP], minutes, 1996). The network, which operated for ten years, was created in the context of an exploding homelessness crisis in Toronto, which was marked by an increasing number of deaths of homeless individuals on the streets in the mid-1990s. Like the other governance networks under investigation, TO-emerg comprised approximately twenty key civil society actors in Toronto – including shelter and housing providers, mental health advocates, homelessness activists, and even academics – together with bureaucrats from the City of Toronto's Shelter, Support, and Housing Administration. One unique feature of this governance network in comparison to the others under study is that it was co-chaired by an elected official – a city councillor. The first co-chair was councillor Jack Layton, and upon his resignation from council, councillors Jane Pitfield and Sylvia Watson took the helm of TO-emerg. During its tenure, TO-emerg was responsible for numerous and substantive policy innovations, including developing emergency shelter protocols, police sensitivity training, and transit policy changes; in addition, the network pushed debates about homelessness onto the Toronto City Council agenda. The leadership turnover caused – or, at the very least, exposed – deep fractures within the governance network membership, causing it to disband in 2006. No similar governance network, with councillor leadership and substantive policy community involvement, has been created since.

Calgary

The Calgary Action Committee on Homelessness and Housing
The mainstream homelessness governance network in Calgary is similar to VAN-main and TO-main in terms of serving as the community advisory board mandated by the federal government's HPI program (now the Homelessness Partnering Strategy), but it is quite distinct from them in other ways. Denoted here as CAL-main, it is familiar to Calgarians today as the Calgary Action Committee on Homelessness and Housing. CAL-main

has had various names throughout its history, but it was first created in 1996 as an ad hoc committee to study the emerging homelessness crisis in Calgary and to make policy recommendations. Over time, it evolved into a large and complex network of civil society actors associated with homelessness and housing in Calgary, as documented by Susan Scott in her book, *The Beginning of the End: The Story of the Calgary Homeless Foundation and One Community's Drive to End Homelessness* (2012). Its full membership exceeds 100, but its executive is composed of a somewhat smaller set of members from diverse segments of the homelessness sector. To this day, CAL-main preserves the numerous working groups that formed to help devise the first Community Action Plan and that serve as "sector groups," each of which independently elects a sector chair to be its representative at CAL-main. Although CAL-main preceded the creation of the NHI, it assumed the role of community advisory board mandated in 1999 by that federal program – that of a local governance network devising policy priorities and making investments on behalf of the federal government in Calgary – and it remains in that role today.

The Calgary Homeless Foundation

The Calgary Homeless Foundation (CAL-CHF) was created in 1998 by local business person Art Smith, who, upon learning of the growing homelessness problem in Calgary, became a tireless advocate and mobilizer for change. CAL-CHF began as a network of business people and community actors, with a very small staff provided in-kind by the province. Initially, the primary role of the organization was to raise money from the private sector to contribute towards assisting the homeless, but CAL-CHF has since evolved into a powerful quasi-government agency that directs federal, provincial, and private funds towards housing and homelessness services. Despite having features like those of a government agency, the organization remains collaborative in nature, with high community involvement and engagement in policy planning and decision making. In 2008, CAL-CHF was tasked with implementing Calgary's aggressive *10-Year Plan to End Homelessness* (Calgary Committee to End Homelessness [CCEH], 2008).

CAL-CHF is larger in institutional heft and mandate than any of the other governance networks under investigation. Somewhat counterintuitively, it does not generally work with the City of Calgary, whose role in dealing with homelessness has, in effect, been taken on by CAL-CHF. Furthermore, because of the uniquely expansive role of CAL-CHF, including fulfilling emergency functions, there is no equivalent in Calgary to TO-emerg and

VAN-emerg. The resulting variation among the properties and dynamics of the governance networks across the cities offers fertile ground for comparisons.[5]

This brief introduction to the governance networks reveals that while each of the equivalent networks in Vancouver, Calgary, and Toronto share similar origins, there are important differences in their institutional roles, memberships, and activities. These differences allow us to isolate the impact of governance network dynamics on the development and implementation of policy. The latitude with which the governance networks were permitted to take shape and evolve offers an opportunity to track a natural experiment in governance and public policy over twenty years.

As important as the properties and dynamics of governance networks are to policy innovation and system coordination, such networks are, of course, not the only pathway to policy innovation and coordination. Since other aspects of politics and governance, such as elected leadership, could potentially explain some of the policy and outcome differences exhibited by the cities, they must also be identified and tracked.

The three cities have interesting variations. First, the leadership of elected officials, particularly mayors (and even premiers), has the potential to be immensely consequential to big-ticket, high-level policy changes. Leadership necessarily varies at the local level and must be tracked over time. In Vancouver, a considerable degree of homelessness and housing policy development is centralized in a single provincial agency (BC Housing), while in Calgary and Toronto it is more or less devolved (with funding transfers) to the local level. Likewise, Vancouver has an integrated and functional regional government system, whereas Calgary and Toronto, because of amalgamations, do not. This difference may have implications for the coordination of homelessness services in the broader urban area. In addition, the electoral systems in Metro Vancouver municipalities are "at-large" (meaning the mayor and council are elected by the entire city), while in Calgary and Toronto the councillors are elected to specific wards. The electoral system in the latter two cities may have implications for the ability of decision makers to implement affordable housing and homelessness support services and may give the NIMBYism of citizens a potentially powerful institutional pathway to resist change. Thus, a focus on analyzing homelessness governance networks over the past two decades does not imply that traditional political and bureaucratic elements are inconsequential. Rather, this focus reflects the fact that governance networks constitute a comparatively understudied element of homelessness governance in Canada and elsewhere.

Methodology

Tracing the influence of governance network structures and dynamics on homelessness policy development requires an examination of the evolution of policy and governance over a considerable period of time. This study begins the analysis in each city in the mid-1990s, not only to capture the early days of the emerging homelessness crisis in Canadian cities but also to set the beginning of the study period at a time before any of the governance networks were created. The mid-1990s provide a policy baseline in Vancouver, Calgary, and Toronto from which to track policy changes attributable to homelessness governance networks and, by doing so, test key precepts of network governance theory.

This approach is consistent with the classic historical institutionalist approach of political scientists Peter Hall (1986), Paul Pierson (2004), and Theda Skocpol (1979), who maintain that the unique institutional features of each city, as well as the sequencing of events and historical timing in that particular context, are significant to policy development. To establish a causal link between governance network properties and certain dimensions of policy development – in particular, policy innovation and system coordination – we must isolate important moments in the governance network creation and evolution and identify corresponding effects on policy. According to political scientist Evan Lieberman (2001), one of the first steps in comparative historical analysis is what is known as *periodization* – that is, dividing up the chronology of the study into analytically and even theoretically consequential periods. Periods are generally marked by variation in a potentially important explanatory factor, whether it be the one we seek to prove as meaningful (e.g., governance network structure, metagovernance changes, or network dissolution) or potential alternative explanations (e.g., local institutional reforms, the leadership of particular actors or organizations, or policy idea diffusion).

Following this method, this study examines three distinct periods: the period before the governance networks were created (pre-1995), the period of the bulk of their existence (1996–2014), and the most recent period (2015–present). Before 1995, none of the eight governance networks was in existence; thus, it is important to establish a policy baseline during this period. Beginning in 1996, the governance networks began to appear – TO-emerg and CAL-main in 1996, VAN-emerg and CAL-CHF in 1998, and the remaining four networks in 2000 – and all of them are analyzed from the date of their creation to 2014, the end of the second period under investigation. The final period is short, but it is critical to examine it as a distinct period, since major changes were made in 2014 to the the federal government's metagovernance of the networks, and metagovernance, as discussed in the next chapter, is an important part of the theoretical framework guiding this analysis.

In the following pages, I present the findings for each city using longitudinal and comparative policy analysis. I have drawn on archival records over a twenty-year period, beginning in 1995, since tracking the development and implementation of policy requires a historical process-tracing approach. The archival documents include meeting minutes and policy documents from all of the governance networks, special task force reports, city and regional council documents, and provincial and federal government policy plans and reports. Complete sets of available meeting minutes for all governance networks under investigation were obtained from the networks' leadership. In addition, more than seventy interviews were conducted with key government and civil society actors in all three jurisdictions to gain perspective on internal policy debates and dynamics within the governance networks and government bureaucracies.

Because investigating network governance requires engagement with ground-level data-collection methods, I used extensive participant observation of governance network policy planning and decision making in all three cities from 2011 to 2015. This enabled me to view the governance network dynamics in real time, including meetings, subcommittee work, and deliberative decision making regarding program investments. Viewing governance networks in action is essential to capturing the properties of network governance that may have an effect on policy development. Being immersed in the institutional setting enabled me to observe the structural forces at work on network actors' daily lives and actions and to collect empirical data on the relationship between structure and agency, as articulated by political ethnographer Jan Kubik (2009). In addition, as suggested by anthropologist Janine Wedel and her colleagues (2005), participant observation is essential to understanding how state policies and government processes are experienced and interpreted by people within networks, whether those individuals represent government, a particular interest group, or another aspect of civil society.

In Vancouver, I was embedded among network members for an intensive five weeks in the winter of 2012, and I made shorter follow-up observational visits from 2012 to 2015. In Calgary, I made multiple week-long visits throughout 2014 and 2015, and in Toronto, I attended bimonthly network meetings over two years, from 2011 to 2013, and made follow-up visits from 2014 to 2015. Participant observation also allowed me to extract data from a unique natural experiment in decision making in one of the Vancouver governance networks; using these data, I was able to examine the differences between investment decisions made by the governance network and those made within the bureaucracy allocating those same investments. I also used investment data from all of the governance networks and municipal governments for a comparative analysis of policy priorities.

This study therefore draws upon a diverse suite of research methods ranging from quasi-experimental quantitative decision-making analysis, to comparative historical policy analysis using archival records, to qualitative analysis based on interviews and participation observation. All of these methods are essential to establishing how and why governance networks matter to homelessness policy development in these cities.

Conclusion

This book is fundamentally concerned with examining the governance issues associated with homelessness in major Canadian cities, particularly the practice and variability of governance processes on the ground. It represents a rare longitudinal comparative analysis of homelessness policy-making in three major Canadian cities. Because homelessness in Canada and elsewhere is rarely viewed through the lens of governance and politics, we are missing information not only about the political dimensions of the distribution of resources in society and the political-economic structures that contribute to homelessness but also about the practicalities of governance in this sector.

Conventional theories in political science and public administration do not adequately explain the variation in homelessness trends and policy that we see across the these three Canadian cities. In this book, I explore how different structures, properties, and dynamics of homelessness governance explain these divergent policy developments in Vancouver, Toronto, and Calgary. In particular, if civil society actors – in this case, shelter and drop-in centre providers, affordable housing providers and activists, mental health and addiction professionals – are included in substantive policy planning and decision making in governance networks, what is the effect on homelessness policy?

In addition to exploring the concrete issue of homelessness governance and policy-making in Canadian cities, *Building a Collaborative Advantage* builds on conversations and theory development in the academic literature related to network governance, deliberative democracy, and metagovernance. It also expands upon emerging theories of network governance in public administration, responding directly to recent calls from scholars such as John Dryzek (2010) and Robyn Keast and colleagues (2014) to more concretely theorize the study of network governance. It is not well understood which institutional and relational features of network governance are most critical to facilitating productive policy deliberations and decision making, and the controlled comparative analysis of eight homelessness governance networks can help clarify this by identifying mechanisms that underlie the causal relationships. This contribution to theory-building bridges the literatures on metagovernance (how the state designs and manages networks), network governance (how properties of networks shape policy development), and deliberative democracy (how policy is shaped through persuasion and brokerage) to construct a generalized model linking network governance to policy outputs. This model, as we will see, can be used to explain the differences in homelessness policy innovation and system coordination in Vancouver, Calgary, and Toronto, but it can also be applied across policy domains. *Building a Collaborate Advantage* draws on and adds to emerging theories of network governance that challenge conventional explanations from political science for policy variation that privilege the individual leadership of elected officials, the intergovernmental relations between different levels of government, and the diffusion dynamics of policy ideas.

This book contributes to ongoing debates on whether governance networks enhance policy innovation and system coordination via persuasion from diverse policy actors (see Borins, 2008; Considine et al., 2009; Paquet, 1999; Strumpf, 2002) or sustain the status quo by promoting compromise and lowest-common-denominator policy (Klijn & Koppenjan, 2004; Scharpf, 1999). How much "policy space" should governance networks be granted by the state metagovernors? Are governance networks truly deliberative in nature? This analysis of developments in three cities shows that it is not merely the properties of the governance networks that shape their impact on public policy development: how those networks are placed in the policy-making arena and managed by the state, what scholars have identified as the metagovernance context, also plays a role (Doberstein, 2013). The metagovernance context determines the arena and the rules of the game, and this context, as we will see, powerfully shapes the policy-making potential and deliberative opportunities of governance networks.

In a broader sense, this book builds on Canadian and international public administration scholarship that challenges the predominant thinking in the West about public administration in the twenty-first century, which favours a leaner public service that is expected to tackle more complex public problems amidst growing expectations of inclusive decision making (Conteh & Roberge, 2013; Leone & Ohemeng, 2011). That there is considerable variation in homelessness policy among Canadian cities strongly suggests that the design and execution of governance institutions matters, and this, in turn, has important public administration implications for other policy issues that also have complex multi-jurisdictional dynamics. Many policy sectors in Canada (including immigrant settlement, health care, economic development, neighbourhood revitalization, urban Aboriginal governance, and homelessness) have seen the emergence of an abundance of new and complex multi-level and network governance institutions in which government and civil society actors jointly engage in institutionalized policy planning and decision making. These governance networks remain underinvestigated by scholars in Canada, despite their increasingly significant role in the policy process. Political scientist Grace Skogstad (2003) reminds us that there is a plurality of conceptions of legitimate political authority in Canada, including state-centred, expert, private (market), and popular authority. Indeed, the contemporary challenge for governing is how to reconcile demands for direct participation with traditional representative democracy. One path forward is that taken by the governance networks examined in the following chapters.

2

Integrated Network Governance

In the domain of electoral politics, particularly in parliamentary systems, the last four decades have seen an indisputable shift towards the concentration of power among a few elites – namely, the first minister and the managers of supporting central agencies (Savoie, 2008, 1999). But in tandem with this shift in authority in high politics, a countertrend in public administration has emerged in certain areas – most apparent in the social policy domain – towards more inclusive and collaborative policy-making and implementation, not only to bridge silos across the bureaucracy but also to leverage the expertise and problem-solving potential of civil society. Designing and facilitating institutional spaces for collaborative policy-making and implementation is a new task for government; it is also viewed by many as an institutional solution to complex governance problems, like homelessness, that cannot be resolved by any single level of government, ministry, or sector acting alone.

Modern challenges of governance extend beyond homelessness to societal issues such as immigrant settlement, the labour market, urban Aboriginal governance, and even health care. Furthermore, governance patterns based on more inclusive and collaborative policy-making and implementation – that is, on governance networks – are by no means limited to Canada. Alex Turrini and colleagues (2010, p. 528) go as far as to say that internationally, "in the public sector, the implementation and management of public programmes through networks has now become more the rule than the exception." Robyn Keast and colleagues (2014, p. 15) likewise claim that since governance networks are increasingly becoming a "cornerstone of contemporary public sector institutional architecture," it is ever more important to understand their performance, effectiveness, and legitimacy.

Thus, a new theoretical framework is needed within which governance networks can be analyzed and evaluated. The framework developed here weaves together concepts and lessons derived from the scholarly literatures on network governance, metagovernance, and deliberative democracy, all of which have staked out normative and empirical claims about the evolution of traditional government institutions and the role of civil society actors in decision making. The framework that I propose transforms these concepts into a more generalized theoretical model to explain how and why governance networks matter to policy development – in particular, to policy innovation and system coordination. This theory of network governance posits that a governance network's degree of institutionalization and inclusiveness is closely linked to policy innovation and system coordination and that the link is made principally through the brokerage relations and persuasion dynamics that are generated from network activity. The effectiveness of governance networks, however, can be compromised by a metagovernance context (how the state designs and manages governance network activity) that is too narrowly constrained and/or is characterized by a contentious leadership style, thereby suffocating the potential dynamism of network governance.

New Forms of Governance

It is uncontroversial to suggest that the practice of governing in many Western democracies has changed in the past thirty years from the state being the dominant actor devising and implementing policy to policy-making being more horizontally distributed among state and civil society agents. To be sure, this is a misrepresentation in both directions: non-state actors have always had considerable influence on government policy (Pross, 1975), and the empirical reality of horizontal governance patterns in a Canadian context, such as governance networks, is by no means universal across policy domains. However, network governance characterizes a growing number of policy domains in Canada, including homelessness, local economic development, immigrant settlement, urban Aboriginal issues, and even health care (e.g., Ontario's local health integration networks). And many of these governance networks are not simply playing small-ball politics: the local health integration network in Toronto is responsible for prioritizing and allocating $4.2 billion annually (Toronto Central LHIN, 2012). This is, of course, an extraordinary example of the type of policy space at play, but many governance networks in other policy areas have significant space within which to create policy and allocate public resources.

The terms used in the literature to describe such governance patterns are varied, including "multi-level governance" (Bache & Flinders, 2004; Horak & Young, 2012; Weiss, 1998), "network governance" (Sørensen & Torfing, 2007a, 2007b), and "new public governance" (Conteh & Roberge, 2013). Canadian public administration scholars have long been attentive to new kinds of arrangements for delivering services flowing from new public management reforms, variously characterized as alternative service delivery (Evans & Shields, 1998; Ford & Zussman, 1997), horizontal management and governance (Bakvis & Juillet, 2004; Phillips & Levasseur, 2004; Sproule-Jones, 2000), distributed governance (Paquet, 1999), and partnerships (Bradford, 2004). Although the terms and concepts employed by scholars in Canada and elsewhere to discuss changing governance patterns vary, they all share a focus on examining the relationships among interdependent public and private actors as they work to address often complex public policy issues in an institutionalized setting.[1]

The changes in political reality from a context in which a sovereign state governs society through top-down central planning towards one characterized more by pluricentric governance based upon interdependence and exchange among state and non-state actors are the result of three concurrent forces: the emergence of organized society, the fragmentation of the state, and the complexity of social and political affairs. In terms of the emergence of organized society, we have witnessed an explosion in the last thirty years not only in the number and importance of collective societal actors and organizations but also in their sophistication as it relates to organization and advocacy (Kenis & Schneider, 1991). The expansion of state influence into more aspects of society has resulted in a fragmentation or "sectoralization" of the state, whereby bureaucracies, policies, and programs are increasingly defined in functionally differentiated terms (Wildavsky, 1974). In addition, social and political affairs have become increasingly complex with the shifting demographics of Canadian society, citizens' changing expectations of their governments, and the emergence of new problems – like homelessness – that have multifaceted origins.

As the state vacated its more or less exclusive role in devising and implementing policy, new public management emerged, an approach that demanded a rethink in terms of the role of bureaucracy and centralized control and one that is biased towards market-based solutions. The new network-based patterns of governance described above are at once the result of a shift towards new public management principles that sought to reduce the lead role of the bureaucracy in managing public problems and a reaction against new public management's market-based principles, which were quickly proven to be incompatible with the complex, multi-level, and consultative features of modern governance (Conteh & Roberge, 2013). The increased complexity of social and political affairs contributed to the greater importance of information to the state in order to make effective policy, and non-state actors are critical sources of that information – from technical expertise to an understanding of causal social mechanisms.

Building a New Theoretical Framework

As various forms of network governance have taken shape in Canada and elsewhere in recent decades, an important question has arisen: What are the implications of these networks – their creation, design, and operation – for governance and policy? Answering that question requires an analysis of governance networks and their performance, which, in turn, requires the construction of an integrated theoretical framework. I propose that integrated governance network theory, as it relates to public policy development, requires the conceptualization of three essential features of governance networks: the mandate of the governance network, its institutional design features, and the actual practice of networking – that is, the deliberative, problem-solving dynamics among network actors.

First, at the macro-level, we must specify how network governance institutions are created, mandated, and managed from above by the state – what is generally referred to as "metagovernance." Second, at the meso-level, we need to specify the structural design attributes of the governance network itself – that is, how these new policy actors are positioned in the policy process. Finally, at the micro-level of individual action, we must conceptualize the behaviour of individual network actors and its relationship to policy development and change – in particular, the transformative potential of the perspectives of those actors as expressed in institutionalized interactions and deliberations. At each of these three levels of analysis, we can draw on theoretical concepts and empirical developments from a number of distinct literatures to build an integrated governance network theory.

From Policy Networks to Network Governance

Devising an integrated model begins with conceptualizing the properties of governance networks that are essential to their operation and performance. Most research on networks in Canada and elsewhere has focused on this meso-level of analysis – the institutional attributes of the network itself – and has engaged in considerable debate about how best to conceptualize this within a theoretical framework.

In the Canadian context, noted public administration scholars Robert Presthus (1975) and Paul Pross (1975) first drew attention to the various relationships between non-state actors and the state. Fifteen years later, political scientists William Coleman, Michael Atkinson, and Grace Skogstad contributed to work on policy networks by conceptualizing four types of networks in Canada based on different state-society relations in the country: pressure pluralist, concertation, corporatist, and state-directed (Atkinson & Coleman, 1989; Coleman & Skogstad, 1990). The typology differentiates networks according to how open (or closed) the network is to policy actors and what role network actors have in the policy process.[2] But according to this school of thought, policy network is a concept that refers to interest intermediation across nations and policy domains, not one that signals a fundamental reorientation of governance by the state. This school of policy network research also has a major shortcoming in that it undertheorizes the relational elements of policy networks: that is, it privileges the structural dimensions of governance and has very little to say about the behaviour of actors within networks, such as bargaining dynamics, policy learning, and resource exchange.

An alternative school of policy network research, the one on which this study builds, conceptualizes networks as new governance arrangements distinct from state hierarchy and markets and is associated with the work of organizational scholars Bernd Marin and Renate Maytnz (1991) and Jan Kooiman (1993) and other, mainly European, scholars. To these scholars, understanding governance requires investigating the evolving relationship between state and society (Pierre & Peters, 2005). At the core of this research is the observation that a shift in the role and authority of the state has occurred since the late 1980s and that, in many policy domains, a mutual dependency among state and non-state actors has coincided with the emergence of cooperation and negotiation as new governing norms. The intellectual origins of this school emerged from interorganizational theorists such as William Dill (1958), who established that conditions in the external environment such as availability of resources, economic factors, and even changing government policy will affect organizations and will lead to changes in their behaviour. State and civil society actors and organizations, then, form policy networks to exchange resources that are relevant to policy – informational and financial resources, for example – as a result of new governance challenges.

Both of these schools of policy network research claim that networks matter to policy development, an idea that was subsequently challenged by a number of scholars. Political scientist Keith Dowding (1995) offered the most prominent critique of the utility of the policy network concept, suggesting that despite many years of inquiry, all that has been provided is a non-rigorous, descriptive account of networks in political life. Furthermore, research attempting to link the attributes of networks to policy outputs was marginal and inconsistent. Likewise, German political scientist Tanja Börzel (1998) argues that typologies of networks and explanations of what causes networks to take the shape they do, while perhaps interesting, have little explanatory power. Mark Thatcher (1998) contends that in order to develop a better theoretical understanding of why networks form, how actor behaviour is enabled and constrained within them, and how all of this relates to policy change, outside theory must be applied. Colin Hay (1995), rather than critiquing the lack of explicit links between network structure and policy development, argues against what he views to be a structural bias to network studies in both schools of thought described above. While some scholars stress the interpersonal aspects of networks (Marin & Maytnz, 1991), the dominant approach among early network scholars was structural in orientation (Atkinson & Coleman, 1989; Coleman & Skogstad, 1990; Marsh & Rhodes, 1992). The structural approach involves mapping the contours of the network structure (e.g., closed/open, tight/diffuse, clustered/non-clustered) rather than focusing on the process and practice of networking. To Colin Hay (1995), this is problematic because a network then tends to be viewed as a static and invariant structure rather than a relational concept or a dynamic process that has emergent properties – that is, an arena where something is produced, such as policy learning or deliberative problem-solving, that would not emerge in different governance contexts.

The critiques launched by Colin Hay (1995), Keith Dowding (1995), and Mark Thatcher (1998) prompted a second generation of network scholarship, overlapping with the first, to develop and test more explicit hypotheses connecting network properties to policy. British governance scholars R.A.W. Rhodes and David Marsh (1992), for instance, found that tight and closed policy networks tend to produce stable policy outcomes, while larger and more open networks are usually associated with unstable policy outcomes.[3] Canadian political scientist Michael Howlett (2002) also discovered a link between network structure and types of policy change: those sectors with networks that are more open to new actors and ideas and thus are more likely to produce change in policy goals and programs. And European scholars Silke Adam and Hanspeter Kriesi (2007) linked kinds of networks to type of policy change by way of patterns of interaction within the network, suggesting that the distribution of power can determine the potential for change, and the type of interaction determines the form of change. Swedish political scientists Annica Sandström and Lars Carlsson (2008) linked network closure/ openness and heterogeneity/homogeneity to the performance of networks. They found that highly dense and centralized networks enhance the process of prioritization and thus the efficiency of decision making and that a higher diversity of actors within a network (and therefore more cross-boundary interactions) enhances the process of resource mobilization and thus improves policy innovation.

These second-generation network studies are characterized by an attempt to assess the performance of institutionalized governance networks across normative criteria, including equity, democracy, goal attainment, productivity, stability, conflict resolution, and learning capacity (e.g., Benz & Papadopoulos 2006; Head, 2008; Klijn & Skelcher 2007; Leach 2006; Sørensen & Torfing, 2003). Thus, the more recent agenda for governance network research has been to link governance networks – that is, more formalized institutions of governance rather than "policy networks" broadly defined – to the effectiveness of policy, efficiency of decision making, and potential for policy innovation. The theoretical framework that I propose here builds on this second generation of research.

The second-generation research makes it clear that two essential properties of a governance network must be conceptualized in theoretical terms: its institutionalization and its inclusiveness. The institutionalization of a governance network captures not only its role in the policy process (e.g., advisory or semi-autonomous, a policy-generation body or a policy-implementation body) but also its meeting frequency and its level of integration with relevant decision-makers in the broader policy community. The second key feature of a governance network is its degree of inclusiveness of diverse actors and organizations from both government and civil society, capturing an essential relational aspect of governance that has been underconceptualized by network scholars. Its centrality in the theoretical framework is based on the claim that a network provides an institutionalized arena for actors with diverse perspectives to share knowledge and experiences and to deliberate about policy solutions (Dryzek, 2007). Conceptualizing (and thus differentiating) governance networks according to the size and diversity of their membership is important because it captures their deliberative potential.

Leading network researchers have observed a trend that has held back the development of a unifying theory of network governance: most scholars have tended to treat networks as undifferentiated and thus have assumed that they are basically the same in structure and design (Keast et al., 2014). This does a disservice to the richness of governance networks and also limits our understanding of how variation in network properties impacts their performance, stability, and accountability, in addition to shaping public policy outcomes. In order to explain the relationship between governance networks and public policy development, then, we must conceptualize the essential structural and relational properties of governance networks, as well as the contexts under which they are created and managed.

From Network Management to Metagovernance

Historically, a key weakness in policy and governance network research has been the lack of context: governance networks have been studied more or less in a vacuum, with a focus on their structures, properties, and dynamics while sidelining an important part of the analysis – the state as a metagovernor of networks. As more collaborative and less hierarchical network governance structures emerge, the state does not fade away; in fact, government maintains key legal and fiscal controls and functions while trying to harness the potential dynamism of the network (McGuire & Agranoff, 2011). An integrated theory of governance networks must, therefore, conceptualize the place of the state in the policy process: How much policy space is a network granted by the state, and how does the state oversee and regulate governance network activity?

In response to this gap, research into network management emerged, recognizing that governance networks – particularly those granted considerable policy space – are generally not self-organizing and in fact require careful management, usually from the state, to function effectively (Meier & O'Toole, 2005). Canadian public administration scholar Evert Lindquist (1992) reflects on the new roles of public servants as "managers" of groups outside of government and on the demand for new management strategies that different policy network configurations impose on government officials.

In a groundbreaking publication, Dutch public administration researchers Walter Kickert and Joop Koppenjan (1997, p. 47) conceptualize the management of networks as "the steering of interaction processes" theorizing that public managers have an important role to play in the performance, stability, and accountability of governance networks. Subsequent studies have tended to focus on two dimensions of network management: the institutional features of management, meaning the rules and structures that steer activity, and the interpersonal features of network managers, meaning the actual practices of managers and how they manage the interpersonal complexity of network governance.

In terms of the institutional features of network management, American public administration scholars Keith Provan and H. Brinton Milward (1995, p. 23) found that networks are most effective "under structural conditions of centralization ... and direct, non-fragmented external control." In effect, this means a powerful and hierarchically empowered network manager, which in some ways challenges the principle of horizontality (of power and influence) of governance networks. Indeed, through empirical research, numerous authors have found a direct trade-off associated with network management: a more formalized and hierarchical network management (e.g., rules that constrain the governance network) may allow for effective steering of activity but may also reduce the dynamism of network governance that can result in new insights, directions, and policy innovations, all of which are more likely with less formalized and hierarchical network management (Keast et al., 2007; Peters & Pierre, 1998; Provan & Kenis, 2008; Rice, 2014; Salamon, 2002).

In terms of the interpersonal features of network management, research has shown that the actual day-to-day practices of network managers can have considerable impact on the performance of a governance network (Agranoff, 2007; Agranoff & McGuire, 2003). According to Dutch public administration researchers Eric Hans Klijn and Joop Koppenjan (2000), "process management" – the management of interactions among network members – is a critical task for network managers, but it is more of an interpersonal challenge than one of institutional design. Process management can range from basic tasks like recruiting membership and chairing meetings to more complex tasks like balancing and coordinating interests at a strategic level. Robyn Keast and Myrna Mandell (2014, p. 36) stress that an effective leadership style, a style that they call "process catalyst leadership," is one "that is able to make connections, to bridge diverse cultures, and that can get participants to be comfortable sharing ideas, resources, and power."

Thus, an effective leader must be able to strategically manage relationships, part of which is attracting and engaging the right people (including those not part of the conventional policy community), and to mobilize resources needed to make the network work.

Network management is fundamentally about trying to achieve, through institutional rules and interpersonal relationship building, the collaborative advantage of network governance while overcoming or avoiding the inertia and fractured decision-making that we would otherwise expect to occur in such a governance context (Doberstein, 2015). While considerable research has been conducted on network management, there is no consensus about how best to manage networks effectively (Bevir & Richards, 2009; Voets, 2014). In fact, the three primary approaches to network management are quite distinct from one another: instrumental (top-down management by the state, preserving an amount of hierarchy), interactive (negotiation and diplomacy among interdependent actors, moving away from hierarchical modes of control), and institutional (rules that set the terms of interaction, focusing on changing relationships among actors, the distribution of resources, and values and perceptions of actors).

The reality is that network management involves all three of these approaches to varying degrees, and this is reflected in the integrated governance network theory advanced in these pages. In recent years, the concept of "metagovernance" has emerged from network management research as a unifying analytical tool to bridge the divide in the literature (Bradford, 2014; Doberstein, 2013; Klijn & Koppenjan, 2012). Metagovernance is a "combination of hands-off tools such as institutional design and network framing, and hands-on tools such as process management and direct participation" (Klijn & Koppenjan, 2012, p. 594, citing Sørensen & Torfing, 2007b). The emerging metagovernance paradigm not only reconciles divisions in the literature with a unifying concept but also introduces new meanings, particularly regarding metagovernance as a way of framing network conditions, thus shaping and constraining the behaviour of actors in networks (Jessop, 2003). This paradigm simultaneously reintroduces the strategic use of hierarchy and demands interactive negotiation and diplomacy among interdependent network actors as a means of promoting governance network performance, stability, and accountability. The metagovernance of a governance network is not about using the heavy hand of hierarchy and control; rather, it is concerned with harnessing the potential dynamism of network governance in the "shadow of hierarchy," in order to conform to traditional understandings of legitimacy and accountability (Bell & Hindmoor, 2009; Heritier & Rhodes, 2011; see also Sørensen & Torfing, 2007a).

Much of the theory-building on metagovernance has emerged from the European context, but Canadian scholars analyzing cases of collaborative governance arrangements have made important contributions that can assist with integrating metagovernance into a theory of network governance. The scholars in Canada who are attentive to less hierarchical and more collaborative governance arrangements have typically analyzed their cases within a multi-level governance framework (see, e.g., Horak & Young, 2012; Peters, 2011; Young & Leuprecht, 2006) and not as cases of network governance with metagovernance dimensions – a theoretical lens that I contend would yield more concrete claims about how and why these new forms of governance matter to policy development, the relative absence of which is the central critique of the multi-level governance literature launched by Jon Pierre and B. Guy Peters (2005). Yet Canadian scholarship offers instructive insights on multi-level governance, particularly in relation to municipalities – insights that are relevant to the theorization of metagovernance in relation to governance networks.

Most of the case studies in the collaborative project "Multi-level Governance and Public Policy in Canadian Municipalities" (2005–12), led by Robert Young, document the various methods by which the federal government has injected itself into municipal affairs on issues like immigrant settlement, emergency preparedness, and urban Aboriginal governance. Despite the wide variation in methodology discovered by the researchers, a common element in many of the cases is that multi-level governance institutions in Canada, while premised on more horizontal relations and collaborative planning by multiple levels of government and civil society actors, tend to remain rather hierarchical in practice, depending on which level of government provides the most significant resources (Horak, 2012). For example, Christopher Leo and Martine August (2009a) examined immigrant settlement in Vancouver and found that the ideological proclivities of key government actors can strongly influence the design of multi-level, collaborative governance mechanisms, often starving them of their purported benefits. Warren Magnusson and Serena Kataoka (2009) studied the same case as Leo and August (2009a) and concluded that while it is often marketed as multi-level and collaborative, immigrant settlement policy-making in British Columbia is, for the most part, siloed, hierarchical, and led by senior governments.

Not all Canadian scholarship on multi-level governance comes to such a dispirited conclusion, however. Political scientist Neil Bradford (2004) argues that since many urban policy issues transcend jurisdictional compartments, they require place-sensitive, holistic approaches that are delivered through networked relations of governments and civil society. He offers urban development agreements in Canada as a promising example of multi-level urban governance that aims to tackle complex policy problems (Bradford, 2008). University of Toronto researchers Meric Gertler and David Wolfe (2004) examine how institutional structures at multiple levels of governance influence the type and scope of local action with respect to regional foresight exercises in several North American cities. While they do not universally applaud instances of multi-level, collaborative-type governance in Canada, the authors find an encouraging example in Ottawa of "institutions of collaboration" that allow for a meaningful exchange among state and non-state actors (p. 62).[4]

Most of the above scholarship from Canada was conducted within the multi-level governance framework, yet the findings powerfully reinforce the importance of the related but distinct theoretical concept of metagovernance. Metagovernance emphasizes that governance networks do not exist in a vacuum: even while they may represent a shift from traditional hierarchical structures, they are always attached to and shaped by the state. Whereas the multi-level governance framework represents an *analytical* framework to guide descriptive inquiry, the metagovernance concept has *explanatory* power – specifically, it helps us to understand and theorize how state management of the governance of complex policy files shapes the performance of that governance.

Two dimensions of metagovernance emerge from the literature as important features that shape the stability and performance of a governance network: the institutional policy space (or autonomy) afforded to the network and the leadership style of the metagovernor. With respect to policy space, a governance network may be given relatively open policy space, in which case it can operate with relative freedom, or it may be given a constrained mandate within limited policy space. Leadership style relates to how a metagovernor's agency and methods of steering can powerfully structure network activities to productive ends if they are cooperative or can result in serious disruption and conflict if they are contentious (Keast & Mandell, 2014). The metagovernance context, therefore, has both structural and agentic dimensions that shape the performance and stability of the governance network.

Governance Networks as Deliberative Systems

With the institutional architecture of governance networks and their meta-governors articulated by theory, one final piece is needed to understand how network governance relates to public policy development: the individual network actors and their interaction with one another within their governance networks. Governance networks are institutional structures, but, perhaps more importantly, they are made up of actors with agency. In fact, this is where the promise of governance networks resides – in the diversity of actors who come together to deliberate and problem solve. Incorporation of the interpersonal, micro-level dimension into the analysis completes the theory of network governance presented here, and for this piece, we draw on an expansive literature, although the topic is rarely associated with network governance: deliberative democracy.

Recall that the central critique of the theoretical and empirical contributions to governance network research to date is that understanding precisely how networks matter to policy remains elusive, one of the chief reasons for this being inadequate theorization (and testing) of *why* network governance may matter to policy development. Beyond predicting when policy change is more likely (e.g., Howlett, 2002), scholars who have studied network governance have generated few testable hypotheses about the relationship between governance networks and dimensions of policy such as innovation and coordination. Part of the problem is that governance network scholars are often too singularly focused on the structure of the network, which, while important, has often predominated at the cost of ignoring what actually goes on inside of governance networks: deliberations, exchanges, and learning among disparate policy actors. In other words, what is missing is an agency-driven explanation for why and how network governance shapes policy (Börzel, 2011; Skelcher & Sullivan, 2008). The contributions of contemporary deliberative democracy theory can help us fill this gap. Indeed, leading deliberative democracy theorists are eager to have their theoretical concepts operationalized in sites of network governance (Dryzek, 2010).

Deliberative models of democracy and governance, like the network governance literature, problematize the aggregation of citizen interests and preferences in the traditional liberal model of representative democracy, suggesting that the atomization of citizenship, interests, and preferences reinforces conflict in the polity, a battleground that systematically privileges some actors over others, resulting in patterns of unjust policy (Chambers, 2003; Mansbridge, 1983; Young, 2000). Several ideals within the deliberative model are relevant to network governance research, chief among them being the principles of inclusion – that a decision is only legitimate if all those affected by it are included in consultation and decision making – and substantive political equality – that all those affected have an equal right and effective opportunity to influence the decision.

Deliberative democracy theorist Iris Marion Young (2000) argues that in deliberative arenas (of which the governance network is an example), the primary activity is not expressing interests or preferences but transforming them through learning or revealing ignorance. Likewise, proponents of citizen involvement in the development of policy argue that if representative democracy were supplemented by public deliberation, individuals might be more likely to revise their opinions through discussion with others (Chambers, 2003; Mansbridge et al., 2010). According to scholars like Iris Marion Young (2000), the deliberative model also holds the promise of creating more just policy decisions and outcomes for historically marginalized groups, whose economic marginalization contributes to their political marginalization under representative models of democracy. This potential for creating just policy makes normative deliberative democracy theory particularly relevant to an examination of homelessness governance networks. Political science researchers like Archon Fung and Erik Olin Wright (2003, p. 3) claim that for issues that involve complex problems associated with poverty, this "empowered participatory governance," whereby community and civil society groups share a role in decision making, can result in more responsive, fair, and innovative policy (see also Fung, 2008).

Although second-generation governance network scholars make claims that are strikingly similar to those made by deliberative democracy theorists, they do not engage deeply with the concepts of persuasion, learning, and trust building in deliberative sites. I argue that these concepts are key to understanding when and *why* governance networks matter to policy. Network governance scholars see governments as typically creating or harnessing governance networks as vehicles to pool resources, resolve knowledge deficiencies, and improve the implementation of programs and services (Agranoff, 2006). Governance networks are seen as advantageous in some policy domains because they bring together a wide range of expertise, knowledge, and resources that not only enables new thinking about complex issues but also lends itself to more successful implementation of policy (Head, 2008). The inclusion of civil society actors, who are generally more connected to the issues on the ground than are public servants, may offer a diversity of lived experience – and therefore information, interpretations, priorities, and perspectives – about what works and is worthwhile in terms of policy (Edelenbos & Klijn, 2006). These are important normative claims from network governance scholarship, and by establishing connections to the deliberative democracy literature, we can better theorize when and why governance networks matter to policy development, test hypotheses with comparative empirical research, and generate new theoretical claims about the causal mechanisms that link networks to policy.

The theoretical framework presented here is informed by two key micro-level concepts, brokerage and persuasion, both of which emerge from the deliberative democracy literature. I propose that these two concepts represent the causal mechanisms that link governance networks with policy innovation and coordination. Causal mechanisms are the specified pathways or processes by which an effect is produced and, in essence, help clarify what the theory is all about (Gerring, 2008). Brokerage and persuasion are thus the basis of the micro-level explanation for why governance networks matter to policy.

Brokerage can be defined as the forging of social connections among previously unlinked persons and sites (Burt, 2005). The theoretical assumption of brokerage as a causal mechanism can be found in the classical political work of John Stuart Mill (1859), who identified the benefit of "communication across lines of difference" (cited in Diana Mutz, 2002, p. 111).[5] For political philosopher Seyla Benhabib (1992, p. 140), interaction with those holding views different from our own is "essential for us to comprehend and to come to appreciate the perspectives of others." Similarly, theorist Charles Tilly (2003, p. 218) contemplates associated causal mechanisms like "encounter" that may cause social boundary changes among actors in a wide variety of "social sites," although he suggests that such mechanisms can, in fact, have the opposite effect, making social boundaries even more pronounced.[6] These seemingly inconsistent findings can be partially reconciled through experimental work by political scientist Diana Mutz (2002, p. 113), who found that one's "perspective-taking ability" (the personal capacity to entertain others' points of view) shapes whether the effects of exposure to differing views leads to a softening or hardening of boundaries or views on issues.

Brokerage relations lower the costs of communication and coordination between unconnected social sites, transforming them by establishing social, political, and economic ties (Lichbach, 2008). Brokerage as a causal process thus captures both resource exchange and trust relations in governance network settings and is a dynamic process in that brokerage may alter relations between policy actors, "allowing collective action to spread along the newly created network pathway" (McAdam et al., 2008, p. 322). Brokerage as a causal mechanism may, therefore, deactivate the previously sharp boundary between policy actors, whether from government or civil society, allowing actors in various silos to interpenetrate, which I theorize drives policy innovation and coordination. Institutionalized and inclusive governance networks provide the venues for boundaries to be dismantled among disparate policy actors as they develop relationships of exchange and trust.

Persuasion, the second proposed causal mechanism at the micro-level in governance networks, provides the other part of the explanation for why networks matter to policy development and implementation. Persuasion as a mechanism is particularly relevant in governance network settings, given that deliberative theory rests on a premise of the transformation of preferences among actors along the path to consensus (Young, 2000). This premise of transformation is implicit in virtually all network research. Yet some, including public administration scholar Evert Lindquist (1992), warn that experts and professionals in such networks can impede learning if public managers do not design institutional arrangements appropriate to the external environment. Scholars nonetheless suggest that governance network activity has consequences for policy because various actors exposed to different experiences, new research, and other activities in other jurisdictions, will promote such experiences and ideas within the network (Mintrom, 1997; Mintrom & Vergari, 1998). Various scholars employ the concept of "policy learning" as a mechanism for understanding change in network or deliberative contexts (e.g., Lindquist, 1992; May, 1992; Sabatier, 1987; Sabatier & Jenkins-Smith, 1993), but this is in fact an indicator of the process of persuasion rather than a mechanism of change.

Highly institutionalized and inclusive governance networks create a venue that facilitates the process of persuasion among policy actors with distinct perspectives and arguments about policy problems and solutions, and the creation of this venue, I theorize, can drive policy innovation and system coordination. Persuasive political speech rests exclusively neither in the domain of rational argumentation nor the domain of emotionally charged pleas, but rather in some combination thereof (Triadafilopoulos, 1999). Indeed, confrontation among diverse actors in a network "can be a potentially productive learning process" (Lindquist, 1992, p. 148). All policy actors have cognitive models – informed by their education, professional, and personal experience – that map causes of policy problems and their best solutions. These cognitive models are subject to confrontation and

FIGURE 2.1   Embedded theoretical frameworks

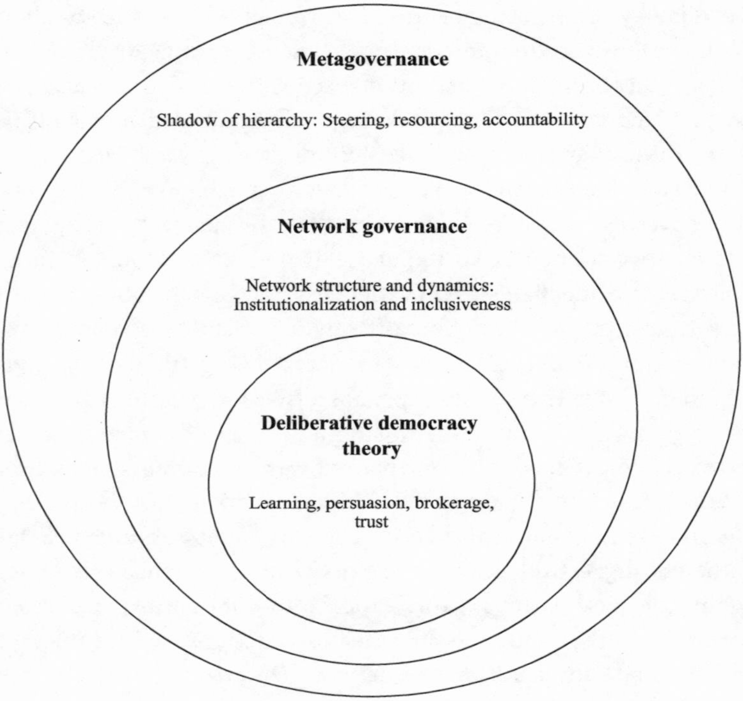

Metagovernance

Shadow of hierarchy: Steering, resourcing, accountability

Network governance

Network structure and dynamics:
Institutionalization and inclusiveness

Deliberative democracy
theory

Learning, persuasion, brokerage,
trust

challenge in deliberative sites like governance networks when diverse actors are tasked with collaborative decision making.

My basic argument regarding causal mechanisms as the linkages between governance network and policy development is this: brokerage and persuasion are emergent and dynamic properties of more institutionalized and inclusive networks, and they stimulate policy innovation and system coordination. Critically, though, while these two mechanisms explain why governance networks matter to policy development, this is all contingent on the metagovernance context.

Figure 2.1 presents the superimposition of theoretical concepts introduced above. Metagovernance, a macro-level concept, refers to the context under which governance networks are designed and evolve. The state, as metagovernor, may provide some decision-making autonomy to governance networks, while maintaining a "shadow of hierarchy" (a concept first characterized by political economist Bob Jessop [1998, p. 38]) to ensure that traditional mechanisms of accountability and democratic legitimacy are retained. Metagovernance is key to differentiating between exogenous and endogenous determinants of network performance – respectively, that which network managers have control over and that which is primarily dependent on participants and their behaviour within the network. Embedded in the overarching metagovernance framework, at the meso-level, is traditional governance network theory, where networks are conceptualized in terms of structural and relational (agency) dimensions as key determinants of policy development. Finally, embedded within traditional theory are concepts derived from deliberative democracy theory, which serve as a guide to the micro-level dimensions of network activity. Deliberative democracy theoretical concepts – learning, persuasion, brokerage, and trust-building – help address a key weakness in network governance theory: the underconceptualization and measurement of the practice of network governance. Networks are fundamentally about people and their relationships, so these need to be central to the integrated framework.

Network Governance and Public Policy

To complete the theoretical framework, we must link metagovernance, network governance, and deliberative democracy concepts to public policy outputs, since policy development and implementation is the primary motivating interest in most governance network research. As already noted, the dimensions of policy that are of primary interest in this study are policy innovation and system coordination, both of which are particularly important in the domain of homelessness, since they have been linked explicitly to an effective policy response. That is, innovative approaches and a coordinated system of programs will most effectively reduce the extent and severity of homelessness (Gaetz et al., 2014; Hulchanski, 2002).[7] Indeed, innovation and coordination are critical dimensions in virtually all policy areas; therefore, this research has application potential beyond the issue of homelessness.

Policy innovation can be defined as the creation or importation of experimental policies that break from conventional approaches to addressing a policy problem. The connection between governance networks and policy innovation rests on the theoretical premise put forward that the inclusion of new and diverse actors in an institutionalized space in the policy process can reset conventional thinking and practices on a policy issue (Borins,

2008; Considine et al., 2009). Public management researcher Fariborz Damanpour (1991), in an early meta-analysis of studies on policy innovation, found that innovation was stifled by a high degree of centralization in the decision-making process (see also Crouch et al., 2004; Lundvall, 1992). Network governance is seen by some as a pathway to collaborative innovation in public policy-making and implementation, an alternative to either traditional bureaucratic management or more market-oriented new public management structures (Hartley, 2005). Others, however, have warned us of the perils of joint-decision traps and lowest-common-denominator decision making when many actors are involved (Klijn & Koppenjan, 2004; Scharpf, 1997).

Policy innovation can include introducing experimental or pilot-tested policies, importing new ideas from other jurisdictions, or simply trying unconventional approaches. Funding more shelter spaces, coordinating food banks, and implementing clean socks programs are not innovative because they typify conventional responses by government and civil society. In contrast, homeless outreach pilot projects, safe-injection sites, and homeless emergency action teams are innovative; not only are they unconventional responses to the problem, but they shift the goal from managing homelessness to reducing it (City of Vancouver, 2009b). For policy innovations to be identified and linked to governance networks across the three cities under investigation, one of the following four criteria must be met: the governance network introduced new policy at the local level, drove policy innovation at a senior government level, funded innovative homeless programs, or initiated new ways of governing and organizing the sector. Policy innovations not linked to the governance networks – that is, introduced by a premier, a mayor, or the bureaucracy – will also be identified to ensure a comprehensive picture of homelessness policy activity during the period under investigation.

In addition to policy innovation, system coordination is a key dimension of the response to homelessness, particularly since many issues or social problems touch (in fact, feed into) the issue of homelessness, including those addressed by the systems of child welfare, criminal justice, and mental health. The coordination of these various systems such that a coherent policy framework exists without major disjunctures or cracks through which vulnerable individuals and families can fall is essential to improving policy outcomes (Doberstein & Nichols, 2016; Foster-Fishman, Nowell, & Yang, 2007; Gaetz, Gulliver, & Richter, 2014). That governance networks can contribute positively to system coordination in complex and multi-level domains is often a fundamental premise of the scholarship, although it is rarely articulated in theoretical terms. Public policy scholar Eugene Bardach (1998, p. 11), in his path-breaking work on interagency collaboration, hypothesizes that "substantial public value is being lost to insufficient collaboration in the public sector." Reflecting on network governance, B. Guy Peters (2007, p. 74) contends that "while individual programs must be made to work well, so too must the assembly of programs in government as a whole. At a minimum the programs within a particular area of policy should work together effectively." Thus, for implementation scholars like Peters, policy (or system) coordination is one of the important tasks for governance networks. Though most network scholars espouse the claim that governance networks can solve coordination problems, some argue that this depends, in part, on network structure and design. As political economist Grahame Thompson and colleagues (1991, p. 15) suggest, "a possible disadvantage for networks is that very large-scale coordination via informal means becomes extremely difficult as the range of social actors expands" (see also Goldsmith & Eggers, 2001).

System coordination is therefore defined as a policy framework that covers the spectrum of needs of the target population – in a service and geographic sense – and whose policies work in a cohesive fashion (i.e., do not work at cross purposes).[8] System coordination will be identified in each governance network examined in the following chapters using the two criteria of policy coordination (the intersecting systems associated with homelessness work harmoniously) and program coordination (the suite of services is consistent with needs and duplication is avoided). System coordination is a critical feature of public policy for both scholars and practitioners, whose aim is not to homogenize policy or reduce experimentation but rather to ensure competence and effectiveness in complex policy domains with many moving parts and institutional silos. Thus, "coordination implies the bringing into a relationship other disparate activities and events" such that "disjunctures can be eliminated" (Thompson et al., 1991, p. 4). Coordination is about smoothing over potentially conflicting objectives and actions of agents and agencies in complex policy fields, but it does not necessarily involve the imposition of a single policy instrument or philosophy. The public administration literature has long engaged with the pathologies associated with institutional silos (Aucoin, 1997; Pierre, 1998), and homelessness is a policy issue involving several levels of government and even more bureaucratic agencies and departments, with a considerable role for the charitable sector and civil society.

Theory and the Eight Governance Networks

We are now in a position to place the governance networks under investigation into the integrated framework that guides their analysis in the forthcoming chapters. The sample of governance networks under investigation here exhibit interesting variation along the dimensions conceptualized in the theoretical framework. This variation is essential to demonstrate and isolate how governance network properties and dynamics stimulate policy innovation and system coordination – the principal aim of this study. Through controlled comparison of the eight governance networks, we can identify the extent to which the governance network – that is, its characteristics and dynamics – is responsible for the most effective homelessness policy responses over the past twenty years.

Network Institutionalization

Recall that a key structural feature of a governance network is its degree of institutionalization, which includes its role in the policy process, its meeting frequency, and its degree of integration with relevant players in the policy community. Existing theory suggests that a highly institutionalized network is more likely to be consequential to policy development than a weakly institutionalized one (Sørensen & Torfing, 2007c). I have chosen five criteria assembled from leading network scholarship (Agranoff, 2012; Holbeche, 2005; Rethemeyer & Hatmaker, 2008) to establish the degree of institutionalization of a governance network. In addition to the three most important criteria – does the network have a decision-making function, a strategic-planning function, and regular meeting intervals (defined as at least six times per year)? – I also examine the official elected leadership and whether the membership represents all levels of government.

Table 2.1 presents the eight governance networks in ranked order according to their degree of institutionalization. VAN-main and CAL-CHF are the most institutionalized, since they both meet regularly with membership from all levels of government and they have decision-making and strategic-planning functions. In contrast, TO-main is the least institutionalized: although it has a strategic-planning function, it suffers from limited government membership and decision-making autonomy, and it does not meet regularly. TO-main, in contrast to all of the other networks, is more of consultative governance network, with its activities heavily constrained by the City of Toronto bureaucracy.

TABLE 2.1
The level of institutionalization of the eight governance networks

Network	Institutional features					
	Decision-making function	Strategic-planning function	Regular meetings (6 times/ year)	Membership from all levels of government	Offical elected leadership	Institutional-ization ranking
VAN-main	✓	✓	✓	✓		Highest
CAL-CHF	✓	✓	✓	✓		Highest
CAL-main	✓	✓	✓			High
VAN-Ab	✓	✓	✓			High
TO-Ab	✓	✓	✓			High
TO-emerg		✓	✓		✓	Medium
VAN-emerg		✓	✓			Low
TO-main		✓				Lowest

Network Inclusiveness

As outlined above, the second critical feature of a governance network is its degree of inclusiveness of diverse actors and organizations from both government and civil society. Differentiating the eight governance networks according to the size and inclusivity of their membership is critical: the more relevant government and civil society players there are at the table, the more likely it is that the governance network can tap into all of the disparate pieces of the policy domain. To generate a measure of network size and inclusivity, I sampled all of the governance network gatherings in 2014.[9] Using meeting attendance records (to ascertain active members), I counted and averaged the network membership over the year and coded members into six organizational categories: government, service provider, other networks, women, Aboriginal people, and youth. Figure 2.2 shows a clear correlation between the size of the network and its diversity. VAN-main, TO-emerg, and VAN-emerg are the largest and most diverse governance networks, with approximately twenty-five active members, followed by CAL-main and CAL-CHF. TO-main and TO-Ab are smaller and less diverse governance networks, with fourteen and nine active members, respectively.

FIGURE 2.2   Average size and diversity of active membership in the eight
governance networks

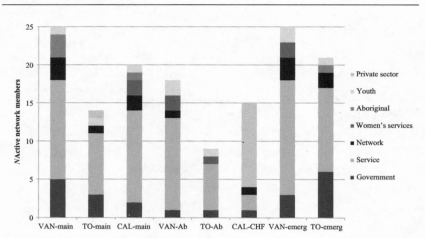

Theory-Driven Hypotheses

The key structural and relational features of governance networks – institutionalization and inclusivity, respectively – can be brought together on
a two-dimensional matrix to generate the hypotheses based on this new
theory of network governance, first in the abstract and then with the eight
governance networks under investigation. Figure 2.3 places inclusivity on
the x-axis and institutionalization on the y-axis and specifies the quadrant
in which we expect to see high policy innovation and system coordination.
The first hypothesis is that more institutionalized and more inclusive governance networks will generate or contribute to more innovative policy,
since more inclusivity means that diverse perspectives and identification
of emerging trends will be advanced, and greater institutionalization will
correlate with more integration into decision structures that can implement innovative policies and programs.[10] The second hypothesis is that
more institutionalized and inclusive governance networks will generate or
contribute to system coordination and policy alignment, since governance
networks that are connected to key sites of decision making and integrated
with other systems will be better positioned to fill service gaps and coordinate the homelessness response more effectively.

Based on these hypotheses and on the above analysis of the eight governance networks, these networks can be placed on the matrix of institutionalization and inclusivity, as illustrated in Figure 2.4.

FIGURE 2.3 Hypothesized linkages between institutionalization, inclusivity, and policy innovation and system coordination

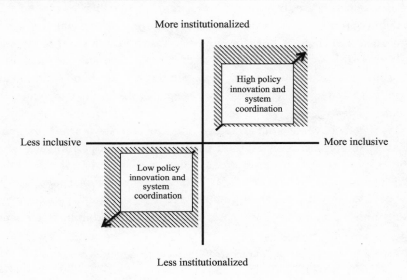

FIGURE 2.4 The eight governance networks mapped according to degree of institutionalization and inclusivity

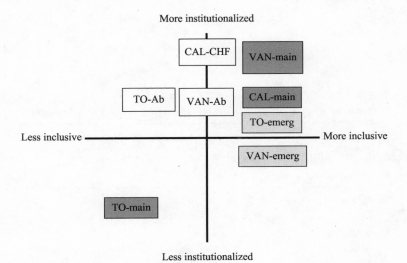

Mapping the eight governance networks according to their degree of institutionalization and inclusivity allows us to put forward specific (and thus falsifiable) hypotheses regarding their relationship to policy innovation and system coordination. As articulated above, however, the metagovernance context is also thought to shape the performance of the governance networks, regardless of their levels of institutionalization and inclusiveness. That is, a particular metagovernance context may foster or stifle policy innovation and system coordination, as represented by the two arrows in Figure 2.5 below.

As noted above, two dimensions of metagovernance appear to be particularly important variables affecting the stability and performance of a governance network: the institutional policy space of the network and the style of leadership (see *Table 2.2*). With respect to institutional policy space, the governance network can be granted a relatively open policy space, operating quite autonomously, or a constrained mandate within limited policy

FIGURE 2.5   The mediating influence of the metagovernance context

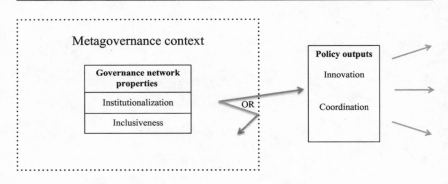

TABLE 2.2
Metagovernance typology based on leadership type and policy space

	Institutional policy space (structure)	
Metagovernor leadership style (agency)	Narrow	Expansive
Cooperative	*Administrative* metagovernance	*Dynamic* metagovernance
Contentious	*Straitjacket* metagovernance	*Volatile* metagovernance

space. The leadership dimension captures the methods of steering used by metagovernors, which can powerfully structure network activities to productive ends if they are cooperative or can result in serious disruption and conflict if they are contentious.

Table 2.2 outlines a typology of metagovernance that captures the central dimensions of the context under which governance networks operate and offers four metagovernance types. Administrative metagovernance provides a governance network with a constrained or narrow mandate and offers leadership that is cooperative and pragmatic and is specified in formal and practical terms. This type of metagovernance facilitates a stable network in terms of function and productivity.

Dynamic metagovernance affords a governance network a relatively unconstrained mandate and encourages a cooperative relationship between the metagovernance leadership and governance network members. Although the metagovernor keeps a hand on the rudder, the network can paddle at its own pace and influence the ultimate destination. The accountability structures in this context serve to monitor activity but do not suffocate the network's activity. The result is a metagovernance context in which the governance network is permitted policy space within which to explore new terrain, but it is kept from driving off a cliff.

Straitjacket metagovernance gives a governance network a constrained or narrow mandate and is characterized by a contentious style of leadership vis-à-vis network actors. This tends to result in strained personal relationships between the metagovernor and the network actors. We would expect governance networks operating in a straitjacket metagovernance context to hobble along rather than thrive. The final category, volatile metagovernance, affords a governance network a relatively unconstrained mandate but is characterized by a contentious style of leadership. We would expect this metagovernance context to have innovative potential, given the expansive policy space, but to be threatened by instability, because of the contentious leadership style.

Why are these types of metagovernance important in terms of theory? As established above, a governance network does not exist in a vacuum: its formation, mandate, structure, membership, and accountability mechanisms are shaped by existing (and evolving) institutional structures and metagovernors, both of which can have a substantial impact on its policy outputs. That is, two governance networks that have similar degrees of institutionalization and inclusivity but that differ in their metagovernance context can produce profoundly different policy outputs. In other words,

FIGURE 2.6 Hypothesized effects of dynamic and straitjacket metagovernance on policy outputs

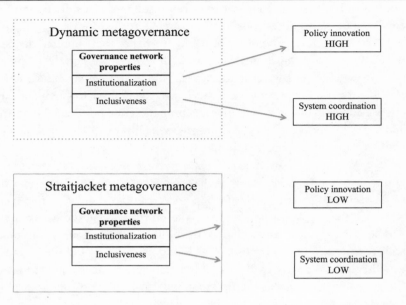

it is not simply the internal features of the governance network that shape its potential to drive policy innovation but also its metagovernance context. This is, however, not explicitly modelled in theoretical terms in previous network governance research.

Figure 2.6 illustrates the potential for the metagovernance context to shape the policy outputs in governance networks. I contend that if the internal properties – institutionalization and inclusiveness – of a particular governance network were held constant, a dynamic metagovernance context would contribute to high policy innovation and system coordination, given the wide policy space and the cooperative leadership style, while a straitjacket metagovernance context would dramatically reduce these policy outputs, since governance network activity would be heavily constrained and contentious.

The other two types of metagovernance – administrative and volatile – are predicted to have a less uniform effect on policy output. Because administrative metagovernance offers the governance network a narrow mandate or policy space, we might expect that policy innovation would be stifled. But the cooperative leadership of administrative metagovernance, which would contribute to system coordination by effectively steering the network towards coherent policy outputs, could encourage policy innovation, despite the narrow space within which the network operates. Put that same governance network in a volatile metagovernance context, however, and the policy output trajectory may change, though in similarly contingent terms. Part of what makes a metagovernance context volatile is the expansive policy space granted to the network, which is likely to contribute to policy innovation. But since the governance network may be in disarray because of the contentious leadership style, policy innovations may be stifled. Because administrative and volatile metagovernance are more contingent theoretical categories than the other two metagovernance types, their causal effects need more empirical examination.

3

Vancouver: Coordinated Regional Networks

Vancouver has long been proclaimed, by a variety of outlets, as the "most livable city" in North America and among the most livable in the world, a proclamation that has received a mixed response of appreciation and eye rolling from Canadians across the land. Notwithstanding the obvious subjectivity and arbitrariness of such city rankings, many Vancouverites are proud of this standing but also recognize that it masks a fundamental truth about Vancouver: it is part of an urban region full of contradictions. Vancouver is the most unaffordable city in Canada in terms of housing, yet it is not merely a city of the wealthy. In fact, estimates of average GDP per capita from Statistics Canada put Vancouver among the lowest of the major metropolitan areas in Canada (Brown & Rispoli, 2014). In the midst of a beautiful natural environment and stunning displays of wealth is a large group of people for whom the "most livable city" declaration constitutes a bizarre parody.

The Downtown Eastside (DTES) of Vancouver is unlike any neighbourhood in Canada. Once the central commercial district of the city, since the 1980s, it has been characterized by an extreme concentration of poverty, drug use, crime, violence, and homelessness. One almost feels transported to another country, much less wealthy than Canada, in this small neighbourhood. Yet the DTES is only the most obvious manifestation of larger problems in society brought on by macro-economic restructuring, laissez-faire government policy, and personal traumas that we, as a society, have allowed to spin out of control. At the time of writing, however, in 2015, the DTES was changing rapidly. In a city characterized most famously by rapturous real estate demand and gentrification, the neighbourhood appears to be next in line. In twenty years, the DTES almost certainly will not be the troubled area we see today but will instead resemble the adjacent ritzy Yaletown and Coal Harbour neighbourhoods. Does that mean that homelessness, extreme poverty, and victimization will have been cured? Hardly.

While homelessness and extreme poverty are concentrated in the DTES, all parts of the larger city and region grapple with these issues – especially since the DTES itself has been trending towards unaffordability and gentrification. The Metro Vancouver region has a homelessness problem, and its unique, decentralized governance context means that cooperation across municipal governments is required to address the issue. If the problem remains unresolved and trends continue, Vancouver's homelessness problem will become adjacent Burnaby's or North Vancouver's problem. Because policy makers in Metro Vancouver know this, they have an interest in collaborating and coordinating their policy responses with a number of governance networks, the development of which is a key focus of this chapter.

I begin the governance and policy analysis of homelessness and affordable housing in Vancouver with an outline of the institutional architecture of governance among all three levels of government. These institutional structures and historical trajectories have shaped the metagovernance that influences the performance and policy outputs of the governance networks operating in this region. By going back to the early 1990s, before any of the governance networks were created, we can establish a baseline from which to measure policy change in Vancouver in the past twenty years. Three key homelessness governance networks have emerged since that time. In this chapter, I identify their contributions to policy innovation and system coordination and measure them against the theory of network governance outlined in the previous chapter.

The Political-Institutional Architecture

Among the many dimensions of homelessness are those related to mental health, drug policy, affordable housing, poverty, criminal justice and victimization, and neighbourhood. This means that the issue is relevant to all levels of government in Canada, but it also reaches across many government departments and ministries within each level (Blau, 1992; O'Reilly Fleming, 1993). As is common in federations, particularly comparatively

decentralized ones like Canada, there is considerable variation among jurisdictions in terms of which level of government possesses key policy levers
and how each level organizes its fiscal relationships vis-à-vis homelessness
and affordable housing.

While the *Constitution Act, 1982,* fails to provide a clear demarcation of
legal jurisdiction regarding homelessness, many of the constituent elements
of the issue are divided among the federal and provincial (and by extension,
local) governments. For example, the federal government possesses unilateral power to legislate on criminal activity and drug policy; the provincial
governments legislate on social assistance, housing, mental health policy,
and child welfare; and the local governments legislate the neighbourhood
dimensions of homelessness, like zoning and provision of housing, shelter, and community services. Some provincial governments have retained
central policy responsibility for homelessness and housing (e.g., British
Columbia and Quebec), while others have downloaded key responsibilities
to the local level (e.g., Ontario and Alberta). Furthermore, the interrelated
nature of many of the forces that contribute to generating and sustaining
homelessness means that the various governments have many intergovernmental policy and fiscal relationships.

The most significant dimensions of policy derived from the federal government relate to affordable housing and homelessness programs through
which cities can gain access to funds. Historically, the federal government
has been a major player in the provision of affordable housing (Shapcott,
2007a). Budget deficits and rising concerns over national debt in the 1980s,
however, coupled with increased implementation of neoliberal ideas surrounding the role of government resulted in a gradually reduced federal
role in affordable housing provision (Carter, 1997). The federal retreat was
completed in 1993, when the Chrétien government's budget withdrew funding for all new affordable housing development (with a few exceptions for
women fleeing violence and on-reserve housing). The policy change was
dramatic: from an annual provision of twenty-five thousand new social
housing units in 1983, the number dropped to zero in 1993 (Hulchanski,
2002). The time period of analysis for the current study begins in 1995, in
the context of full federal retreat from affordable housing provision.

Despite existing in the same federal constitutional context as Ontario
and Alberta, British Columbia has used rather different institutional structures for and policy approaches to the issue of homelessness over time, including a different response to the 1990s federal government spending cuts.
At that time, the province was led by an NDP government committed to

an interventionist role for government in social policy, although it adopted welfare reform and a tightening of social assistance eligibility characteristic of centre-right parties in other jurisdictions. The BC response to the federal government withdrawal from affordable housing was to maintain some construction of such housing by contributing more provincial funds.[1] The most critical government institution as it relates to homelessness and housing in British Columbia is not a ministry or department but a Crown agency called BC Housing (established in 1967), whose mandate is to fulfill the provincial government's commitment to the development, management, and administration of subsidized housing (BC Housing, annual reports, 2014). BC Housing provides subsidized housing options across the housing continuum, from emergency shelters, transitional supportive housing (to support those with mental health and addiction issues), and independent social housing to rent assistance in the private market (BC Housing, annual reports, 1997, 2010, 2014). In short, BC Housing controls the vast majority of housing and homelessness expenditures in the province, but the agency partners with municipal governments to leverage resources for major projects and programs.

At the local level, the institutional architecture in Vancouver is likewise distinct from that of Toronto and Calgary. In additional to municipal government, there is a regional government system, the Greater Vancouver Regional District – more commonly referred to as Metro Vancouver – which comprises twenty-one municipalities and one First Nations government in the Lower Mainland. Metro Vancouver was not involved in homelessness in 1995, but as we will see, its role in this issue has become more substantive in the last twenty years. The City of Vancouver is the largest city in Metro Vancouver, and it has, historically, been the most active one in the homelessness policy domain, although cities such as Surrey have increasingly become active on the issue in recent years. The City of Vancouver has long used its zoning and regulatory powers over land use to assist in the development of affordable housing. In 1988, for example, the City introduced a policy called "inclusionary zoning," which requires major rezoning of lands to multi-unit residential use to include 20 percent affordable housing (either 20 percent of units developed or the equivalent in cash to a city fund). The City estimates that this policy has created 1,360 units of affordable housing, although this number could have been much higher (3,450 units) if the City did not allow developers exemption from this policy if the 20 percent requirement makes the project economically unfeasible (City of Vancouver, 2009a, 2010a). The City of Vancouver has long funded community centres and services that support vulnerable citizens, both in the Downtown Eastside (e.g., the Carnegie Community Centre) and elsewhere.

Establishing a Baseline: The 1995 Policy Context

Although all levels of government are touched by homelessness, in Vancouver, as in other Canadian cities, the year 1995 was characterized more by a policy vacuum than a multi-level response to homelessness. The federal government had just walked away from its four-decade-long commitment to building affordable housing in Canada, the BC government was struggling to maintain its investments but could not keep up, and there was no policy plan at any level of local government in Metro Vancouver. And in just a few years, Vancouver, like all other major Canadian cities, would face an unprecedented homelessness crisis.

A major research task force commissioned by the BC government documented many significant systemic policy gaps at the turn of the millennium: no comprehensive regional or municipal housing or homelessness policies or plans, insufficient and restrictive emergency shelter spaces, a rapid loss of rooming housing due to redevelopment, few effective discharge protocols and resources at state institutions like correctional and mental health facilities, and few prevention-based mechanisms related to homelessness (Eberle, 2001). The minimal policy framework that was in place was focused on emergency shelters, with the charitable sector pulling most of the weight. And finally, decision makers had very little demographic or situational data about the homeless population that could help them craft policy responses. If one were to characterize a policy framework in human terms, this would be Vancouver's policy at rock bottom, and the exploding homelessness crisis on the streets in the late 1990s – although unfortunately not unique to Vancouver – was its ugly result.

Creating Governance Networks

At the onset of the homelessness crisis in Vancouver, homeless shelter providers, in 1998, formed a regional network, the Greater Vancouver Shelter Strategy (VAN-emerg; GVSS, in citations), to coordinate an emergency response to homelessness, particularly during the winter months, when shelter spaces were increasingly filled beyond capacity. The principal task in the early years of VAN-emerg was to increase communication and coordination among shelter providers to ensure that services were accessible to target populations during inclement weather (GVSS, minutes, 2005). The creation of the network was driven from the service sector level, although BC Housing has provided in-kind secretarial support and local governments have provided research and coordination funds to assist in the operations of the network (GVSS, minutes, 2006). In contrast to both VAN-main and VAN-Ab, VAN-emerg is less of a policy-focused network and more of a coordination network, but over the years, it has expanded its mandate and role in the region (GVSS, minutes, 2010; GVSS, 2012). The need to strategize and coordinate during cold and wet weather remains a priority, but the mandate of the network now extends to more general policy planning and coordination of shelter services (year-round), systematic service tracking to inform decision makers, and the promotion of sharing resources and expertise among shelter providers. Membership consists of nearly thirty organizations – all of which are actively involved in meeting emergency shelter needs, whether in providing, funding, or otherwise associating with shelter services – as well as local and provincial government bureaucrats.

From a metagovernance perspective, while it is not an allocator of funds, VAN-emerg nonetheless requires metagovernance resources and steering to bring the various actors together, to marshal data, to issue reports, and to coordinate the activities of the shelter providers in Metro Vancouver. Historically, the provincial government, via BC Housing, has been a core source of funding for VAN-emerg, providing funds to operationalize the network and making in-kind contributions in the form of administrative tasks, meeting space, and the production and analysis of statistics for VAN-emerg and the shelter sector.[2] BC Housing is, therefore, the metagovernor for VAN-emerg. There are two principal means through which VAN-emerg influences policy vis-à-vis the metagovernor: responding to and implementing BC Housing policy and shaping BC Housing policy development.

Although BC Housing does not, in a formal sense, control VAN-emerg activity, it is able to steer some of its activity by virtue of the network's key role in the shelter sector, as well as through its funding of VAN-emerg activity (GVSS, 2010). BC Housing, as the metagovernor, is a key member of the network; it is involved in all VAN-emerg meetings and important subcommittees, effectively steering the network from the inside. Steering is generally done informally, in contrast to the other networks, which also have bureaucrats involved in the network, but some steering is also conducted through formal administrative structures like contribution agreements[3] and other contracts to keep the network activity in a space that can be controlled by the metagovernor. The relationship between BC Housing (the metagovernor) and VAN-emerg is enhanced because high-level BC Housing bureaucrats were previously employed by agencies associated with VAN-emerg and thus understand the internal dynamics of the network and have high trust relations with VAN-emerg members.[4] As a result, VAN-emerg operates in a dynamic metagovernance context, which is hypothesized to facilitate policy innovation and system coordination.

VAN-emerg may have been the first homelessness governance network to take shape in Vancouver, but it is not the only one. The federal government, having seen some alarming trends in the growth of the homeless population in major Canadian cities since its decision to withdraw almost completely from affordable housing provision, decided to tiptoe back into the issue in a very targeted manner and with modest investments. The Regional Steering Committee on Homelessness (VAN-main) is a governance network initially created under the auspices of the Government of Canada's National Homelessness Initiative, launched in 1999, which mandated the formation of a community advisory board (i.e., a governance network), consisting of civil society and government members, to create a community plan to address homelessness and to access and allocate federal funding (Greater Vancouver RSCH, 2003). VAN-main has an expansive and diverse membership that includes representatives from local, regional, provincial, and federal government administrators; health authorities; charitable groups and foundations; Aboriginal peoples; and service providers. No elected officials are actively involved in the governance network. Since 2010, VAN-main has been formally attached to the Metro Vancouver regional government, based on the recognition that homelessness exists in the broader metropolitan area (not just the City of Vancouver) and that a regional approach is required to make effective policy interventions (Greater Vancouver RSCH, 2007).

The design of the National Homelessness Initiative (renewed under Prime Minister Stephen Harper in 2007 and renamed the Homelessness Partnering Strategy) was heavily influenced by the newly appointed federal coordinator on homelessness, Claudette Bradshaw, who, in 1999, travelled the country and heard from homelessness advocates, service providers, and local governments that communities should play a key role in crafting the homelessness response, with the federal government serving as a funder and capacity enhancer but not as the key government in charge (Doberstein, 2012; Smith, 2004). As a result, Bradshaw developed the federal intervention such that the role of civil society actors would be institutionalized alongside local government actors, via local governance networks (what the

NHI called community advisory boards), to prioritize and allocate federal government dollars (rather than a direct transfer of federal funds to provinces or municipalities). Access to this money thus required the formation of a local governance network consisting of diverse civil society actors ranging from shelter and affordable housing providers, to mental health organizations, to advocacy groups. This network was to exchange ideas on policy responses to end homelessness in the specific locality and was required to develop a community plan to address homelessness, a plan that would set out the strategic priorities and serve as a framework to determine funding allocations to specific programs and services. Notwithstanding this federal government requirement, the national framework had considerable flexibility in terms of the design of these governance networks and the activities in which they engaged, accepting the unique governance context and policy priorities identified in each locality. This metagovernance flexibility becomes very apparent when we compare VAN-main with CAL-main and TO-main. The existence of these three networks, all of which have functioned as the NHI-mandated Community Advisory Committee since 2000, provide an opportunity to analyze a natural experiment in governance that has unfolded since that time.

Most importantly from a metagovernance perspective, cities in Greater Vancouver are afforded flexibility in the design of their governance network institutions. The NHI allowed cities some choice among several models for the administration of the program. They could form a "community entity" (usually via a prominent community group or the local government itself) and assume full decision-making autonomy as well as full legal and financial liability for homelessness investments, or they could choose the "shared delivery" model, whereby the Government of Canada would receive recommendations from the local governance network and formally vet and approve programs and services; rarely, if ever, does the federal government veto decisions from the local level. Vancouver chose a different model from Toronto and Calgary, and these early decisions around governance relationships reflect policy legacies of the provincial governments and have shaped how power is exercised within the governance network vis-à-vis the associated municipal government. In contrast to most other large cities in Canada, which define the boundaries of the "community" as the municipality (Toronto and Calgary included), the approach in Vancouver is unique in its regional scope. That is, federal funds allocated to Vancouver are distributed throughout the twenty-one municipalities of Metro Vancouver rather than to a single municipality, as is the case for Toronto and Calgary.

Thus, rather than the City of Vancouver conducting homelessness policy planning and implementation within its boundaries, a group of regional and municipal government and civil society actors, which I call VAN-main, was formed as required by the Government of Canada, its metagovernor. VAN-main was established based on the recognition that homelessness exists in the broader metropolitan area and that a regional, coordinated approach is required to make effective policy interventions (Greater Vancouver RSCH, minutes, 2003). From 2000 to 2011, VAN-main operated under the "shared delivery" model rather than the "community entity" model, which was adopted by Toronto and Calgary in 2000 but was used by VAN-main only after 2011.[5] The only practical consequence, for our purposes, was that until 2011, the Government of Canada held final decision-making authority in Metro Vancouver, whereas in Toronto, that authority was transferred, by administrative agreement, to the City of Toronto, and in Calgary, it was delegated by the City to the Calgary Homeless Foundation, a private sector foundation created the year before the NHI's launch by energy sector executives concerned with homelessness in the city.

The most important consequence, as we will see in the next chapter, is that the TO-main homelessness-related policy priorities and allocations had to be consistent with those of Toronto City Council, which functions as the network's community entity, whereas in Metro Vancouver, the City of Vancouver was only one of approximately thirty government and civil society members on VAN-main. The pressure for TO-main to conform to Toronto City Council policy helps to explain certain policy choices and governance patterns of TO-main over the years. Effectively, the federal government program in Toronto was municipalized and the one in Calgary privatized, yielding different metagovernance contexts than the one in which VAN-main operated, which affords more autonomy to the governance network. Therefore, one significant structural difference shaped by the metagovernance contexts is that TO-main has historically been more constrained in its policy space than have VAN-main and CAL-main. VAN-main operated in a dynamic metagovernance context, with an empty policy space at the regional level and the ability to carve out its own identity and role, whereas TO-main was inserted into an administrative metagovernance context, with a pre-existing and active policy space in Toronto.

The third governance network that emerged in Vancouver was the Aboriginal Homelessness Steering Committee (VAN-Ab), which, like VAN-main, was created in 2000 in conjunction with the federal government

National Homelessness Initiative. In addition to requiring the formation of community advisory boards, the NHI required the creation of governance networks of Aboriginal civil society actors to develop and implement local strategies for Aboriginal homelessness.

The metagovernance of VAN-Ab by the Government of Canada demonstrates just how powerfully a metagovernance context shapes governance network performance and stability. While the local Aboriginal homelessness governance networks were created under the same framework as VAN-main, the federal government designed them differently. Concerned that local Aboriginal community organizations would not have the capacity to organize, strategize, and implement homelessness policies and programs without an existing institutional base (like a municipal government), the Government of Canada simply attached the Aboriginal homelessness component of the NHI to an existing federal labour-market-focused program called the Urban Aboriginal Strategy (UAS).[6] The Aboriginal homelessness networks thus served as an enhancement to existing Aboriginal governance networks in selected cities.

This choice by the federal government to funnel the Aboriginal homelessness funding through an existing delivery structure with a labour market focus rather than through a structure exclusively dedicated to homelessness proved to severely and inappropriately constrain the activities of local Aboriginal decision makers (Human Resources and Social Development Canada [HRSDC], 2003). This was true across the country, not only in Metro Vancouver. Basic rules and operating procedures set forth by the metagovernor had large consequences. For example, since the Aboriginal homelessness funding flowed through the administrative institutions and rules designed for labour market programs, the local Aboriginal homelessness governance networks were only able to set policy and allocate funds to homelessness services and programs with a labour market dimension; they could not allocate funds to housing projects or programs. As a result, across Canada, only 20 percent of Aboriginal-dedicated NHI funds were allocated by July 2002, compared to 85 percent of the funding granted to community advisory board governance networks, like VAN-main (HRSDC, 2003). Thus, there was a fundamental disconnect between what Aboriginal organizations on the ground proposed within local governance networks as relevant services and programs to address Aboriginal homelessness and what the metagovernor allowed these networks to prioritize and fund. We will see that this straitjacket type of metagovernance seriously impinged on VAN-Ab's ability simply to operate, let alone innovate public policy.

To the credit of the metagovernor, when Government of Canada bureaucrats learned of this disconnect and dysfunction (which they had created) caused by Aboriginal homelessness funding being situated within a labour market program, it changed the administrative framework to be similar to that of the community advisory board homelessness governance networks (Smith, 2004). But even under the new terms and conditions of the Aboriginal homelessness funding stream, vestiges of the previous metagovernance framework remained, and new complications were introduced. Unlike the community advisory board governance networks, the Aboriginal networks were not required to develop a community plan that would guide investments and track progress, and there was no dedicated funding for Aboriginal communities early on to conduct the planning and research needed to make informed choices, although some managed these tasks by channelling program funds for this purpose (HRSDC, 2003, 2009). With the first renewal of the NHI in 2003, the federal government formally separated the Aboriginal homelessness governance networks from the Urban Aboriginal Strategy and henceforth provided dedicated planning funds similar to the community advisory board homelessness governance networks (HRSDC, 2009; Leo & August, 2006, 2009b).

Like VAN-main, the Aboriginal homelessness governance networks are principally metagoverned by bureaucrats and administrative mechanisms rather than by elected officials. A recurring theme in the Aboriginal governance networks is the difficulty they encounter navigating the bureaucratic channels efficiently and effectively. In Vancouver, the relationship between VAN-Ab and federal bureaucrats has been strained over the years. These tensions are the result of VAN-Ab wanting the decision-making autonomy that the NHI is designed to provide and federal bureaucrats needing to ensure that the process, as defined by the metagovernor, is respected. After the initial conflict and dysfunction, the next major conflict arose when local federal bureaucrats became concerned that a truly community-wide process of governance and decision making was not occurring at VAN-Ab and threatened to intervene to reconstitute the membership and governance structures. VAN-Ab membership disagreed with this view and with the heavy-handedness of the Government of Canada (Aboriginal Homelessness Steering Committee [AHSC], minutes, 2002). The conflict was eventually smoothed over, after months of crisis meetings, but it left a lasting distrust and resentment, particularly from VAN-Ab members, who felt that the metagovernor did not respect their autonomy to set policy priorities and make investments (AHSC, minutes, 2002). Even after the structural redesign that came with the renewal of the NHI in 2003, VAN-Ab operates in a constraining administrative metagovernance context rather than in the freer dynamic context that VAN-main enjoys (AHSC, minutes, 2010, 2011).

Applying Theory to Vancouver's Networks

The features of the three Vancouver homelessness governance networks can be distilled along two lines: their internal properties (degree of institutionalization and inclusiveness) and their external properties (their metagovernance contexts). Recall where these three networks lie on the matrix of internal properties: VAN-main is more institutionalized and more inclusive, VAN-emerg is less institutionalized and more inclusive, and VAN-Ab is more institutionalized and neither more nor less inclusive (see Figures 2.3 and 2.4 on page 43).

But situating the Vancouver governance networks on the internal-property matrix gives us only a partial picture. As discussed above, the metagovernance context may have a powerful mediating effect on the performance of governance networks, irrespective of their levels of institutionalization and inclusiveness. Depending on its characteristics, a metagovernance context may foster or stifle policy innovation and system coordination. Figure 2.6 (page 46) articulates this theoretical relationship by contrasting the potential effects of dynamic and straitjacket metagovernance on the outputs of governance networks. Table 3.1 places Vancouver's governance networks in their metagoverance contexts.

With this description and analysis of the three Vancouver networks in mind, we can now determine whether these networks function according to

TABLE 3.1
Metagovernance contexts of Vancouver governance networks

Metagovernor leadership (agency)	Institutional policy space (structure)	
	Narrow	Expansive
Cooperative	*Administrative* metagovernance (VAN-Ab: 2005–15)	*Dynamic* metagovernance (VAN-main, VAN-emerg)
Contentious	*Straitjacket* metagovernance (VAN-Ab: 2000–04)	*Volatile* metagovernance

the predictions of the theory outlined in Chapter 2. This involves tracking policy changes – in particular, policy innovation and system coordination – from 1995 to 2015 and linking them to the governance networks.

Policy Innovation and System Coordination from 1995 to 2015

In measuring and tracking policy innovation and system coordination, it is important to recognize that these policy changes can occur in a variety of ways: for example, they can involve changes in legislation, regulations, funding priorities, or ways of organizing the collective response to homelessness. Policy innovation can thus be both output- and process-oriented (Considine et al., 2009): that is, innovations in the organization of the sector and modes of decision making are as relevant as legislative and regulatory policy outputs. Likewise, system coordination can have a policy dimension (Are policies cohesive?) as well as a program dimension (Is the package of services consistent with needs and is duplication avoided?). Furthermore, innovative policy and system coordination does not occur primarily because of governance network activity; it can also occur through traditional bureaucratic and elected official channels.

Examples of policy innovation and system coordination from 1995 to 2015 were identified by triangulating legislation, policy statements, meeting records, and interviews with key stakeholders at all levels of government and civil society. For each of the three Vancouver governance networks, we examine the policy innovations first, followed by the system coordination.

VAN-main

Integrated governance network theory predicts that VAN-main will generate high levels of policy innovation and system coordination, since it is not only the most institutionalized and inclusive of all the homelessness governance networks under investigation, but it also operates in a dynamic metagovernance context. This prediction is borne out: VAN-main's policy innovation, in the form of new governance approaches or ways of organizing the sector, has been profound. The first major innovation was the reconceptualization of the homelessness problem in Vancouver in regional terms, manifested in the region-wide homelessness policy plan (Greater Vancouver RSCH, 2003). As City of Vancouver planner and former VAN-main member Celine Maboules recalled, "homelessness was not just a [City of] Vancouver problem" or, even more narrowly defined, a Downtown Eastside problem, which were the dominant frames prior to this reconceptualization.[7] Many VAN-main members, when interviewed, pointed to this reconceptualization as one of the earliest and most power- ful innovations of VAN-main.[8] Until this reconceptualization, it was only the City of Vancouver that took homelessness seriously at the local gov- ernment level; the other twenty municipalities in Metro Vancouver had no official policy and offered few, if any, services (Greater Vancouver RSCH, minutes, 2002, 2003). The regional reconceptualization "is actually an innovation ... because the region was otherwise quite fragmented insti- tutionally," said Peter Greenwell, a former planner at Metro Vancouver.[9] Kingsley Okyere, former manager of the Homelessness Secretariat at Metro Vancouver, also noted that other than the City of Vancouver, "no local government was willing to admit the magnitude of the problem in the Lower Mainland."[10]

Not only was the problem no longer simply a Downtown Eastside issue, but, as VAN-main member and former executive director of Lookout Emergency Aid Society Karen O'Shannacery noted, the "regional di- mension and organization brought community people to the table be- cause its scope was big and the potential to create change was big."[11] The most concrete manifestation, on a policy level, of this new governance innovation was that prior to VAN-main, none of the municipalities had homelessness plans, whereas by 2015, nearly all of them had an explicit strategy. Michael Anhorn, former member of VAN-main, also noted a major increase in homelessness awareness: "Few deny homelessness in their Metro Vancouver community; that's a radical change that I really do believe RSCH [VAN-main] has driven, which means they have raised awareness at both the staff levels and the political levels in the municipalities."[12]

This policy innovation is directly related to the positive homelessness out- come trends we see in Metro Vancouver. Over time, services and programs have shifted from a downtown, emergency bias towards a balanced regional coverage of services that avoids pulling individuals out of their home com- munities into the Downtown Eastside, according to Kingsley Okyere.[13] This is confirmed when we consider recent Homelessness Partnering Strategy (HPS, formerly NHI) investments by geography and contrast them with investment patterns in Toronto, as depicted in Table 3.2 below. In Metro Vancouver, we see a tendency to overinvest in the suburban areas at the expense of the core (which the City of Vancouver generally prefers, so as to

TABLE 3.2

HPS investments in Vancouver and Toronto, by area, 2011–14

Area	HPS investments, 2011–14 (% share)	Share of homeless population (%)
Vancouver	44	60
Surrey	16	15
New Westminster	12	5
Maple Ridge	8	4
Other in Metro Vancouver (*n* = 7)	19	16
Toronto (old city)	74	66
North York	15	18
Scarborough	8	5
Etobicoke	4	11

Source: Generated by the author from RSCH (approved applications), 2012; Social Services and Housing Administration, 2012; Greater Vancouver RSCH, 2012b; City of Toronto SNA, 2009.

avoid being a magnet for those seeking services), whereas in Toronto, the investment scheme remains very focused on the downtown core.

Another governance innovation with policy implications (and also a key example of system coordination) at VAN-main is the Metro Vancouver Investors Table, formed in 2012. This idea was the result of learning from Calgary's experience: the Calgary Homeless Foundation is similar to the Investors Table in terms of institutionalization and inclusivity, but the Investors Table is arguably more expansive because it also brings together government and charitable funders in the city so as to leverage more effectively the money spent in the homelessness sector. The formation of a group like this in Metro Vancouver is particularly important not only because of the decentralized authority in the region but also because the provincial government retains key spending and policy authority and thus needs to be brought into discussions and collaborations to achieve funding cohesion.

Meeting minutes from VAN-main reveal that members longed for a more strategic response within the fragmented system of homelessness funders. Individual funders were unlikely to join a partnership in which their autonomy as decision makers might be compromised, but persuasive arguments from the VAN-main membership (many of whom are service providers who feel the system fragmentation most acutely) inspired the funders to join together to coordinate investments. Led by VAN-main, the major funding players in the region – including VAN-main, the Vancity Community Foundation, United Way, the Streetohome Foundation, the Surrey Homelessness and Housing Fund, and BC Housing – meet four times per year to coordinate their homelessness response through the Investors Table. Two of the purported benefits of the Investors Table are the provision of a more centralized site to align homelessness funding more strategically with needs and the opportunity to work together "to generate supplementary resources to address homelessness" (Greater Vancouver RSCH, minutes, 2012). While it is too early to assess the performance of the Investors Table, two key parts of its mandate are to provide leadership on a common vision for funding strategies in Metro Vancouver and to develop a new joint funding stream to complement federal government funding for facilities, programs, and services to end homelessness. If fully implemented, this joint funding stream would represent a considerable innovation in terms of partnership funding, as well as a noteworthy achievement in terms of system coordination (Greater Vancouver RSCH, minutes, 2012). A key measure of success of the Investors Table in the coming years will be the degree to which the independent funders collaborate such that funding priorities shift and realign to fill identified housing and service gaps.

One of the earliest policy choices made by VAN-main was to introduce a homeless count across the region every three years in order to better understand the scale of the problem demographically and regionally so as to assist with policy planning and program evaluation (Greater Vancouver RSCH, 2002). Such counts are now common in cities; in fact, they are now mandated by the federal government for cities that receive federal funds, but this was not the case in the early 2000s. Meeting records and interviews suggest that VAN-main members, although aware of the limitations of the count, were eager to get some hard numbers and that it was the bureaucracy that was less eager to put hard numbers on the exploding homelessness crisis, since those numbers could very well embarrass their political masters (Greater Vancouver RSCH, minutes, 2006). The first homeless count in Vancouver, in 2002, was among the first in Canada (Calgary led in this particular area with a less sophisticated count in the 1990s), and it has since been replicated in cities across the country, including in Toronto. A homeless count is a one-night snapshot that captures the number of homeless in a region by sending hundreds of volunteers out into the streets and shelters to count and collect demographic and situational data from homeless individuals.[14]

The survey and demographic data in the Vancouver count are more comprehensive than in Calgary, where only basic data on the homeless population are collected.

Vancouver's triennial count is important not just for smart planning and for guidance on directing funds but also for generating awareness in municipalities outside of the City of Vancouver that homeless people do exist in their area; citizens and political actors then become less able to credibly deny a policy problem. That nearly 30 percent of the street homeless population was situated in the suburb of Surrey in the 2005 homeless count sent a powerful message to the surrounding municipalities that this was not in fact just a problem in the Downtown Eastside. The planning and execution of the triennial homeless count in Metro Vancouver is truly a community-wide effort led by VAN-main, one in which the sector and the region as a whole are invested in the results. Following the 2005 count, homelessness suddenly became the number one issue for municipal voters in the region, and it has remained the primary issue in the 2008, 2011, and 2014 local elections (Vancouver Sun, 2008, 2014; Justason Market Intelligence, 2014).[15] This is in contrast to Toronto, where the issues of homelessness and housing continually fail to break beyond being the number one issue for more than 10 percent of voters, despite a more significant homelessness problem than Vancouver (Church, 2014).

Another VAN-main innovation that many members point to as a key reason why homelessness and affordable housing has the attention of voters and political leaders in Metro Vancouver is the creation of an annual Homelessness Action Week (HAW) in 2006 (Greater Vancouver RSCH, minutes, 2006). HAW is an event requiring months of planning at VAN-main, as well as engagement from the broader policy and service community; it involves creating media events and information sessions throughout Metro Vancouver to raise awareness of the issue of homelessness, in addition to implementing a massive mobilization of pop-up service tents across the region. Drawing attention to the severity of the homelessness problem was never going to come from elected leaders or from within the bureaucracy of the municipalities; thus, the members of VAN-main developed HAW as a key plank of their policy work in an effort to create change at the local and provincial level. In the early years of VAN-main, the principal goal was to obtain municipal proclamations of HAW to generate local government policy momentum, but now this annual event has grown into a much more ambitious endeavour. For example, VAN-main has organized or supported documentaries of homelessness experiences, advertising campaigns, educational video games for high schools, and engagement with business improvement associations.

HAW is a one-of-a-kind event in Canada in terms of scale and has had several tangible policy implications. First, establishing HAW in Metro Vancouver led the BC premier to adopt HAW province-wide in 2007 and every year thereafter. Second, a new permanent drop-in centre was launched in Burnaby (historically, a difficult suburb in which to gain traction on homelessness issues) directly as a result of the 2006 HAW (Greater Vancouver RSCH, minutes, 2006). Third, the 2008 HAW introduced an innovation from San Francisco called Project Connect, a pop-up service that offers homeless persons a one-stop shop to access needed services: hundreds were served in the first year of Project Connect in Vancouver. Project Connect is about direct and rapid service provision, not simply referrals, and VAN-main created a manual for, and offers support to, community agencies wanting to create a Project Connect event.[16]

According to community volunteers associated with HAW programming, it is one of the most important events of the year, particularly for the community housing tables – locally organized networks of homeless service providers across Metro Vancouver, nine in total, including the Tri-Cities Homelessness and Housing Task Group, the Surrey Homelessness and Housing Task Force, and the Burnaby Homeless Task Force – since it allows service agencies to build connections with those in need of services and to raise awareness of the issue among citizens.[17] VAN-main has not only been the core organizing force of HAW since it was first launched in 2006 but is also an anchor of leadership and support for the community housing tables across the region, helping to set them up, advising on local efforts, and integrating them into the work and advocacy at a pan-regional level.

Policy innovation can also be measured according to the investments made by the governance networks in programs or services offered to those who are homeless or at risk of homelessness. VAN-main has exhibited considerable innovation in terms of investments that have resulted in new types of homeless services: being willing to fund "risky" programs or services, being the first to fund low-barrier homeless shelters (no requirement to be clean or sober), and initiating the Extreme Weather Response in the region. Low-barrier shelters are an important piece of a harm-reduction approach, which rejects holding back services until individuals meet certain behavioural standards (e.g., being sober). Prior to the harm reduction-based paradigm that now pervades Vancouver, most homelessness services had an abstinence-based approach as a result of government policy, which served to exclude those who were most vulnerable and most in need of services. VAN-main and VAN-emerg led this paradigm shift in Vancouver, which also resulted in major changes in BC Housing policy across the province and in homelessness policy across the country.

In terms of a willingness to fund riskier programs, several VAN-main members who have served on the decision teams for funding allocations, as well as Michelle Ninow, a consultant who had served as a facilitator of decision making at VAN-main, suggested that VAN-main has been willing to take a chance on less proven service models and organizations that a bureaucracy would be unwilling to consider.[18] Michael Anhorn, a former manager at BC Housing was even more direct, suggesting that VAN-main was able to pilot initiatives that were seen as far too risky for BC Housing to fund and that after the risky projects were executed, it "shaped BC Housing's thinking – it just lessened the risks" and made it more feasible to expand and scale up such policy innovations.[19] An illustrative example is VAN-main's funding of Extreme Weather Response (EWR) planning in the region, a policy first conceptualized by VAN-emerg.[20] The EWR was a policy innovation created by VAN-emerg and designed to get Metro Vancouver municipalities to create community plans and protocols for occasions of extreme (cold) weather, which would typically mean the provision of additional emergency shelter space for street homeless to shield them from inclement weather. This was made possible in part by the willingness of VAN-main membership to fund innovative projects and programs but also by the close working relationship between VAN-main and VAN-emerg, each of which have emissaries in the other's network. That VAN-main was the first to fund EWR in the region may seem unremarkable in a narrow sense, but bureaucrats at BC Housing confirm that prior to this, like other innovations such as low-barrier shelters, EWR was an untested mechanism and therefore not feasible for BC Housing to implement and fund; after its successful piloting by VAN-main (with VAN-emerg driving it), BC Housing was able to take it over and fund it more substantially, according to Michael Anhorn.[21]

As we will see in the next chapter, this pattern is not evident in the Toronto case; interview respondents in Toronto claimed that the City bureaucracy is comparatively impenetrable and risk averse. A significant feature distinguishes VAN-main from the traditional bureaucratic decision-making in the TO-main context: in Vancouver, the decision makers are a diverse set of community and government actors, and community members demonstrate a tendency to be much less risk-averse than government bureaucrats tend to be.

A survey of homelessness policies and programs in the region linked to VAN-main also lends evidence to network governance theory as it relates to system coordination. Metro Vancouver's triennial homeless count and annual Homelessness Action Week are examples of system coordination among major players in the region, and VAN-main pioneered both in its unique capacity as the regional voice for homelessness in Metro Vancouver. The homeless count has grown into an institutionalized and powerful example of regionally coordinated activity among the Metro Vancouver municipalities and service providers. The regional homeless count is viewed by those in the sector, such as City of Vancouver housing planner Celine Maboules, as critical not only for a comprehensive and standardized count methodology in Metro Vancouver, but also because "[suburban] municipalities are not going to do their own counts, so without RSCH [VAN-main], I don't know how the municipalities would have the capacity or political will to fund and conduct their own count. In that way, RSCH [VAN-main] is a great coordinating centre."[22] Thus, the region-wide homeless count as a policy choice made visible a policy problem not previously articulated or accepted, and it has directly resulted in suburban mayors in Richmond, Coquitlam, and Surrey, for example, accepting the argument that homelessness in their cities needs to be addressed with affordable housing and services, according to Kingsley Okyere, the former manager of the Homelessness Secretariat of Metro Vancouver.[23]

Likewise, the annual Homelessness Action Week (HAW) coordinates government and civil society action to raise awareness of homelessness and paths towards solutions in media-savvy ways. Pulling together all the major policy players once a year for a week of sustained advocacy and awareness building is a major operation in Metro Vancouver, and although more events like this are popping up across Canada (e.g., Victoria and Calgary), they have never existed or been proposed in Toronto, where TO-main is tightly controlled by the municipal bureaucracy. According to some VAN-main members, HAW is creating more change than would be expected by the funds they allocate towards homelessness programs because it is building towards change at both the local and senior government level. One former VAN-main member, Celine Maboules, claimed, "It has really become something people know about, they understand it, there is a great communication strategy around it, lots of organizations are getting involved. We have way more connections with some of our neighbourhoods that were less involved a couple of years ago."[24] More recent HAWs have extended beyond advocacy and issue awareness into direct and coordinated service provision, with pop-up services via Project Connect events, which attempt to establish linkages in the service system for homeless individuals.

The other major example of system coordination for which VAN-main is chiefly responsible is the adoption by local municipalities in Metro Vancouver of the VAN-main master policy planning document for the region, the *Three Ways to Home* plan, along with the development of their own localized homelessness plans using *Three Ways to Home* as a model. By 2015, VAN-main had obtained the endorsement of the plan by nearly all of the twenty-one municipal councils in Metro Vancouver. VAN-main has also been successful in shaping local municipal homelessness plans. For example, the City of Vancouver's *Homeless Action Plan* created in 2005 and its follow-up plan in 2012 were designed using "the same framework as the regional plan," including prioritizing according to the three areas of income, housing, and support services (City of Vancouver, 2005, 2; 2012). Largely as a result of years of engagement with VAN-main, other municipal homelessness plans in the region are similarly consistent with the *Three Ways to Home* plan, including those of Surrey, New Westminster, and the North Shore, according to former chair of VAN-main Alice Sundberg and former Homelessness Secretariat manager Kingsley Okyere.[25]

The municipal homelessness plans differ to the extent that each municipality experiences its own localized pressures with regard to homelessness, but they all exist within the overarching policy framework established by VAN-main. This means that the constituent municipalities are all paddling in the same direction as VAN-main and that homelessness policy in the region is cohesive. VAN-main member Annie Maboules, who is also a planner from the District of North Vancouver, identified clear causal links between their actions and those of the municipalities and suggested that VAN-main can take credit for spurring the region's municipalities to develop homelessness policies.[26] When asked hypothetically about outcomes if VAN-main had never been created, all interviewees strongly predicted a much less developed and coordinated homelessness response in the region, with one City of Vancouver bureaucrat suggesting, "I think there would be much less activity around homelessness in other parts of the region. I think that would be the biggest thing. There would be much more focus on [the City of] Vancouver, much more focus on the Downtown Eastside – that's been one of the key pieces of RSCH [VAN-main], is helping people understand that homelessness isn't just a Downtown Eastside issue."[27]

In contrast to the more centralized bureaucratic model in Toronto, VAN-main is not a central intake for homelessness funding in the region, yet it has built, from the ground up, informal mechanisms to achieve high levels of investment and system coordination. This has been done primarily by developing strong relationships with municipal bureaucrats who work on homelessness issues, placing them on decision teams for investment allocations alongside community actors, and with other government funders (like BC Housing) and private community foundations throughout the region. VAN-main is a diverse mix of individuals who together bring to the table distinct perspectives and a breadth of knowledge of what is occurring on the ground (in the community and on the streets) and what is coming down the policy pike (from government).

What may appear to be a recipe for endless debate and fractured decision making is actually reported (and witnessed through extended periods of researcher observation) to be a fairly efficient context under which to make decisions that are coordinated and cohesive and that avoid duplication of or gaps in services. A prominent community service provider in Metro Vancouver, Karen O'Shannacery, admitted, "Most of us individually do not know the package of services in all regions, so having all types of service providers, government, and other funders at the table can help us get an idea of what is coming down the pike."[28] Likewise, government is not always aware of what is working or emerging at the ground level; thus, the community role in decision making is viewed as essential to produce a package of coordinated and cohesive programs. The former bureaucratic manager of VAN-main suggested that the advantage of including community and service providers in decision making is that "they will know immediately as to whether there is a duplication or if it reinforces an existing project."[29] Furthermore, by including private foundations – like the Vancity Foundation, the Streetohome Foundation, the Vancouver Foundation, and United Way, all of which also fund many homelessness services in the region – in policy planning and decision making, VAN-main can internalize funding trends to avoid duplications and service gaps.

Although VAN-main does not enjoy the structural advantage that exists in the City of Toronto in terms of a centralized institutional framework for homelessness policy and programs at the local level, it has managed to weave activities together in other formal and informal ways. VAN-main also engages in further coordination within the region in ways that TO-main and the City of Toronto bureaucracy do not. Because Metro Vancouver engages with the other major governance networks in its jurisdiction, the

Greater Vancouver region is characterized by a significantly more coordinated policy and programmatic framework than is Toronto. VAN-main and
VAN-Ab have integrated policy documents (TO-main and TO-Ab do not),
and VAN-main members invite VAN-Ab to help them make decisions on
Aboriginal homelessness programs (an opportunity not provided to TO-Ab
by TO-main or the City of Toronto). In addition, there have been a number of joint planning sessions involving all three Vancouver homelessness
governance networks working in partnership to coordinate policy and advocacy (e.g., the Joint Task Group on Shelter Service Planning in 2002). The
more recent creation of the Metro Vancouver Investors Table by VAN-main
is another example of coordination, in this case of the investments by government and private foundations.

VAN-Ab

VAN-Ab is a moderately institutionalized and inclusive governance network that initially operated in a very constrained metagovernance context,
as explained earlier. As predicted by the integrated governance network
theory, the history of VAN-Ab in terms of policy innovation and system
coordination is mixed. The network has several innovative features with
respect to new governance approaches and ways of organizing the sector.
Despite not being required to do so by the federal NHI program, VAN-Ab
created the first ever Aboriginal community plan to address homelessness
in Metro Vancouver, thus filling what VAN-Ab members believed to be a
major gap in municipal and provincial policy frameworks. Local politicians
and municipal bureaucrats were largely unaware of the particular challenges of the Aboriginal population, and in this environment, VAN-Ab members were committed to carving out a culturally sensitive policy framework.
But the real innovation was in how the community plan was conceptualized and presented to the Aboriginal population and the broader public.
The community plan template offered to communities by the Government
of Canada was considered inappropriate by VAN-Ab members, many of
whom thought it was too technocratic, sterile, and inaccessible to their constituents, according to former chair Patrick Stewart.[30] Instead of using that
template, VAN-Ab crafted a community plan in narrative form, telling a
story about how homelessness has affected the community and articulating
the policy priorities that network members considered most important.
Only ten pages long, it is concise, clear, and powerful – in distinct contrast to the impenetrable federal government community plan templates

and forms, which extend far beyond one hundred pages, including several appendices. One can imagine how much more feasible it would be for an overburdened Aboriginal service provider to read and engage with a concise, narrative-based community plan than to wade through a lengthy, jargon-filled one.

Another of VAN-Ab's governance-based innovations with clear policy implications is the flexibility with which the governance network solicits homelessness program and service proposals from Aboriginal community agencies. Because VAN-Ab members recognize that many Aboriginal community agencies are very small and lack capacity to generate sophisticated program proposals that would be likely to impress policy professionals, they have changed their process to be more accessible to Aboriginal community service providers. One major innovation is that VAN-Ab invites Aboriginal agencies that have submitted homelessness program proposals to engage in an informal interview with governance network members; this allows the agency to orally communicate its arguments for the proposed program and humanizes the process through a discussion among program proponents and decision makers. This type of process is virtually unimaginable in a municipal bureaucratic context. VAN-Ab leadership feels that these modifications are more consistent with Aboriginal peoples' oral traditions and also serve to help Aboriginal organizations with a lower capacity to generate professional program proposals, allowing VAN-Ab members to assess the programs more clearly based on the potential benefit to the Aboriginal homeless population rather than on an organizational capacity to produce a sophisticated program proposal.

In terms of new policies to the jurisdiction, VAN-Ab shares credit with VAN-main (and VAN-emerg) for the success of the homeless counts in Metro Vancouver and the annual Homelessness Action Week. All three networks work in partnership to make these now institutionalized activities as comprehensive and influential as they are. VAN-Ab is particularly helpful in the homeless count, providing advice and operational assistance to the coordinators, who attempt to execute the count in ways that are sensitive to Aboriginal people's experiences, and functioning as a central part of the dissemination and articulation of the results. VAN-Ab has also developed a strong presence at Homelessness Awareness Week events in recent years, including at the Project Connect event that involves pop-up one-stop service provision. More generally, the network ensures that Aboriginal people's homelessness experiences are prominent in the week's events. These efforts have contributed to change at other levels of government, including acquiring funding for Aboriginal-specific shelters and housing programs from BC Housing and the City of Vancouver.

Like VAN-main, VAN-Ab is tasked with both planning policy and allocating funds to homelessness programs. In this regard, VAN-Ab, like VAN-main, is willing to fund programs and services that would be deemed too risky by government bureaucrats, either because the service model has not been tested widely or it falls outside of the conventional frame of homelessness or because the organization involved has low capacity. But other than the willingness to entertain risk, VAN-Ab's policy innovations have been minimal. Members of VAN-Ab claim that the narrow policy space they are granted and the limited funds offered to them (less than $1 million annually) constrain their ability to innovate and force them into a reactive and emergency-focused response to homelessness.[31] In theory, policy innovations do not necessarily have to cost a lot of money, so this claim may not stand up to scrutiny. But the highly constrained nature of the metagovernance of VAN-Ab in the early years clearly tied their hands by restricting their ability to make investments in areas they deemed essential.

In terms of system coordination, the presence of Aboriginal community service providers at VAN-Ab assists the network in avoiding duplication of services and major service gaps, according to former chair Patrick Stewart.[32] After visiting each governance network in Vancouver (VAN-main, VAN-emerg, and VAN-Ab) to see them in action, I observed one common feature that was immediately evident: the function that the governance network serves to keep communication channels open regarding available services in the community, which allows members to strategize as to how to fill gaps, redirect clients during disruptive periods, and shuffle resources to maintain a coordinated system of services. While VAN-Ab meetings take about a half a day of members' time every month (and more often for members of subcommittees) – which is substantial for many overburdened and understaffed civil society organizations – most active members claim that this is essential to understand the service system and to react to shifting dynamics on the ground. VAN-Ab member Paulette Seymour confirmed the efficacy of the VAN-Ab meetings: "Yes, it takes away from our time, but at the same time I don't have the time to go and visit and sit down with whomever in Surrey and learn what sort of homeless and housing programs are out there."[33]

VAN-Ab performs this coordinating function better than TO-Ab does: because of VAN-Ab's formal connections to the other governance networks, it is able to make more links to the activities out in the community. Indeed, the major difference between the coordination performances of VAN-Ab and TO-Ab is the stronger links between VAN-Ab and the major players in the homelessness domain in the region, especially VAN-main and VAN-emerg. This was not anticipated as a feature of institutionalization within the integrated governance network theory, although B. Guy Peters (2007) suggests that "networks of networks" may be required to coordinate complex policy files. As described earlier, VAN-Ab not only was invited to help determine the policy priorities of VAN-main with respect to the homeless Aboriginal population but is also an integral decision maker in the allocation of VAN-main funds towards Aboriginal homelessness programs, a type of collaboration not common across the country.

VAN-emerg

VAN-emerg, TO-emerg, and CAL-CHF, are different from the other five homelessness governance networks in that unlike the others, which were created in a top-down fashion by government and given clear mandates, they were created from the bottom up at the community level and had to fight for policy space and for influence on policy development. TO-emerg and VAN-emerg, however, have significant institutional differences, with TO-emerg being formally linked into the Toronto City Council committee system and having city councillor leadership and VAN-emerg having no formal integration into key sites of decision making. Thus, integrated governance network theory predicts that VAN-emerg will be less well-equipped to drive policy innovation and promote system coordination. But even without being formally institutionalized – that is, without dedicated policy space or funds to allocate – VAN-emerg has developed a close and mutually beneficial relationship at the bureaucratic level with the major decision makers in BC Housing, the most significant government player in homelessness and housing in Vancouver, through which the network has exercised its influence.

VAN-emerg has contributed to several innovative governance approaches or ways of organizing the sector since it was created in 1998. While VAN-main and VAN-Ab were innovative in conceptualizing homelessness planning and policy development on a regional scale, it was VAN-emerg that set the model in 1998 with its regional scope in emergency homeless shelter planning. While it was concerned with a much narrower issue than VAN-main or VAN-Ab, it was certainly the first to organize on a regional scale. In 1998, the shelter system was not only a woefully undersupplied patchwork but also a disorganized and competitive system marred by bitter jealousies

(GVSS, minutes, 2003). The early goals of the conveners of VAN-emerg were to dismantle the competitive structure of the system by bringing the actors together and to work together to coordinate and expand the system, particularly outside of the downtown core (Pratt, 2001). VAN-emerg is chiefly responsible for helping to create and coordinate shelter services outside of the Downtown Eastside and the City of Vancouver, and as a result, shelters now exist in nearly every Metro Vancouver municipality. "We have everything coordinated and planned from North Vancouver to Hope" (125 km from the City of Vancouver), said VAN-emerg member, and prominent homelessness advocate Judy Graves, in part because the network developed a training program for new shelter operators in the region.[34]

In addition to year-round shelter development, another of the network's innovations, VAN-emerg has helped organize and craft Extreme Weather Response (EWR) plans covering fifteen Metro Vancouver municipalities (GVSS Extreme Weather Task Group, minutes, 2007). To get some suburban municipalities to develop and implement an EWR required that they acknowledge they had street homeless persons in their jurisdiction, which, in the late 1990s, was indeed a tall order. According to a former high-level BC Housing bureaucrat, Michael Anhorn, VAN-emerg getting municipalities to acknowledge a need for an EWR plan paved the way for additional homelessness programming, the need for which previous municipal administrations would never have conceded.[35]

Another key policy innovation initiated by VAN-emerg in the region was improved data collection in all of the region's homeless shelters in order to track service provision year-round (GVSS, 2012). This was an enormous task, not least because most shelter providers were so understaffed that collecting data on clients was virtually unfeasible. Yet VAN-emerg pushed shelters to develop policies of standardized data collection that would allow data to be aggregated in order to paint a comprehensive picture of shelter-use patterns year-round and to capture demographic shifts in the shelter population. This innovation powerfully shifted decision making, not only at VAN-main but also at BC Housing, when VAN-emerg identified new trends like youth and seniors increasingly occupying the shelter system (BC Housing, 2006; BC Housing, annual report, 2010).

VAN-emerg members believed that this type of data collection was essential for shelter planning in terms of both locating services and making the case, in data-driven terms, to local and provincial government decision makers for the increasing demands on the shelter system. Over time, the standardized data on use patterns could be aggregated on a monthly basis, a precondition to building a reliable real-time database for shelter use across the whole region. A similar system of shelter-statistics compilation exists in Toronto, but the critical difference is that it is managed centrally by the City bureaucracy rather than by an independent organization like VAN-emerg, and some segments of the homelessness service community do not trust the statistics produced by the City, given the political incentives to undercount.[36]

VAN-emerg has achieved limited innovations in investments because its primary function is not as a funding allocator (unlike all of the other governance networks investigated here) but as a policy development and coordination network. Yet by leveraging its relationship to VAN-main, VAN-emerg was able, in its early years, to get financial support for the regional Extreme Weather Response (EWR); it also won a big victory when BC Housing and the City of Vancouver eventually began to support the EWR program in a comprehensive fashion (BC Housing, 2006; BC Housing, annual report, 2010). Local governance network activities can also motivate policy innovations at senior levels of government, and in this respect, VAN-emerg has been particularly successful. One of the key arguments made by VAN-emerg, in addition to extreme weather shelter needs, was that year-round shelters need to be more than warehouses for homeless people at night. Instead, shelters should be given the resources to be open twenty-four hours a day, to have daytime staff to implement programming to help people break the cycle of homelessness, and to have meal-provision capabilities.

In the mid-2000s, the provincial government engaged in a shelter-policy review. According to a senior BC Housing official, VAN-emerg ideas and advocacy played a major role in bringing these issues to the attention of key decision-makers, resulting in some dramatic changes to how BC Housing funded shelters. Changes were made to maximum-length-of-stay policies and other inflexible rules that were more burdensome than effective, and BC Housing shifted to a low-barrier model for shelters, according to Michael Anhorn.[37] VAN-emerg revealed, through data collection and member experiences, that policies that put up barriers to shelter use were counterproductive to helping individuals break the homelessness cycle, and the network gradually brought nearly all shelters to adopt a low-barrier model; now, as Judy Graves explained, "everybody competes to have the lowest barrier, and that is really good."[38] Several interviewed VAN-emerg members, including former BC Housing representatives, claimed that the influence of VAN-emerg on provincial shelter-policy development could not have been achieved without engagement from BC Housing at the network level, where BC Housing would appreciate realities on the ground, and without the ongoing dialogue about and deliberation of solutions at the VAN-emerg table.[39]

In terms of system coordination, the most significant coordination successes that resulted primarily from the work of VAN-emerg are related to creating and sustaining Extreme Weather Response plans among the Metro Vancouver municipalities and standardizing shelter services and data collection. The value to shelter providers of standardized and coordinated data collection cannot be understated; because of this innovation, VAN-emerg (with the assistance of BC Housing) is now able to track emerging issues in the shelter system and react with much greater speed and effectiveness than in previous periods. The standardization of shelter services and coordinated collection of data is likewise a success of TO-emerg, whose primary concern in the early years was pressing the City administration to coordinate the patchwork of homelessness services and to collect and share reliable data on shelter-use patterns. The coordination achievements of TO-emerg, TO-main, and TO-Ab, however, are limited compared to those of the triad of VAN-main, VAN-Ab, and VAN-emerg, the actions of which have had considerable impact on the coordination of the sector in terms of policy and programs.

As noted above, VAN-emerg, TO-emerg, and CAL-CHF were created in a bottom-up fashion, primarily by community actors, in contrast to the other governance networks, and as a result, these networks focused primarily on the coordination of the community sector and services on the ground rather than on the policy of government – though as noted above, they have advanced change in this area as well. But more so than the other networks under investigation, the members of these three governance networks devoted considerable time to sharing with the community information about emerging issues and devising informal (and immediate) strategies to address shifting service needs and gaps in the sector (GVSS, 2007b; GVSS, minutes, 2010). One of the reasons why VAN-emerg was created was the lack of knowledge among shelter providers of each other's work. Early VAN-emerg convener Karen O'Shannacery describes the situation when VAN-emerg began its work:

> There were numerous shelters, and they are all working in isolation, various requirements and organizations turning away people. I mean, none of that

information was readily available. I mean, we didn't even know how many shelter beds that actually existed around the region.[40]

The type of coordination achieved by VAN-emerg is somewhat intangible in policy terms, but it is evident in meeting records, which show community actors sharing emerging patterns (more youth this year than last, more concurrent disordered individuals presenting, fewer women accessing shelters), deliberating over possible causes for these trends (Why do women not feel safe accessing shelters?), and often coming to quick decisions regarding service referrals or in-house policy changes to address new and emerging needs. The disaffection and discouragement faced every day by front-line community service providers trying to solve a big problem with limited resources is ameliorated by governance networks like VAN-emerg, according to respondents to internal surveys; one network member claimed, "Often I find there's nowhere else to share frustrations, and glean from others' experience and expertise. I come out from these meetings and I feel encouraged" (GVSS, 2008).

When assessed against the theoretical model, VAN-emerg has performed better than expected, given its lack of formal institutionalization in any site of decision making. Despite this low level of institutionalization, VAN-emerg has been responsible for considerable innovative and coordination, which has been facilitated by the dynamic metagovernance context in which it operates, and particularly by its very close and productive relationship with its metagovernor, BC Housing. Clearly, then, the metagovernance context can make or break a governance network in terms of performance.

Network Governance and the Collaborative Advantage

Network governance institutions are justified on the basis of what organizational scholar Chris Huxham (1993) calls the "collaborative advantage" – that is, because of their deliberative process among actors with diverse perspectives, they have the potential to solve policy problems that could not be resolved by an organization or a government department acting alone.

In addition to strategic policy change, a key test of the importance and collaborative advantage of governance networks to policy development is the examination of how such networks allocate funds and make investments in services. That is, are the investment decisions that emerge from these governance networks substantively different from those that are produced by more traditional bureaucratic policy makers? This question is often difficult to answer in a systematic way, given the empirical challenges associated with accessing data, assessing investment decisions, and predicting how things might have unfolded in the absence of a governance network.

With some creative use of data, however, we can estimate the efficacy of networks in this regard using decision-making data from VAN-main. In 2012, VAN-main invited local homelessness and housing service providers to apply for funding of programs for up to two years and received a total of eighty-seven proposals; this amounted to nearly $30 million in program support requests, although VAN-main had only $11 million to allocate. The proposed programs included the provision of outreach services, shelter and supports, transitional housing, mental health and addiction treatment, life skills programs, and youth safe houses across the Vancouver area. VAN-main was formally responsible for deciding how to make the investments, although parallel to their deliberations and decision making was a group of bureaucratic staff from the Metro Vancouver regional government who individually reviewed, scored, and deliberated on all eighty-seven proposed programs in order to provide administrative support for the network's decision making. Network actors and bureaucrats separately evaluated and scored *precisely the same homelessness program proposals*, using the same fifteen criteria, which provided comparative data that could be analyzed to reveal similarities and differences between the two groups, extrapolate to counterfactual scenarios of decision making (i.e., what if just the bureaucrats made investment decisions?), and track how the deliberative process affects policy choices in collaborative governance networks. This context therefore offers built-in analytical controls for comparing how bureaucrats (who represent traditional public administration decision-making) and governance network actors like those in VAN-main conceptualize policy problems and solutions.

The comparison between the decision making of VAN-main members and bureaucrats supports the following conclusions (see also Doberstein, 2015). First, network actors and bureaucrats have distinctive knowledge and perspectives, which manifested in very different scores for the same program proposals. Second, if only bureaucrats were in charge, nearly 50 percent of the decisions would be made differently. And third, deliberations within VAN-main resulted in the different perspectives of the governance network and the bureacrats converging to shape the policy choices and program investments.

Another noteworthy finding emerged from a comparison of the differences in scoring among network actors with the differences among bureaucrats for each proposed program. Network governance theory would lead us to expect that network actors would be more likely to disagree among themselves on the merits of a particular homelessness program than would a group of bureaucrats, because network members are more diverse, coming from very different perspectives and parts of the homelessness sector (e.g., shelter provider, mental health professional, person with lived experience, United Way funder, etc.), whereas bureaucrats, who share similar professional training and norms, are more alike (Fung, 2008; Head, 2008).

One way to measure the degree of difference in scoring among network actors and bureaucrats is to calculate the average standard deviation for each program within each group. As expected, network actors displayed more than twice the standard deviation as that of bureaucrats (18 percent and 8 percent, respectively; see Doberstein, 2015), meaning that for each proposed program, network actors' individual scores were much further away from the group's mean than were individual bureaucrat scores from that group's mean. This strongly supports the idea that network actors indeed bring more diverse perspectives to their policy analysis than do bureaucratic actors, who, according to the data, tend be more homogeneous. Approaching homelessness policy from diverse perspectives does appear to be a key component of generating policy innovation and of the collaborative advantage of governance networks.

Policy Change Derived from Other Sources

The policy innovation and system coordination of the three homelessness governance networks in Metro Vancouver do not, of course, constitute all of the policy activity in the region during the period under investigation. Mayors and city councils, and even premiers, also play a substantial role in driving homelessness policy change. In order to put the empirical findings from the governance networks into context and determine the appropriate scope of related theoretical claims, it is essential to document policy innovation and system coordination derived from outside of those networks.

In Vancouver, several notable innovations have been initiated by non-network actors. The most remarkable of these was the Vancouver Agreement, which was signed in 2000 and discontinued under the Harper government in 2010. The Vancouver Agreement was a tripartite agreement between the federal, provincial, and municipal governments in which a formal partnership, a decision-making structure, and funding arrangements were created with the aim of tackling complex and intersecting social and economic problems in an urban context (City of Vancouver, 2001; Doberstein, 2011). The Vancouver Agreement focused primarily on the Downtown Eastside, a neighbourhood that faces health crises related to HIV and drug use, highly concentrated poverty, infrastructure decay, and crime.[41] A key product of the Vancouver Agreement was Insite, the first supervised safe-injection site in North America, which required delicate manoeuvring by all three levels of government, given the criminal, health, and public safety dimensions. Insite is funded primarily by the provincial government, but it was advanced by key leaders at the City of Vancouver – most notably, the mayor at the time, Philip Owen. Insite is an innovative harm-reduction program for those with drug addictions; its intention is to draw these people in from the streets to encourage them to inject in a safe and clean environment, where detox and counselling services are also available. Harm reduction is one of the pillars of the four pillar strategy (the others being prevention, treatment, and enforcement) adopted by the City of Vancouver in 2001 (City of Vancouver, 2001; MacPherson, 2001). The philosophy of harm reduction, and of safe injection sites specifically, has enormous consequences for those among the homeless population suffering from addictions, and the model has since been replicated across the country.

Like his predecessor, Mayor Gregor Robertson of Vancouver has also been an influential innovator, especially in terms of housing policy (City of Vancouver, 2001). In 2012, the City of Vancouver began implementing its ten-year *Housing and Homelessness Strategy* (City of Vancouver, 2012), which involves the City assisting with the construction of social and supportive housing and leveraging its power over zoning to incentivize affordable housing development. Robertson is notable among mayors in Canada for championing homelessness as a key priority, famously promising in his first mayoral campaign in 2008 to end street homelessness by 2015. While he has not succeeded in accomplishing this ambitious goal, the City administration has tried innovative approaches to incentivize private sector development of affordable housing.

For example, in response to Vancouver's extremely low vacancy rate for rental housing units, the City of Vancouver initiated a two-year pilot project in 2009, the Short-term Incentives for Rental Program, to encourage private sector development of rental housing in Vancouver and to increase the supply of affordable rental housing over time (City of Vancouver, 2009a). The incentives include reduced property taxes, development cost charge waivers, reduced parking requirements, and density increases (City of Vancouver, 2010b). This program has since been expanded into the Rental 100: Secured Market Rental Housing

Policy to encourage development projects in which 100 percent of the units are residential rentals; the goal is to create five thousand new affordable rental units in Vancouver by 2021, although if historical patterns are repeated, the number of actual units constructed will be much lower (City of Vancouver, 2009b).

Although private charitable foundations like United Way and the Salvation Army have existed for many years in Canadian cities, providing funds and critical services to the homeless population, Vancouver has another innovative private foundation with an explicit mandate to address homelessness. The Streetohome Foundation was created as a partnership of the Vancouver Foundation, the Province of British Columbia, and the City of Vancouver. Streetohome created a ten-year plan focused on marshalling resources to build permanent affordable housing (rather than shelters). The foundation also created the Vancouver Rent Bank with the aim of preventing homelessness by offering emergency loans to individuals threatened with eviction. Streetohome is particularly innovative in that it leverages expertise and funds from the private sector as part of the solution to solving homelessness: at the time of writing (2015), it has raised more than $25 million from the private sector and has contributed capital towards the completion of a number of major social housing developments, with the City providing the land and BC Housing the majority of the capital and operating funds (BC Housing, annual report, 2014).

In the Vancouver context, several attempts to reorganize and better coordinate the collective government response to homelessness have been made without the primary involvement of the governance networks examined. Most prominent among these are the major task forces created at the provincial and municipal levels that were tasked with studying the system-wide policy framework, documenting service gaps, and making recommendations for a more integrated and effective policy framework. The Premier's Task Force on Homelessness, Mental Illness, and Addictions (2004) and the (Vancouver) Mayor's Homelessness Emergency Action Team (2009) were the most substantive exercises focused on revealing coordination challenges on this complex policy file and on making recommendations to the relevant political actors. Although task forces such as these do bring in diverse actors for consultation, their approach is very different from that of network governance in that they are created to operate for short periods of time with very defined tasks and are dismantled after reporting recommendations. Therefore, although they might achieve the coordination of policy planning, translating their recommendations into action depends on the extent to which elected officials and bureaucrats faithfully implement them.

In Vancouver, the coordinating effect of the task forces was uneven. The Premier's Task Force on Homelessness, Mental Health, and Addictions was established in 2004 to identify integrated strategies to address homelessness throughout British Columbia, and it led to the creation of the provincial strategy called Housing Matters BC, a comprehensive plan across the housing spectrum, from shelters to independent private market home ownership. The creation of Housing Matters BC also coincided with BC Housing becoming the centralized provincial agency for housing and homelessness, although a subsequent provincial Auditor General's report in 2009 concluded that the provincial homelessness response still suffered from coordination challenges due to a lack of an explicit homelessness policy strategy (BC Auditor General, 2009). That said, BC Housing is a major player, perhaps the most important player, in homelessness policy in the province. While suffering from coordination challenges, it provides over $200 million annually towards emergency shelters, rent supplements, and affordable housing preservation (provincially owned single-room-occupancy buildings) and construction in Metro (BC Housing, annual report, 2014). As noted above, BC Housing may be slow to move at times, but it has demonstrated a willingness to adopt innovations coming from the local level and to be a partner in system coordination.

The Mayor's Homelessness Emergency Action Team, created in 2009 shortly after the election of Mayor Gregor Robertson, was composed of fourteen members – including city councillors and staff, housing stakeholders, and private sector representatives – and was given a ninety-day period to come up with a coordinated plan for rapidly moving homeless people off the streets and into secure shelter over the winter and linking them to more permanent housing. While this task force made important linkages across sectors – including shelters, health, and police – it was limited to the City of Vancouver, one of twenty-one municipalities in Metro Vancouver, and thus cannot be considered a coordinated plan consistent with the reality of the policy problem in the region.

Clearly, then, some policy innovations and system coordination in Vancouver are attributable to agencies other than the governance networks under investigation, and identifying these helps us to measure the scope of the policy influence of governance networks. Key elected and bureaucratic leaders within Vancouver, championing new ideas of harm reduction in the case of Vancouver drug policy, drove these innovations. It is clear that political leadership has, in different periods, been able to drive the issue of homelessness onto the public agenda with great policy consequence. Yet policy changes derived from the highly institutionalized and inclusive governance networks (in particular, VAN-main) are more numerous and, in some cases, more consequential to improving the policy and service landscape for homeless individuals in Vancouver.

Theoretical Implications

This analysis of the homelessness governance networks in Vancouver yields findings that generally conform to integrated governance network theory, which predicts that the more institutionalized and inclusive governance networks will generate or contribute to more substantial policy innovation and system coordination. The Vancouver networks, especially VAN-main, are highly institutionalized and inclusive and are associated with numerous examples of policy innovation and system coordination that flow directly from their activities.

The analysis also shows that the metagovernance context, as theorized, has a powerful mediating influence on the performance of the governance networks. This will be most powerfully demonstrated in the next chapter, where VAN-main and VAN-emerg (both operating in a dynamic metagovernance context) are contrasted with TO-main and TO-emerg (subject to administrative and volatile metagovernance, respectively). It is, however, also clearly evident in the policy development at VAN-Ab, which began under a straitjacket metagovernance context and then operated under administrative metagovernance, a change that directly corresponds with increased policy innovation and system coordination.

VAN-main has successfully reconceptualized the policy issue and reorganized the sector in regional terms, pioneered new policies, supported new funding approaches and programs, and driven innovations at other levels of government. Network governance can drive policy innovation principally because the diversity of the actors at the policy-formulation and decision-making table can reset conventional thinking on an issue. The identification of emerging issues and potential responses, in particular, is the key contribution of civil society actors in governance networks, a task for which government, being weak and slow to react, is not well suited. Former BC Housing manager Michael Anhorn explained it this way:

> It's way too easy as a government bureaucrat to sit in our office and look at stats and think you know what's happening [on the streets] is because

of this or that. And, in part, that is because your statistics will only tell you what you measure, whereas service providers are in it day-to-day, and they will recognize trends that are happening before the statistics can identify them.[42]

While public servants tend to possess valuable research and analytical skills, including cost-benefit and risk analyses, that are essential to support decision making, they often have little experience with the issue at hand and may not be in a good position to assess the effectiveness or suitability of a proposed policy or program, particularly if it is based on an unconventional idea. For example, involving youth who have had lived experience of homelessness in VAN-main policy planning and decision making created administrative challenges, but many respondents claimed it solved a major information gap among decision makers. According to Alice Sundberg, a long-time VAN-main member and former chair,

> We got really great, positive input on issues that we were not sure about. We were thinking, "Well, this is kind of strange as an idea, but would that really work?" And then the youth would say, "Oh yeah, that program works great. So I think that without that link to the actual consumers, we just don't have the same level of understanding of the actual experiences.[43]

Governance network members in Vancouver suggested that civil society actors were significantly less risk-averse and asked tough questions about the status quo policy framework.[44] A governance network is not simply about throwing diverse policy actors into a room to vent about their pet issues; rather, a network reinforces the deliberative ethic whereby diverse actors come together to learn, exchange, debate, and problem solve. The agency of governance network actors is thus a key driving force behind policy innovations.

A relatively high degree of institutionalization is an important structural feature for policy innovation because the governance network needs to be connected to the policy process in order to implement innovations successfully. A highly inclusive network is clearly less likely to contribute to policy innovation if it is situated in an activist's basement and remains unconnected to actual levers of public decision-making. A former VAN-main member and current City of Vancouver housing planner, Dan Garrison, echoed this sentiment, emphasizing that the role of the network "wasn't so much developing the innovation as it was pushing through the adoption of those innovations once they were developed."[45]

The analysis of the Vancouver governance networks generally lends evidence to the part of the integrated governance network theory that postulates that more institutionalized governance networks will generate or contribute to superior system coordination, although there are instructive empirical deviations. The connection between governance networks and policy coordination rests on the theoretical premise that in complex policy fields, creating institutionalized space for diverse policy actors to exchange knowledge and resources will help eliminate disjunctures in the policy framework by placing the activity in system-wide terms (Thompson et al., 1991). A notable governance feature in Vancouver is the close working relationships among the three governance networks. VAN-main enjoys success with regard to policy and program coordination not just because of its willingness to engage with key players but also because it works in concert with VAN-emerg and VAN-Ab in planning policy and making decisions on key investments and strategies, a feature that is not apparent in the Toronto context, as we will see in the next chapter. The surprising finding that superior coordination in Metro Vancouver is owed, in large part, to collaboration among the three governance networks lends credibility to governance scholar B. Guy Peters's (2007, p. 73) claim that policy coordination is not fostered within a "single, lonely network" but rather by relationships between networks.

Many of the policy and governance achievements over the past twenty years are threatened by very recent changes in metagovernance. In 2014, the Government of Canada dramatically altered the federal Homelessness Partnering Strategy (HPS, formerly NHI) program that forms the backbone of VAN-main and VAN-Ab activity. What was once a program lauded for its flexibility and adaptability to local contexts and conditions was reshaped along a much narrower policy frame and agenda by the Harper government, which introduced strong constraints and restrictive mandates on governance networks like VAN-main and VAN-Ab that not only direct their financial investments but also restrict the policy and advocacy activities in which they are permitted to engage as part of mobilizing a comprehensive response to homelessness. This dramatic revisioning of the federal program has had mostly deleterious effects on the operations of local homelessness governance networks. According to a briefing note drafted by VAN-main to the Metro Vancouver regional government, "the future of RSCH [VAN-main] is at risk" for a number of reasons, chief among them being restrictions on the use of HPS dollars for administrative and project management support (Greater Vancouver RSCH, 2014b). The memo suggests that these meta-governance changes compromise nearly all of the innovative and coordinating activities outlined in this chapter, including Homelessness Action Week, support for the community housing tables, and the innovative "risky" pilot programs championed and supported by VAN-main when it had wide latitude in its decision-making role (Greater Vancouver RSCH, 2014b). As we will see in the next two chapters, these recent changes in metagovernance, which have shifted the context for all governance networks into straitjacket metagovernance, are causing major problems for all HPS-affiliated local homelessness governance networks.

4

Toronto: Bureaucratized Municipal Governance

Toronto is a megacity with a mega homelessness problem. In 1995, more than three thousand citizens occupied emergency shelter beds (not counting those sleeping outside) on any given night. This was a stunning statistic at the time, when there were no more than a few hundred homeless individuals in Vancouver and Calgary. And the number in Toronto has grown: in 2015, more than four thousand people used emergency shelters on any given night. In the mid-1990s, as is still the case, Toronto shelters were either too full or so undesirable that many homeless individuals would sleep outside, and in the winter months, this proved fatal for far too many. The Homeless Memorial at the Church of the Holy Trinity near City Hall lists more than seven hundred names representing those who have died since 1985 from exposure, usually in winter, or from an illness caused primarily from being homeless. Organizers concede that these are only the ones they were able to identify; thus, the memorial certainly underestimates the deaths associated with homelessness in Toronto.

With twenty-five people, on average, dying each year from being homeless in Toronto, it is no surprise that community activists mobilized in 1998 to declare a "state of emergency" that constituted a "national disaster" requiring immediate humanitarian relief (Toronto Disaster Relief Committee [TDRC], 1998, p. 3). The homelessness crisis was particularly acute in Toronto because the federal government cuts to affordable housing were compounded by simultaneous provincial government cuts to housing and social services, opening up a major breach in the social safety net for the most vulnerable.

Locally, mayors in the region were also relatively unsympathetic. Toronto's first mayor after amalgamation, Mel Lastman, famously proclaimed during the 1997 mayoral campaign that there were "no homeless people in North York," his formerly autonomous municipality, only to be contradicted one day later when a homeless woman was found dead at a North York gas station. Awareness and understanding of homelessness did improve over the next five years: in 2002, then Toronto city councillor Rob Ford declared, "This is an insult to my constituents to even think about having a homeless shelter in their ward [Etobicoke North]" (Toronto Star, 2013).

Perhaps in part because of the chronic difficulty of getting local political leadership to sit at the table on the issue of homelessness, Toronto has strong roots of community activism and protest movements around homelessness. The role of community activists in helping to craft the response to the homelessness crisis would be contemplated and refined in an interesting and unique homelessness governance network – one that was formally attached to Toronto City Council but possessed considerable power and legitimacy to push for policy change at the local level. Toronto advanced many important policy debates and changes in the late 1990s and early 2000s, but the city has since lost its position on the cutting edge, following the collapse of genuine processes of community inclusion and dialogue in the policy process.

This chapter begins with an outline of the institutional architecture of governance in Ontario and Toronto, as it relates to homelessness and affordable housing. Once again, we will travel back to the early 1990s, before any of the Toronto governance networks were created, to establish a baseline from which to measure policy change over the past twenty years. Tracking the emergence of the three homelessness governance networks and identifying their contributions to policy innovation and system coordination shows that these governance networks – which are weakly institutionalized, relatively non-inclusive, and constrained by a restrictive metagovernance context – have produced limited policy innovation and system coordination in last decade. Homelessness policy-making in Toronto is essentially municipalized in the City bureaucracy, which contrasts with the institutionalized and inclusive governance patterns in Vancouver.

The Political Institutional Architecture

As noted in the previous chapter, homelessness, as a multi-dimensional issue, is relevant to a number of government departments and ministries within each level of government. Cities within a federal system of government like

Canada share similarities by virtue of their common constitutional framework, but they may also diverge quite sharply at times, given the flexibility inherent to federalism. The Government of Canada's presence in homelessness and affordable housing in Toronto is much the same as in Vancouver: as described above, the federal government stepped away from its historical role in the provision of affordable housing in the mid-1990s. But despite co-existing in a similar federal policy context, the governments of Ontario and British Columbia have demonstrated rather different institutional and policy approaches to the issue of homelessness over time.

The Government of Ontario's policy response to housing and homelessness in the mid-1990s can best be described as laissez-faire. In contrast to British Columbia, which tried to maintain investment in social housing, the role of the Ontario government in addressing these matters was downplayed and the private market privileged: all new social housing was cancelled by the Harris Conservatives in 1995, including projects that were already under construction (Hackworth & Moriah, 2006). In 1998, the Tenant Protection Act was modified heavily in favour of landlords, some scholars argue, as a purported mechanism to stimulate new rental construction (Shapcott, 2001). In addition, the Harris government, immediately upon taking office, reduced social assistance rates by 21.6 percent, including the portion of social assistance provided for housing. The provincial Conservatives believed that with some tax incentives and regulatory changes, the private market would most efficiently provide housing to satisfy all market demand (Hackworth & Moriah, 2006). This did not materialize, since it did not take account of loss of rental housing due to demolition or conversion; in fact, there was a net loss in rental units from 1995 to 2001 (Shapcott, 2007b). The years between 1995 and 2000 marked the most extended period without government funding for new affordable housing in fifty years, with virtually no non-profit housing developed in Ontario in this period (Ontario Nonprofit Housing Association, 2007). Maintenance of existing social housing was subject to cuts in spending and subsequently downloaded to municipalities (Shapcott, 2001).

Some provincial governments retained central policy responsibility for homelessness and housing in the face of mid-1990s budget cuts from the federal government (e.g., British Columbia and Quebec), while others downloaded key responsibilities to the local level (e.g., Ontario and Alberta). In 1995, as part of the Harris agenda, the City of Toronto, like all other municipalities in Ontario, was subject to the successive downloading of responsibility and funding for affordable housing and homelessness. In that year, the City jointly funded hostels, shelters, and drop-ins with the province on a 20:80 basis (Golden, 1999). This amounted to forty-six shelters, most of them community run, with a total occupancy of approximately four thousand beds.[1] What is clear about the 1990s context is the emergency bias of the policy and programming offered by governments and community organizations in Toronto (Golden, 1999). Another institutional player was Metro Toronto, a regional government covering the municipalities of Toronto, Scarborough, York, East York, and Etobicoke.[2] Metro Toronto was not heavily involved in homelessness in 1995, although it was responsible for the Metro Toronto Housing Corporation (MTHC), an affordable housing agency. In 2002, the MTHC became the Toronto Community Housing Corporation (TCHC), an agency of the recently amalgamated City of Toronto. Funded in part by the Government of Ontario, the TCHC had control over fifty-eight thousand units of various levels of affordable housing. The agency, however, was another victim of the forced amalgamation by Premier Harris, who had promised that the devolution of affordable housing provision to the local level would be "revenue neutral." The devolution imposed costs on the local level that are in part responsible for the extreme backlog in repairs and maintenance of TCHC buildings in Toronto, with an estimated $100 million gap in needed repairs annually (City of Toronto, 2009b).

Establishing a Baseline: The 1995 Policy Context

The issue of homelessness cuts across all levels of government, but the obvious trend in the 1990s was one of downloading responsibility to the municipal level. In Toronto, however, homelessness was rising within a policy vacuum in the mid-1990s. The federal government had just ended its long commitment to affordable housing, the provincial government had downloaded most of the important related policy files of affordable housing and mental health to the local level, and there was no policy plan at any level of local government in Metro Toronto. Within a few years, Toronto was facing a homelessness crisis, to which a local advocacy group responded by declaring a "state of emergency" (TDRC, 1998).

Clearly, there were significant policy gaps in Toronto in 1995. By the end of the decade, the Mayor's Homelessness Action Task Force, chaired by Dr. Anne Golden, had documented the systemic policy gaps: no comprehensive regional or municipal housing or homelessness policies or plans, insufficient and restrictive emergency shelter spaces, rapid loss of rooming housing due to redevelopment, few effective discharge protocols and resources at state institutions like correctional and mental health facilities, and few prevention-based mechanisms related to homelessness (Golden, 1999). The minimal policy framework that was in place was focused on emergency shelters, with the charitable sector pulling most of the weight. And finally, decision makers had very little demographic or situational data about the homeless population that could help them craft policy responses. Just as in Vancouver, this was Toronto's policy rock bottom, and the exploding homelessness crisis on the streets in the late 1990s was indeed a "disaster" (TDRC, 1998). While there were some differences in their respective approaches, Toronto, Vancouver, and Calgary were in a similar place in 1995 in terms of policy and programs. This would soon change, as each city carved out a unique path in the areas of governance and policy.

Creating Governance Networks

In 1996, at the onset of the homelessness crisis in Toronto, the Toronto Advisory Committee for Homeless and Socially Isolated Persons (TO-emerg) was formed by a group of community service providers and activists who, mobilized after a series of homeless deaths on the streets, demanded that the Metro Toronto Council issue emergency funds to stem the crisis on the streets, according to early convenors and housing advocates Cathy Crowe and Beric German.[3] The Metro Council was persuaded of the urgency of the situation and formally established TO-emerg, co-chaired by a councillor and a community leader, to advise the Metro Council on how to allocate $600,000 of emergency funds. Shortly after its creation and more deaths on the street, the TO-emerg mandate expanded from advising Metro Toronto staff and council on emergency issues to include prevention and long-term homelessness issues (ACHSIP, minutes, 2002). Metro Toronto Council – and after amalgamation, Toronto City Council – institutionalized the governance network by inserting it into a reporting and decision-making structure that fed, via council subcommittees, into City Council. Membership included approximately thirty individuals from the homelessness service sector, housing providers, and even academia and was also equipped with policy analysts from the Metro and later City bureaucracy to conduct research, produce reports, and manage the network on a day-to-day basis, according to former City of Toronto bureaucrat Barbara Emmanuel.[4]

The mandate of TO-emerg expanded over time from an emergency shelter focus to a broader advisory status on all issues related to homelessness in Toronto. It was tasked with advising staff and council on policies, programs, strategies, and actions related to homelessness, as well as reviewing existing services, working to improve collaboration among community agencies, and promoting long-term and prevention-oriented solutions (ACHSIP, terms of reference, 2002). Key activities of TO-emerg were identifying emerging issues that members encountered on the ground, deliberating on potential solutions, and presenting those solutions to key bureaucratic and political decision makers. Much of this activity was productive in terms of policy, because it was linked into the council committee system, a key metagovernance feature that added credibility to the work of the network. TO-emerg harnessed this legitimacy to gain audiences with councillors and high-level bureaucrats in order to push for their issues and educate these City officials on the gaps in the system. Richard Barry, former assistant to councillor Jack Layton, suggested that TO-emerg was as much an advocacy force to keep the community engaged and help spread awareness by politicizing issues as it was a policy-oriented network.[5]

In addition to the role of TO-emerg in allocating funds, having an elected city councillor as co-chair of the network was an enabling resource that brought many to the table, since it elevated the status of the network and increased the perception that policy changes could be made.[6] An elected official leading the governance network had both practical and strategic benefits. The practical benefit was that issues and policies that TO-emerg wanted to advance could be brought to council and media with amplified attention (ACHSIP, minutes, 1998). Strategically, councillor leadership legitimized the activity and advice of the governance network to such an extent that senior bureaucrats would routinely appear in network meetings to explain proposed policy changes and seek advice and endorsement (ACHSIP, minutes, 1998, 1999, 2002, 2003). According to former member Richard Barry, TO-emerg "would have done nothing of consequence without the councillor co-chair," in part because of the skilful leadership of the councillor but also because of the network's place as a committee of council, providing it with an institutional basis.[7] The dimension of metagovernance that stresses the agency of political actors – not just the structural attributes of the network's mandate and policy space – is the defining feature for most former members of TO-emerg, and it powerfully explains both the network's surprising level of influence on homelessness policy and its demise.

Jack Layton was the councillor co-chair of TO-emerg from 1996 until his resignation from City Council in 2002. Former members recall Layton's skilfulness in this metagovernance role: he had immense trust in the community (most importantly, among more radical elements), yet he also learned over the years how to most effectively gain unlikely allies.[8] In one illustrative example, Mayor Lastman famously declared that there were absolutely no homeless people in North York, thus precluding the need for investment. Layton knew this to be false, but rather than castigate him in public, he presented the evidence to the mayor in private, convincing him that he had made a mistake and that he could make the controversy go away by seriously getting behind the work of TO-emerg.[9]

The importance of the councillor co-chair, from the perspective of metagovernance, came into even clearer view when Jack Layton left council in 2002 and was replaced by Councillor Jane Pitfield, a conservative-leaning councillor with a distinct vision of homelessness issues and solutions. From the beginning, Pitfield did not enjoy the trust of the majority of the community members of TO-emerg, given her positions on the issues, and she lost whatever goodwill she enjoyed because of how she metagoverned the network. Trust began to unravel when Pitfield, having lost policy debates within the governance network, refused to bring forward to City Council the majority position, according to several former network members.[10] Conflict reached a breaking point when Councillor Pitfield advanced an anti-panhandling bylaw at council, which was so offensive and counterproductive to many community members of TO-emerg that they marshalled twenty-eight of thirty-two members to declare no confidence in her (ACHSIP, minutes, 2006). This had no effect because the metagovernor was put in place by City Council, not by TO-emerg membership, and at this point, many of the community members resigned in protest and never returned. The governance network was disbanded in 2006 and remains so today.

Although TO-emerg was the first significant homelessness governance network to take shape in Toronto, it was not the only one. Like VAN-main, Toronto's Community Reference Group (TO-main) was created when, in 1999, the federal National Homelessness Initiative mandated the creation of local governance networks (what the NHI called community advisory boards) in order to set policy priorities and allocate federal dollars. Recall that the Government of Canada allowed considerable flexibility in terms of the constitution of these local networks and their fiscal and policy relationship to municipal decision makers. Whereas VAN-main, because it was organized at the regional level (and in a policy vacuum), had relatively open policy space, TO-main was inserted into the existing Toronto City Council policy framework, chiefly because much of the recently downloaded provincial power related to homelessness was already in place within the City bureaucracy. Thus, TO-main was immediately constrained by local political institutions in a way that VAN-main was not.

The City of Toronto chose to establish itself as the "community entity" with the responsibility to implement a community plan and allocate funds accessed through the NHI; as a result, the City administration (rather than the federal government, as in the case of Vancouver until 2010) is the actual metagovernor of TO-main.[11] As in Vancouver, the existing local governance context in Toronto uniquely shaped decisions on how to structure and manage the newly mandated homelessness governance network. After amalgamation in 1998, Toronto, unlike Vancouver, effectively became a municipal government with regional scope, and this shaped what was perceived to be the appropriate approach at the municipal level. Furthermore, whereas in British Columbia, provincially funded homelessness policy and administration is centralized in a Crown agency, BC Housing, in Ontario, the policy and administration for homelessness is entirely devolved to municipal government bureaucracies. As a result, City of Toronto officials were already administering major homelessness programs funded by the provincial government, and it was believed that the City could more efficiently coordinate homelessness programs and project funding by acting as the metagovernor of the local governance network under the NHI program (Carter & Polevychok, 2004; City of Toronto, 2003a). TO-main was thus created as the governance network required by the federal government; it consisted of representatives of civil society groups and the private sector (e.g., major landlords), but it had a much smaller membership and lower meeting frequency than its counterparts across the country. It was mandated with providing ongoing advice and identifying funding priorities for the federal government investments.

The metagovernance picture in Toronto is thus distinct from that in Vancouver for these two governance networks, TO-main and TO-emerg. Whereas the federal Social Development Minister was the final decision maker regarding policy priorities and investment decisions at VAN-main until 2010, when Metro Vancouver took over this role, it is the Toronto City Council that plays this role for TO-main. The most important consequence is that the TO-main policy priorities and allocations must be consistent with those of Toronto City Council, whereas this is not the case in Vancouver, where the City of Vancouver is one of approximately thirty government and civil society members on VAN-main. The metagovernance context in Toronto, where the NHI has essentially been municipalized, thus results in pressure on TO-main to conform to City Council policy, which helps to explain certain policy choices and governance patterns of TO-main. In contrast, in Vancouver, the municipal metagovernance context affords VAN-main considerably more autonomy.

One of the core elements of the metagovernance of networks is the "enabling resources" – the spending power or bureaucratic resources of governments that are used to encourage actions they wish to promote. Such investments have both enabling and constraining effects: the resources offered by the metagovernor allow the governance network to exist and to be relevant to the community, yet they also constrain the activities of network participants, both government and civil society. The distinct enabling and constraining dynamics of resources in TO-main emerge from the local structures in which the governance network resides. While the federal funds available to Toronto for dealing with homelessness and affordable housing are significant (approximately $20 million annually), they are a drop in the large bucket of funds that the City of Toronto spends or administers (from its own tax base or on behalf of the provincial government) on homelessness and housing in Toronto.[12] Therefore, TO-main was intentionally designed by the City to be a governance network that has the very narrowly defined role of satisfying the mandate from the federal government to establish some sort of community-based network. TO-main was not designed to determine or influence broader City Council priorities with respect to homelessness, which was, in part, the task of TO-emerg until it disbanded in 2006.

One significant structural difference, then, between TO-main and VAN-main is that TO-main, shaped by its metagovernance context, has been more constrained in its policy space than VAN-main has been. Unlike VAN-main, which has essentially operated in an empty policy space at the regional level and has carved out its own identity and role, TO-main was inserted into a pre-existing and active policy space in Toronto. In addition, a high-level City bureaucrat chairs TO-main (City of Toronto, 2003a); several respondents called him a "super-bureaucrat" to signal his influence, which is so strong that the network essentially functions as a rubber stamp for the bureaucracy's homelessness agenda.[13] Thus, the approach by the City of Toronto metagovernor of TO-main is fundamentally more about ordering relations in the broader homelessness community than it is about drawing on diverse expertise. This is significant because the federal NHI program was initially conceptualized as a community-driven, participatory model of governance, not as a municipal government program (Smith, 2004). City of Toronto bureaucrats maintain, however, that they use TO-main as an important consultative body for the broader work City Council faces with respect to homelessness.

The third homelessness governance network that emerged in Toronto in the early 2000s was the Urban Aboriginal Homelessness Review Committee (TO-Ab). Created in conjunction with the National Homelessness Initiative, it is the precise equivalent of VAN-Ab. The NHI, recognizing the high rate of homelessness among Aboriginal people, as well as their unique needs and cultural norms, required the creation of governance networks of Aboriginal civil society actors to develop and implement a local strategy for Aboriginal homelessness in major cities, including Toronto. The historical relationship between the Government of Canada and Aboriginal Canadians means that metagovernance of Aboriginal governance networks – how such networks are created, structured, and held accountable – is especially important to conceptualize.

In its early years, TO-Ab was just as negatively affected as VAN-Ab was by the botched metagovernance of the Aboriginal portion of the NHI. The choice by the federal metagovernor to funnel the Aboriginal homelessness funding through the existing Urban Aboriginal Strategy (UAS) program, which has a labour market rather than a homelessness focus – proved to severely and inappropriately constrain the activities of local Aboriginal decision makers (HRSDC, 2003). As with VAN-Ab, there was a fundamental disconnect all across the country between what Aboriginal organizations on the ground, as members of local governance networks, proposed as relevant policies, services, and programs to address Aboriginal homelessness and what the governance network was permitted to prioritize and invest in by the metagovernor.

TO-Ab has undergone significant transitions since the launch of the NHI in 1999. Like VAN-Ab and the other Aboriginal homelessness governance networks across Canada that were created under the program, TO-Ab was constrained by the initial UAS framework, but there were larger problems as well (UAHRC, minutes, 2009). For a number of years, there were concerns within and outside of the Aboriginal community that the governance network was not sufficiently representative, transparent, and accountable to the broader community. In contrast to VAN-Ab, the governance network had few members and met very infrequently. This was increasingly viewed as problematic by federal government metagovernor, who expected that the community plan and funding allocations would represent the collective ideas of the broader Aboriginal community in Toronto. Eventually, a number of Aboriginal organizations asked the Government of Canada to step in and construct a more transparent process with clear lines of accountability.[14] The federal government responded to this request, and the current iteration of TO-Ab is more transparent, meets regularly, and operates with more accountability to both the Aboriginal community and the Government of Canada, although it still struggles with small membership, according to a long-time network member.[15]

Like VAN-main and TO-main, the Aboriginal homelessness governance networks are principally metagoverned by bureaucrats and administrative mechanisms rather than by elected officials. A recurring theme with the Aboriginal governance networks, vis-à-vis the federal government metagovernor, is the difficulty they encounter navigating the bureaucratic channels efficiently and effectively. In Toronto, as in Vancouver, the relationship between TO-Ab and federal government bureaucrats has been strained over the years as the result of a tug-of-war over decision making, with TO-Ab wanting more autonomy and bureaucrats needing to fulfill certain requirements of the metagovernor.

Most significantly, the relationship became volatile and tense because of what several TO-Ab members claimed were "culturally insensitive" metagovernors, who spoke down to Aboriginal community members and were inflexible in the supervision and management of the network, according to long-time network members Jennifer Abbott and Frances Sanderson.[16] The conflict and tension reached a "breaking point" and "almost needed a mediator at one point when firm lines were drawn in the sand" by both sides, according to one TO-Ab member.[17] To the credit of the federal metagovernor, a breakthrough came when the government "offered an olive branch by abandoning the rigid box" in which they had placed TO-Ab and instead "started to bend the box," which changed the policy space in which TO-Ab operated, according to Frances Sanderson.[18] But the conflict re-emerged in 2014, when the Government of Canada once again shrank the policy planning and decision making space of the Aboriginal homelessness governance networks.

Although most TO-Ab members claim that the relationship with the metagovernor has been better in recent years than in the past, they cite several remaining issues that hold them back from achieving their task of reducing Aboriginal homelessness in Toronto. First, many TO-Ab members are aggrieved that although the City of Toronto (via TO-main) allocates 20 percent of their federal funds towards Aboriginal programs and services (in addition to the funds that TO-Ab is allowed to prioritize and allocate on its own), TO-Ab has no role in the decision making regarding Aboriginal policy priorities or allocations (UAHRC, minutes, 2010). City officials argue that other Aboriginal groups in Toronto participate in their priority setting, but many TO-Ab members contend that an exclusively Aboriginal group like theirs should be making decisions for Aboriginal people in Toronto, as equivalent groups do in Hamilton and Vancouver.[19] A second grievance regarding the metagovernance of their activity is that when the federal government sends an emissary to participate in TO-Ab meetings to provide information and advice, it sends junior officials "with no real power."[20] All of the TO-Ab members are executive directors of their organizations and are able to make key decisions on behalf of their organizations at network meetings, yet the junior representatives of the federal metagovernor often do not have definitive answers to questions or are not in a position to give even tentative approval to proposed TO-Ab activities.

Applying Theory to Toronto's Networks

Like the Vancouver networks, the key features of the three Toronto homelessness governance networks fall into two categories: their internal properties (institutionalization and inclusiveness) and their external properties (their metagovernance context). As depicted in the matrix in Figure 2.4 (page 43), TO-main is comparatively less inclusive and less institutionalized – in stark contrast to VAN-main, which is strongly inclusive and institutionalized. While TO-Ab and TO-emerg are both somewhat institutionalized, they differ in terms of inclusivity, with TO-Ab being less inclusive and TO-emerg more inclusive. TO-emerg is significantly more institutionalized and inclusive than TO-main, although, as mentioned, it suffered from severe conflict in its later years, causing it to dissolve.

As in the analysis of the Vancouver homelessness governance networks, it is critical to take the metagovernance context into account here. The metagovernance context, as previously discussed, has a mediating effect on the performance of the governance networks: that is, it could foster or stifle policy innovation and system coordination, regardless of the networks' internal characteristics. Table 4.1 shows the metagovernance context for each of the Toronto homelessness governance networks according to the metagovernance typology established in Chapter 2.

TABLE 4.1

Metagovernance contexts of Toronto governance networks

Metagovernor leadership style (agency)	Institutional policy space (structure)	
	Narrow	Expansive
Cooperative	Administrative metagovernance (TO-main, TO-Ab: 2005–15)	Dynamic metagovernance (TO-emerg: Layton years, 1996–2002)
Contentious	Straitjacket metagovernance (TO-Ab: 2000–04)	Volatile metagovernance (TO-emerg: Pitfield years, 2002–06)

FIGURE 4.1   Theoretical relationship between metagovernance type (dynamic and volatile) and policy outputs

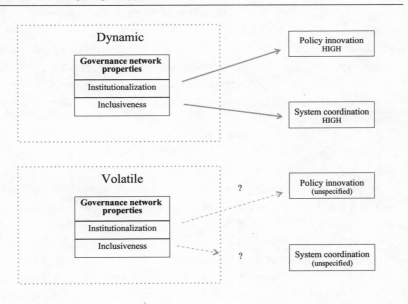

Figure 4.1 above contrasts dynamic and volatile metagovernance in terms of their theoretical relationship to policy development – specifically, policy innovation and system coordination; this contrast, as we will see, helps to explain both the early policy achievements and the downfall of TO-emerg.

Recall that predicting the effects of volatile metagovernance is more difficult than predicting those of dynamic or straitjacket metagovernance. We might expect that the wide policy space granted to a network operating in a volatile metagovernance context would contribute to policy innovation, but if the metagovernance leadership is contentious, the resulting disarray could stifle policy innovation. The case of TO-emerg allows us to examine empirically the potential theoretical effects of this contingent metagovernance type.

We are now in a position to track policy changes in Toronto from 1995 to 2015 and to link them to the three governance networks so as to determine the extent to which the Toronto homelessness governance networks conform to integrated governance network theory.

Policy Innovation and System Coordination, 1995–2015

The tracking of policy innovation and system coordination in Toronto over the period in question follows the same method as that described in the previous chapter on Vancouver's networks. As we will see, the Toronto homelessness governance networks exhibit fewer and less substantive policy innovation and system coordination in the past twenty years than those in Vancouver. The remainder of this section documents the policy innovation and system coordination accomplishments of each of Toronto's three networks.

TO-emerg

TO-emerg is unique among the eight homelessness governance networks examined in this book, largely because it was led by an elected politician – a city councillor. (At times, two city councillors co-chaired the network.) TO-emerg skilfully harnessed the resulting institutional legitimacy in innovative ways and represents the most institutionalized and inclusive homelessness governance network in the Toronto set. For example, as an advisory network of City Council, it was empowered to send motions to council subcommittees, which, if passed, would go to City Council. This was a powerful mechanism to get homelessness issues not only on the council agenda but also into the broader public domain. One particularly innovative approach of TO-emerg was to use its capacity to advise council to initiate a coroner's inquest upon the death of a homeless person, which was typically due to inclement weather conditions. A coroner's inquest was an effective and legitimized means through which to have public authorities affirm that a lack of safe shelter and services was resulting in the deaths of homeless Torontonians. There were so many homeless deaths that TO-emerg created an inquest response team to act as a consultative body to the City in response to the coroner's recommendations. This inquest approach was innovative because at a time when few homelessness programs existed, TO-emerg used and publicized an institutionalized and legitimatized reporting pathway between the coroner and the City bureaucracy in the pursuit of enhanced services and shelters for the homeless population. The move was strongly resisted within the bureaucracy, according to meeting records, because the coroner's conclusions exposed significant homelessness policy gaps.

In terms of innovations that represent new policies in the jurisdiction, TO-emerg's impact was due to its institutionalized advisory capacity, which was linked into the council committee system. TO-emerg had its own sub-committees related to evictions, transportation, shelters, police education, service needs, and mental health and addictions, and on several occasions, the network's identification of emerging issues on the ground was fed into the council committee system and resulted in innovative pilot projects or new City policy. For example, on the issue of evictions, TO-emerg was able to initiate a rent-bank pilot project in 1997 for women with children in danger of losing their housing. The rent bank provided short-term loans to individuals on an emergency basis to cover rent shortfalls (ACHSIP, minutes, 1997). Other examples of policy innovation include the co-production of a homelessness policy for the Toronto Police Department to guide police officers in their interactions with the homeless population, which was subsequently approved and implemented by the Police Services Board, as well as supplemental emergency dollars to fill service gaps in an especially cold winter (ACHSIP, minutes, 1996). TO-emerg was thus a major policy innovator during its tenure – a much more significant presence and driver of change than TO-main, as we will see shortly.

In terms of innovations in the investments made by TO-emerg, the network was granted a small envelope of funds ($600,000) in its early years to allocate to emergency needs, but its principal mechanism to extract funds was in its capacity to advise council to create or expand homelessness services. One particularly noteworthy program innovation directly linked to TO-emerg is the Toronto Transit Commission's On the Move pilot program, which began as a TO-emerg research project in the late 1990s to understand the transportation needs of the homeless population. The research revealed tremendous barriers to homeless people getting around and accessing services, barriers that were causing them to remain trapped in their current status.[21] TO-emerg pressed for a pilot program to provide transit tickets for distribution at agencies serving the homeless, which was accepted and then later approved on an ongoing basis. VAN-main is only now beginning to deal with similar issues in Metro Vancouver, showing how innovative TO-emerg's initiative was.

What is perhaps the most significant homelessness policy innovation in the country, in terms of its effect on senior government policy development, originated at TO-emerg: the creation of the National Homelessness Initiative (NHI) by the federal government in 1999 (through which VAN-main, TO-main, VAN-Ab, and TO-Ab emerged). The NHI began with key members of TO-emerg advocating for the declaration of a "disaster" in Toronto regarding the rapidly rising number of deaths of homeless people living on the street. TO-emerg members were initially hesitant to pursue the emergency-declaration avenue, since they feared it could be manipulated into a police-driven response that would involve rounding up homeless people, but they were persuaded that the problem was reaching crisis levels. TO-emerg sent the disaster declaration through the City's committee system, and it was approved by City Council in late 1998 and, subsequently, by the Federation of Canadian Municipalities. Big city mayors began actively lobbying the federal government, which resulted in Prime Minister Chrétien appointing a federal coordinator on homelessness, Claudette Bradshaw, to engage in nation-wide consultations on how to address homelessness. The consultative process led to the announcement of the NHI in December 1999.

The standardization of shelter services and the coordinated collection of data are also successes of TO-emerg, whose primary concern in the early years was pressing the City to coordinate the patchwork of homelessness services and to collect and share reliable data on shelter use patterns. The coordination among TO-emerg, TO-main and TO-Ab, however, is limited compared to that among the equivalent Vancouver network triad, the actions of which have had considerable impact on the coordination of the sector in terms of policy and programs.

In Toronto, one City staff member formerly involved with TO-emerg suggested that this type of system coordination among homelessness networks is a critical part of effectively implementing policy, not only by reducing the competitive nature of the sector but also "by getting everyone to use the same language and think about things in similar ways." It also allows those working at ground level to make a stronger case to decision makers, because they all frame the problem in the same way, which is critical to issue mobilization.[22] And one cannot discount the positive effect of system co-ordination on front-line community service providers, who face the possibility of disaffection and discouragement every day as they try to solve a big problem with limited resources.

One of the first objectives of TO-emerg after it was created in 1996 was to help generate the Extreme Cold Weather Alert system in Toronto (similar in purpose to the Extreme Weather Response developed in Vancouver by VAN-emerg), creating protocols and policies for the emergency deployment of extra resources during periods of inclement weather when it is dangerous to remain outside. This involved creating 170 additional relief shelter spaces and opening two warming centres. In partnership with churches that had been operating an Out of the Cold program chiefly (at first) with their own resources, TO-emerg helped to formalize the process, which also involved the City. TO-emerg members were central to the Extreme Cold Weather Alert system, created and implemented by the City of Toronto in partnership with Toronto Public Health, yet were only able to get the extra shelter spaces engaged at -15° C. Minutes from a meeting of Metro Toronto's Advisory Committee on Homeless and Socially Isolated Persons reveal that most committee members considered this temperature threshold to be much too low, declaring that "the measures in place are not sustainable" – that is, even -5° C is still far too cold to sleep outside safely (ACHSIP, minutes, 1997). When TO-emerg collapsed, the City of Toronto took over exclusive policy planning around cold weather determinations and rules, and while it has, in many ways, competently managed the system, recent changes have sparked considerable critique from the service and activist community. Meeting records from 2002 state that among TO emerg members, "there is a lack of faith in the City calling cold alerts that are meaningful and that will protect people" (ACHSIP, minutes, 2002). This is a concern that homelessness activists still have today.

The City recently shifted responsibility for the Extreme Cold Weather Alert system to Toronto Public Health and sustained the temperature threshold at -15° C (without windchill; City of Toronto, 2014), despite the fact that TO-emerg members, years earlier, were arguing for a threshold just below 0° C, which is the standard that VAN-emerg uses in Vancouver (ACHSIP, minutes, 2002). One can deduce from 1997 TO-emerg meeting records why this change was resisted years later: at that time, in response to TO-emerg efforts to raise the temperature threshold, network members heard that "[Toronto] Public Health is concerned that if the temperature is set higher, alerts would be called too frequently and people may no longer see the situation as critical" (ACHSIP, minutes, 1997). While the standard is currently set at -15° C, Toronto Public Health is expected to exercise discretion to engage the protocols in warmer temperatures if windchill, snow, and/ or sustained cold periods make it untenable to be outside. In recent years, critics have suggested that Toronto Public Health has not used its discretion wisely: they have identified periods colder than -15° C when the extra shelter beds and spaces were not engaged, which also tragically coincided with nights when homeless individuals were found dead on the street from exposure. Former TO-emerg members claim that the power to use the cold weather protocol resides with City bureaucrats, who mechanically implement the rules without an appreciation for the experience on the ground.[23] Recall that in Vancouver, VAN-emerg is responsible for determining when the Extreme Weather Response will be triggered, not the bureaucracy. In response to widespread criticism in the winter of 2014, Toronto City Council, just after placing the authority with Toronto Public Health, announced that they were reviewing the procedures and policies related to cold weather.

TO-Ab

It is particularly important to track the Aboriginal homelessness governance networks in Vancouver and Toronto in terms of policy achievements, because of the principle of Aboriginal self-governance as well as the claim that the unique needs of the Aboriginal homeless population will not be understood adequately by non-Aboriginal bureaucrats and elected officials (Ward, 2008). TO-Ab was created as mandated by the National Homelessness Initiative program, and it is responsible for determining homelessness policy priorities and allocating related expenditures for the Aboriginal community. VAN-Ab and TO-Ab thus share a similar origin and mandate, yet VAN-Ab has a much larger membership than TO-Ab does and is much more integrated into mainstream institutions that allow it to extend its influence further.

TO-Ab has not engaged in radical, process-oriented governance innovations like those of VAN-Ab, such as interviewing service agencies proposing homelessness programs. The Toronto network, however, has adopted a much more flexible policy with regard to funding Aboriginal homelessness programs in Toronto than the City bureaucracy. It should be noted that when assessing the Aboriginal governance networks, the most valuable comparison is not so much to each other (VAN-Ab vs. TO-Ab) but to a (hypothetical) situation in which none of these Aboriginal governance networks exist and all Aboriginal homelessness policies and programs are prioritized and funded through city bureaucracies. In this regard, TO-Ab is a much leaner and more flexible decision-making structure than that of the City (or of any bureaucracy). TO-Ab, for example, accepts program proposals from Aboriginal community agencies on an ongoing basis, not just during a funding cycle, which is characteristic of bureaucracies. Not only does this policy recognize that community organizations' ideas and needs do not always align with funding patterns suitable for government, but it also means that the network can very quickly make a decision on a program proposal. According to one long-time TO-Ab member, it can cut right through the proposal, something the City bureaucracy cannot do: "The problem with the City, they don't know us, and they don't know our capacity to deliver a program. We do know our capacity. And so, when our people bring the proposal, it is usually two or three pages. That's it."[24]

TO-Ab does not have a formal role in the production of the Toronto homeless count, called the Street Needs Assessment. There is also no equivalent to a Homelessness Action Week in Toronto, to which TO-Ab could contribute. Yet TO-Ab has been innovative within its own (albeit narrow) policy space. As with VAN-main and, to a lesser extent, VAN-Ab, there is evidence that TO-Ab allocates resources to Aboriginal organizations and homelessness program models that would be considered too risky by bureaucrats because the organization putting the proposal forward may not have the perceived capacity or experience to effectively execute the program, or because the proposal is not sophisticated enough to be competitive with organizations that have professional grant writers (e.g., United Way, Salvation Army, etc.).

The support of programs associated with increased risk is manifested not only in how TO-Ab members appear to conceptualize the problem of homelessness and the appropriate solutions but also in the very tangible sense of how they allocate expenditures. Having observed nearly a dozen TO-Ab meetings from 2011 to 2013, I can report that in both respects, there are clear differences between TO-Ab members and City officials. Examples of programs funded by TO-Ab that one would not expect (and TO-Ab members confirmed) City bureaucrats to relate to homelessness include daycare services for at-risk single mothers, cultural programming for at-risk Aboriginal youth, and programs for Aboriginal youth discharged from foster care.[25] Why is there a difference between TO-Ab members and bureaucrats in this regard? Steve Teekens, the chair of TO-Ab, offered his take: "I really relate to why they ended up where they are and I know with a lot of bureaucrats it seems like a big mystery to them as to why people end up on the streets."[26] This sentiment was echoed by other TO-Ab members, for whom homelessness is not simply an economic issue of poverty and un-affordable housing but is also related to feeling alienated from one's culture and to lacking self-esteem and self-worth. The chair of TO-Ab confirmed, in a qualitative sense, that many Aboriginal homelessness programs have been funded by TO-Ab that would not have received money under City of Toronto procedures. TO-Ab, however, is willing to work with Aboriginal agencies to develop service models and accountability mechanisms to get the program off the ground.[27]

Although the unique governance mechanisms employed to foster policy innovation for Aboriginal peoples are critical to this analysis, it is also important to examine the actual policies and programs funded in or-der to identify differences between Aboriginal governance networks and traditional bureaucracies. That is, do Aboriginal governance networks set priorities and allocate resources in more culturally sensitive and cultural-ly appropriate ways than non-Aboriginal, professional bureaucrats would? While TO-Ab does not display the governance methods of VAN-Ab, one can easily identify distinct and culturally appropriate programs funded under TO-Ab's leadership, as compared to programs supported by the City of Toronto.[28] When asked whether different programs would be funded if City bureaucrats rather than TO-Ab were the decision makers, several TO-Ab members unequivocally said yes. Frances Sanderson, a long-term TO-Ab member, emphasized that bureaucrats are generally good people, but "many of the services that we fund are not ones that the City would have or the federal government or the provincial – they would not have because they don't know. They never look past the top layer."[29] By "top layer," Sanderson meant the conceptualization of the issue of homelessness, in particular its causes and solutions, which is rather narrowly defined in bureaucracies and expansively defined among many Aboriginal people.

An example of homelessness programs that TO-Ab has funded illus-trates this difference. An Aboriginal organization asked TO-Ab to fund daycare services, to which it agreed on the basis of rising numbers of home-less or at-risk Aboriginal women and children. Based on the initially tepid response from the Government of Canada metagovernor of the network and on historical City of Toronto investment patterns, the City would be very unlikely to support this as a response to homelessness. Yet Aboriginal decision makers in Toronto conceive of homelessness in much broader and systemic terms, recognizing the positive impact of Aboriginal daycare services for both the homeless mother and child. In fact, this broader "systems" approach to addressing homelessness is increasingly being adopted by non-Aboriginal leaders in homelessness research and is considered the cutting edge of policy (Gaetz, Gulliver, & Richter, 2014).

TO-Ab is tasked with both planning policy and allocating funds to Aboriginal homelessness services and programs; as with VAN-Ab, the presence of community service providers assists the network in avoiding duplication of services and major service gaps. Yet, as discussed in the analysis of Vancouver's governance networks, VAN-Ab performs this coordinative function better than TO-Ab does because of VAN-Ab's formal connections to the other governance networks. The lack of analogous connections in Toronto is not for a lack of trying on TO-Ab's part, however. TO-main allocates 20 percent of its total federal funds to Aboriginal homelessness – double the share than VAN-main parcels out – yet TO-Ab members are not invited to participate in policy development and decision making regarding investments in Aboriginal homelessness programs.

The result of this disconnect is that TO-main (in essence, the City of Toronto), flush with Aboriginal homelessness funds, allocates them according to priorities developed in-house, and TO-Ab, which has a significantly smaller funding envelope, is limited to funding small and more patchwork homelessness programs. TO-Ab does not have sufficient funds to execute the development of a capital project like a supportive housing building; as a result, the network's decision making is biased towards service provision, which means taking reactive rather than preventative measures to address homelessness. Decisions about the allocation of Aboriginal funds would be much more coordinated and cohesive if TO-main and TO-Ab developed a closer relationship in priority setting and decision making, like that of VAN-main and VAN-Ab.

TO-main

TO-main is perfectly analogous to VAN-main in terms of its formation and mandate, derived from the National Homelessness Initiative, yet it has not produced significant policy innovations or system coordination. TO-main is much less institutionalized and inclusive than VAN-main, which, according to integrated governance network theory, suggests that TO-main's potential to generate and implement policy innovations will be more limited because of the lack of diversity of network actors and the relatively narrow policy space. TO-main members are also not permitted to make decisions on funding investments; as we saw with VAN-main, increased decision-making ability can lead to considerable innovation.

Indeed, over the past fifteen years, TO-main has not contributed to new governance approaches or to ways of organizing the sector in Toronto. Whereas the Vancouver networks moved into a vacuum of governance and policy activity and thus had an opportunity to grab policy space, in Toronto, City officials quickly placed TO-main into a relatively narrow policy-planning box. Therefore, the fairest comparison to VAN-main, in terms of generating policy innovations, is the City of Toronto bureaucracy, since it controls the important governance levers and TO-main is, in practice, more of a consultative network than a governance network. One TO-main member, wishing to remain anonymous, confirmed that in terms of policy development, network members "are basically presented with a fait accompli, with some opportunity to comment, but the important decisions have already been made."[30] When asked about this, City of Toronto officials, who also wished to remain anonymous, defended these actions by claiming that much community consultation had already been done when TO-main was created in order to access funds through the NHI; this consultation had been achieved through the 1999 Mayor's Homelessness Action Task Force and the numerous service planning reference groups at the City.[31] It is important to note, however, that the Homelessness Partnering Strategy (formerly the NHI) is not designed as a mechanism for traditional "consultations" with community but rather for promoting an alternative form of governance that actively involves civil society in policy planning and decision making.

TO-main is thus distinct from most other local homelessness governance networks in the country created through the NHI in having had its wings clipped so early in the process; as a result, it has not had an identifiable influence on governance approaches or ways of organizing the sector in Toronto. Although it formally advises the City of Toronto on the approximately $18 million per year of federal funds that it receives from the Government of Canada, it is not involved in the decision making and has a low (some have suggested non-existent) profile in the community. Thus, it has not contributed governance innovations, unlike the governance networks in Vancouver and Calgary (discussed in the next chapter).

In terms of policy innovations in the form of the introduction of new or pioneering policies, VAN-main and TO-main (and the City of Toronto bureaucracy) are, once again, quite different. The City of Toronto followed the lead of Vancouver and other North American cities with its own systematic homeless count in 2006, called a Street Needs Assessment (SNA), and this has been replicated every three or so years. Unlike Metro Vancouver, where the homeless count is entirely conceptualized and executed by VAN-main, the Toronto SNA was not driven by TO-main but by the City bureaucracy, in consultation with a select number of civil society representatives (City of Toronto SNA, 2009). This example reveals a common theme with respect to homelessness governance networks in Toronto. The City bureaucracy controls all streams of government funding allocated to homelessness in a consolidated department – Shelter, Supports, and Housing Administration – that is willing to consult with the community but retains the authoritative role in centrally planning and executing homelessness policy and programs. TO-main is, by design, not sufficiently institutionalized to yield any substantial impact on policy or the allocation of resources. The difference between consultation and network governance is subtle but real. Consultative networks like TO-main allow for diverse perspectives to be communicated to government decision makers, whereas governance networks like VAN-main embody a diverse and more collective process of problem definition, deliberation on appropriate solutions, and creative collaboration and exchange of ideas for new approaches to the sector.

Policy innovation can also be measured according to the investments made by governance networks in services offered to persons who are homeless or at-risk of homelessness. In Toronto, this is where we find the central policy innovation during the period under study: the Streets to Homes (S2H) program, piloted in 2005 and expanded in 2008. The S2H program is based on the Housing First model, which emphasizes the provision of housing to the street homeless as a first stabilizing step, at which point supportive services are offered. It is difficult to overstate the importance of this innovation, initially piloted in New York City, since it turned on its head the dominant philosophy on how to address homelessness. According to the Housing First approach, individuals should not have to meet behavioural or other standards in order to be housed. This model, which focuses on the most chronic street homeless population, has since been taken up by the Government of Canada as the core homelessness policy underlying the Homelessness Partnering Strategy (HPS) program for 2014 to 2019. The main mechanism used to rapidly house homeless individuals in Toronto is mobile multi-disciplinary outreach teams, who locate and connect with the chronically homeless and provide them with rent subsidies to find housing in the private rental market, with cooperation from landlords.

The S2H program was initially very effective, reducing the number of chronically homeless individuals on the street by 50 percent in just three years, but in subsequent years, the numbers returned to 2006 highs (City of Toronto SNA, 2013, 2009). TO-main in Toronto is connected to the S2H innovation only in a tangential sense: the federal funds on which TO-main formally advises the City of Toronto first supported the pilot program and, as of 2010, funded a considerable share of the expanded program (City of Toronto, 2010). It was the City of Toronto bureaucracy that drove this policy innovation, based on evaluations of a similar program in New York City. S2H was, in fact, controversial in the community. It was argued that using a rent-subsidy model to house individuals would pull individuals out of the downtown core to areas where housing is cheaper but where few services exist to help these individuals to stabilize their lives.[32] Critics also contend that it is a program that finds support among the downtown business and tourism sectors because it "cleans up the streets of the core" but that it simply pushes the problem elsewhere.[33] Yet it is also a program that puts emphasis on those who are most chronically homeless and thus in need of housing, support, and services, and it has a strong record of success for individuals who are able to access the program, so it is cynical to conclude that it is simply a conspiracy to clear the downtown core of unsightly individuals.

It should also be noted that a policy innovation in one city might not be appropriate for another, depending the economic features of the city. For example, S2H would be much less effective in Vancouver because it is based on a rent-subsidy model, which is most effective in a context of a relatively high vacancy rate in the private rental housing market. That vacancy rate in Toronto was 4.3 percent in 2005, when the program was launched, whereas in Metro Vancouver, it was 1.4 percent, and in the City of Vancouver, 0.7 percent, making an S2H model much less attractive in those jurisdictions (Canada Mortgage and Housing Corporation [CMHC], 2011; Falvo, 2010). Researchers argue that in a Vancouver context, purpose-built subsidized affordable housing is more cost-effective in the long run (Falvo, 2010). City officials in Toronto acknowledged that the S2H model works well when the private market housing vacancy rate is high, as it was in 2005, but it faces challenges at low vacancy rates, which characterizes the current context in Toronto. As a result, the City began engaging in a "refocusing" of the S2H program in 2015, according to a City of Toronto official, with a plan to place more emphasis on follow-up services for those who have been unsuccessfully housed through S2H multiple times.[34]

Integrated governance network theory predicts that TO-main will contribute relatively little to policy coordination, since it has no autonomous decision-making function and limited intergovernmental and civil society membership, and it is not formally connected to other governance networks in the city. Since TO-main is effectively a consultation network for the City of Toronto bureaucracy, it does not have the distance from the local government bureaucracy that VAN-main is afforded. Policy at the municipal level, however, is well coordinated administratively but strikingly uncoordinated in other areas, particularly with respect to Aboriginal homelessness. The policy activity of TO-main, to the extent that it exists, is fed into the City bureaucracy, which is the centralized planning authority for homelessness policy development in Toronto. All the funds from the federal, provincial, and local governments flow through the City bureaucracy; this is very different from the situation in Metro Vancouver, where policy planning and fund allocation remain fragmented across local governments within Metro Vancouver (the Metro Vancouver regional government) and coupled with a major policy role for the provincial government via BC Housing.

When the National Homelessness Initiative was announced in 1999, Toronto, like other cities, was required to create a community advisory board as a prerequisite to accessing federal funds. The community advisory boards were mandated with bringing together various local government and community actors to develop, from the ground up, a community plan to address homelessness. The City, however, already had an established policy framework for homelessness (City of Toronto, 2003b) and, according to City bureaucrats, an extensive consultation process for the production of their homelessness priorities. TO-main, then, was not needed in the same way as community advisory boards might have been needed in other municipalities in Canada, according to City of Toronto officials.[35] The City explicitly stated the expectation that the priorities "approved" by TO-main would arise from pre-existing municipal policies and processes – not from deliberations within the community – and that the federal funds acquired through the NHI would "enhance and complement various new initiatives" (City of Toronto, 2003a).

One City of Toronto official also claimed that it would be "undemocratic" to allow community members to collectively devise policy priorities and recommend investment decisions, since these responsibilities rest with the elected members of City Council.[36] The counterargument, offered by some Government of Canada bureaucrats and community members, is that the NHI (and the HPS) is supposed to be a community-driven program, not a municipal program (HRSDC, 2003). It was not designed to be a supplemental fund for municipalities but rather an incentive for community actors and government to come together in a collaborative fashion to address homelessness. If the Government of Canada had wanted the City to simply spend NHI funds according to its existing policy priorities, it would have transferred money directly to the municipalities or indirectly through the provinces rather than through a complex administrative system that requires the formation of a community-based governance network to develop a policy plan and allocate funds.

That said, in terms of system coordination – at least of mainstream homelessness policies and programs – Toronto's policy framework is, on the surface, already coordinated by virtue of its administrative centralization in the City bureaucracy. But, as one City of Toronto official reported, a recent revamp of the City's housing and homelessness policy framework in 2014 was premised on an acknowledgment that "we had each piece working reasonably well, but not as a cohesive whole."[37] Toronto's policy coordination in terms of Aboriginal homelessness is also quite weak, in part because of the City failing to engage with TO-Ab in aligning policy priorities and jointly planning investments for homeless Aboriginal people in Toronto. When asked to describe the relationship between TO-main and TO-Ab with regard to Aboriginal policy planning, a TO-Ab member, who wished to remain anonymous, claimed it is "next to non-existent."[38]

Despite the lack of engagement on the part of the City of Toronto bureaucracy with TO-Ab on Aboriginal homelessness policy planning, the centralized nature of funding allocation, with all homelessness funds flowing through the City, allows for a built-in system of coordination of investments and homelessness programs (at least for non-Aboriginal investments), although this comes at a cost: several respondents in the community referred to the City as an impenetrable bureaucratic force.[39]

Although VAN-main does not enjoy the structural advantage that exists in the City of Toronto in terms of a centralized institutional framework for homelessness policy and programs at the local level, it has managed to weave activities together in other formal and informal ways. VAN-main also engages in coordination within the region in areas that TO-main or the City of Toronto bureaucracy does not. That is, VAN-main engages in productive ways with the other major governance networks in the same jurisdiction, and in this vein, Metro Vancouver has a significantly more coordinated policy and programmatic framework than does Toronto. As already mentioned, VAN-main and VAN-Ab have integrated policy documents, unlike

TO-main and TO-Ab, and VAN-main invites VAN-Ab to help in making decisions on Aboriginal homelessness programs, an opportunity not provided to TO-Ab by TO-main or the City of Toronto.

Policy Change Derived from Other Sources

As in Vancouver, there were a number of policy innovations and examples of system coordination in Toronto between 1995 and 2015 that were not derived from TO-main, TO-Ab, and TO-emerg. Perhaps the most consequential such innovation was the 1999 Mayor's Homelessness Action Task Force, led by the CEO of United Way, Dr. Anne Golden. The task force report, informally known as the Golden Report, was arguably a pivot point for housing and homelessness awareness in Toronto, and in Canada more generally, as a result of the substantial media attention it received. Task forces themselves are not inherently innovative, but this one drove policy innovations for several reasons. It was initiated by Mel Lastman, a conservative mayor of Canada's largest city, and was provided the resources to commission research and produce a comprehensive set of recommendations at the municipal, provincial, and federal levels, which would provide an important catalyst for other jurisdictions. While many of the top line recommendations were never implemented by the City of Toronto, including instituting a Facilitator for Action on Homelessness (a high-profile point person to push and implement the agenda), and several innovations like the Annual Report Card on Homelessness (City of Toronto, 2003b) were quickly phased out, the Golden Report had substantial and direct influence on senior levels of government. Some credit this task force, as well as Federation of Canadian Municipalities lobbying (initiated by TO-emerg), with applying the needed pressure to the Chrétien government to launch the NHI in late 1999 (Layton, 2008).

The most recent policy innovation in Toronto that is not attributable to the three governance networks is the Toronto Housing Charter, a key plank of the Housing Opportunities Toronto Action Plan 2010–2020 and the first of its kind in Canada when it was adopted in 2009. The charter, designed to guide City Council and City bureaucracy in the provision of services and programs, contains several policy statements related to the right for all to non-discriminatory, safe, and affordable housing in all neighbourhoods (City of Toronto, 2009a). While the charter does not constitute a legal obligation on the part of the City of Toronto to provide safe and affordable housing for all its residents, it represents an aspirational framework to enhance housing and services for the homeless in Toronto. The City of Toronto also uses tax credits or refunds as policy instruments to encourage the development of private affordable rental housing, but as in Vancouver, these tools are not consistently invoked (Hulchanski & Shapcott, 2005). More recently, the City of Toronto approved the development of the Housing Stability Service Planning Framework to shift its work towards "an integrated, client centered, outcome-focused service system," one that better links the emergency responses to homelessness with the administration of social housing, largely in response to faltering progress at reducing homelessness in recent years (City of Toronto, 2014, p. i).

Perhaps the most significant innovation in Toronto has been the Streets to Homes (S2H) program, as described earlier, which placed Toronto among the first in Canada to adopt the Housing First approach as a response to homelessness. This approach has since become a mandated feature of the federal government's Homelessness Partnering Strategy. While TO-main funds a considerable portion of the S2H program, it was the City of Toronto bureaucracy that drove this policy innovation, based on a similar program in New York City.[40]

A central piece of the S2H program is the Streets to Homes Assessment and Referral Centre (SHARC), a coordinated access and assessment centre, opened in 2010, that serves as a one-stop shop to link homelessness individuals to housing and appropriate services and that is considered by the City to be "an anchor for all downtown street outreach work" (City of Toronto, 2015). Quite remarkably, SHARC is open 24/7 and is staffed by individuals with knowledge about and connections to all relevant services across the city, including housing, counselling, food provision, and even identification cards. While SHARC's forty beds are intended to serve as a temporary respite for individuals in the event that their link to housing is delayed, media reports and street outreach workers claim that SHARC is increasingly being used as a shelter because of the limited capacity elsewhere in the system (Spurr, 2013). Yet because of the combination of SHARC and Central Intake, a 24/7 telephone service staffed by counsellors to assess and link clients to appropriate services, Toronto can fairly be described as coordinated at the level of intake, which serves to benefit clients who may lack information about the suite of services available to them around the city.

Although, as described earlier, S2H turned on its head the dominant philosophy on how to address homelessness, shifting resources to this model in Toronto was (and still is) controversial among major elements of the service community, mainly because it is viewed by some as a cynical attempt to clean up the downtown core and spread visible homelessness out to the periphery. It probably never would have made it through the governance networks. In fact, TO-emerg strongly opposed the piloted S2H program, in part because it uses rental subsidies rather than purpose-built affordable housing and tends to pull homeless individuals out of the downtown core, where most services for the homeless are located; some argue that this disconnects individuals from the services they might need.[41] S2H does, however, find support among Housing First advocates, who claim that while it is not perfect, the program actively targets the most vulnerable – the chronically homeless. From a theoretical perspective, it also demonstrates that governance networks do not enjoy exclusive ownership over driving policy innovations; sometimes the bureaucracy is required to make hierarchical and coercive decisions in order to try new approaches that may go against established interests in the sector. But although S2H has successfully housed thousands of individuals since it was first piloted ten years ago, occupancy of emergency shelters has grown to four thousand on any given night, and shelter staff report that many are using the shelter system as their long-term housing, suggesting that S2H leaves many unattended.

Toronto was the first city to give full support to Housing First, and City officials were so convinced of its effectiveness in reducing homelessness after the first few years of operation that they began to plan for the closure of homeless shelters in Toronto. They expected the problem of homelessness to evaporate with the implementation of Housing First, and they believed that shelters did nothing to address homelessness. Homelessness activists and service providers, a bit taken aback by what they thought was a naïve belief in Housing First as a silver bullet, strongly resisted the closure of shelters. This was prescient, since a few short years after S2H was launched, while many had been housed, the homelessness shelter occupancy was creeping up, and by 2015, it was the highest it had even been. This effort to close shelters would probably have been resisted and reconceptualized if Toronto had had a diverse homelessness governance network that was deliberating over these issues. As a result of recent trends in the shelter system, the City of Toronto has now done an about-face and is actually proposing to increase the number of shelters and beds, suggesting that shelters have a role to play in the broader Housing First policy framework – a claim that has been made for years by homeless activists and many in the service community.[42]

Another example of a policy innovation that was driven principally from outside the governance networks examined here is the recent proposal to create an LGBT-specific homeless shelter in Toronto. The homelessness governance networks, in particular TO-emerg, were sites of the earliest conversations about generating policy responses that were more sensitive to the unique needs of the LGBT population, which, according to some estimates, constitutes up to 25 percent of the homeless youth population and which suffers from discrimination in the shelter system (Abramovich, 2012; Hunter, 2008). In fact, if TO-emerg had continued to operate, its research and advocacy work in this area would probably have continued and the creation of an LGBT shelter would have occurred much earlier. At the time of writing, in 2015, fifty-four LGBT shelter beds, probably in two separate facilities, have just been approved by City Council thanks to both strong research demonstrating the need and sustained advocacy. According to the City of Toronto, the LGBT safe shelter space will "offer youth a chance to stabilize their lives, learn new skills, access education, employment and housing supports, all while living in a safe and supportive environment" (Patricia Anderson, quoted in Watson, 2015). The first of its kind in Canada, the LGBT shelter is a major win for the community, and advocates suggest it will be a key resource to assist LGBT individuals to move out of current vulnerabilities and to help them establish connections to services that can assist them (Abramovich, 2013).

There are several examples in the period from 1995 to 2015 in Toronto of attempts to reorganize and better coordinate the collective government response to homelessness that were not made primarily via the governance networks examined here. Most prominent among these are major task forces created at the provincial and municipal levels that were tasked with studying the system-wide policy framework, documenting service gaps, and making recommendations for a more integrated and effective policy framework. In the Toronto context, the Provincial Task Force on Homelessness, in 1998, and the Mayor's Homelessness Action Task Force, in 1999, were the most substantial. Task forces take a very different approach from that of network governance: they are short-lived, have defined tasks, and are dismantled after issuing reports and recommendations. Therefore, while the policy planning coordination piece is present, translation into action depends on the extent to which elected officials and bureaucrats faithfully implement the recommendations.

For example, the landmark Mayor's Homelessness Action Task Force, chaired by Anne Golden, revealed major coordination challenges and service gaps in the Toronto context. The task force's first recommendation was for the City to institute a Facilitator for Action on Homelessness, who would be the point person for integrating the system, yet council never created this position (Layton, 2008). Likewise, although the task force recommended the creation of an annual "report card," which would measure the progress of the City's actions on homelessness, this was discontinued after a couple of years. That said, the Mayor's Task Force did provide the broad framework under which City policy on homelessness was administered in subsequent years (City of Toronto, 2000).

The Provincial Task Force on Homelessness also had an impact on homelessness system coordination, since it recommended that the municipal level be exclusively in charge of administering services and programs relating to homelessness (though the province would still transfer funds), creating the Municipal Service Managers model (Carroll, 1998). As a result, homelessness policy development and implementation in Toronto is highly centralized within the City bureaucracy, with all federal, provincial, and municipal dollars flowing through the same City department. This has the advantage of having a "single window" for all homelessness services and programs in Toronto, which may lend itself to system coordination but does not guarantee it. In fact, the recent revamp of City policy on housing and homelessness is intended to address what the City describes as "a prescriptive, uncoordinated, and at times conflicting framework of funding programs" (City of Toronto, 2014, p. 4).

Mayors and councils in Toronto have rarely expressed much interest in homelessness policy, much like Calgary but in contrast to the prominent examples in Vancouver described in the previous chapter. Toronto's first post-amalgamation mayor, Mel Lastman, famously declared that no homeless people existed in North York, and thus, policy and investment was not necessary. The most promising mayor to give attention to homelessness and affordable housing in Toronto was David Miller (2003–09), but those interviewed in the community responded with nearly uniform disappointment in this regard. While Streets to Homes was piloted and expanded under his watch, it was implemented alongside fairly regressive bans on sleeping in public spaces and attempts to ban panhandling in the city. These policies are of the reactionary kind and obviously do not in any way resolve the fundamental problems that drive homelessness (Shapcott, 2005). The conservative mayor Rob Ford did not make addressing homelessness an explicit priority, other than the promise to appoint a homelessness task force (which was never created), and at times, he mocked the significance of the issue: as a councillor, he remarked that it is "an insult to my constituents to even think about having a homeless shelter in their ward" (Toronto Star, 2013).

Theoretical Implications

This analysis of the governance networks in Toronto provides evidence for the theoretical model outlined in Chapter 2, which predicts that more institutionalized and inclusive governance networks will generate or contribute to superior policy innovation and system coordination. On the one hand, the Toronto homelessness governance networks that continue to operate, TO-main and TO-Ab, have low levels of institutionalization and inclusiveness and, as expected, provide few examples of policy innovation and system coordination that flow directly from their activities. On the other hand, TO-emerg, the first homelessness governance network, which was institutionalized within the council system, developed numerous policy innovations in Toronto from 1996 to 2006, when it dissolved as a result of conflict among membership and a new metagovernor.

As is now clear, the Toronto and Vancouver political contexts have been quite different, with Vancouver largely avoiding mayors who were at best disinterested in and at worst hostile to innovative and thoughtfully coordinated homelessness policy, but this political difference alone does not explain the variation in the governance networks between the two cities. In fact, TO-emerg was one of the most successful homelessness governance networks of those examined thus far, despite the fact that it operated in a volatile metagovernance context that caused it to unravel after only ten years of operation.

TO-emerg, despite its short tenure, had a significant policy impact, which is what network governance theory predicts: in addition to meeting regularly and performing a strategic planning function, the network was institutionally anchored in elected official leadership, without which, according to former members, TO-emerg would have achieved little. Yet its less formally institutionalized comparator network, VAN-emerg, had much more lasting and substantial policy influence over the period of study. This is, in part, because VAN-emerg remains active, while TO-emerg dissolved quite spectacularly in 2006 because of its volatile metagovernance context. Bringing together diverse actors is the key task of metagovernors, since disagreement is what drives policy innovation and reveals service gaps that need to be resolved with better coordination, but the skills and approach of the metagovernor are essential ingredients. Comparatively open policy space and contentious metagovernance – the features that define volatile metagovernance – can be toxic when healthy disagreement and deliberation transforms into backstabbing and distrust among members and managers, as the TO-emerg experience demonstrates.

Trust is a key variable accounting for the difference between TO-emerg and VAN-emerg: for example, some TO-emerg members were very quick to take policy disagreements between factions within the membership and the bureaucracy or elected officials to the streets in protest, whereas VAN-emerg membership has determinedly never taken this radical option. Several former TO-emerg members and bureaucrats referenced the degradation of trust over time – "I didn't trust them as far as I could throw them"[43] – while VAN-emerg members and BC Housing bureaucrats emphasized the trust that has developed from years of cooperative, albeit challenging, collective problem solving.[44]

Network governance theory suggests that more institutionalized and more inclusive governance networks will generate or contribute to more innovative policy. The data from and policy analysis of the homelessness governance networks in Toronto lends evidence to this relationship. The weakly institutionalized and less diverse TO-main has contributed to policy innovation only in the most marginal sense. Even when comparing VAN-main to the City of Toronto bureaucracy, which sidelined TO-main in favour of itself, the policy innovations from the more institutionalized and inclusive governance network of VAN-main surpass those of Toronto, notwithstanding a couple of notable policy innovations that have emerged from the City bureaucracy. Even if TO-main were to have a highly inclusive roster of civil society and government actors, it would be unlikely to drive policy innovations because, severed as it is from the City's decision making, it is the least institutionalized network in this study. Contrast that to TO-emerg (when it existed), which was highly institutionalized by virtue of its advisory relationship to City Council and councillor leadership and was able to push major policy innovations from a position of influence. It should be noted that TO-main is highly coordinated within the City bureaucracy's policy frameworks, which are substantial because the City is the dominant player, but policy and system coordination largely ends there. There is effectively no relationship between TO-main and TO-Ab, and even before its dissolution in 2006, TO-emerg was not meaningfully engaged with either TO-main or TO-Ab.

The benefits of diversity in policy planning and decision making in governance networks comes into clear view when we compare the inclusive governance mechanisms at VAN-main to those at TO-main. As mentioned, TO-main is significantly less diverse, with no Aboriginal representation, and the City administration restricts TO-main to a consultative role in the strategic planning, with the network having no role in decisions regarding the allocation of funds to homelessness services and programs.[45] Without

Aboriginal perspectives at TO-main and with no formal or informal relationship with TO-Ab, the policy priorities from TO-main display little
sensitivity to unique Aboriginal needs. This is evidenced by the 2007 community plan to address homelessness put forward by TO-main, which suggests, without further explanation, that it is "anticipated that the priorities
and projects that come forward for the Aboriginal allocation will fall into
the six broad objectives outlined in the City's HPI Plan," referring to the
City's general homelessness plan (Community Reference Group [CRG],
2007, p. 6). Recall that TO-main has, notably, carved out 20 percent of its
total federal funding allocation for Aboriginal homelessness services and
programs, but there are no procedures to include the perspectives represented by TO-main in the City's actual decision making. In the Vancouver
context, the practice of VAN-main inviting VAN-Ab to help make decisions
regarding VAN-main's investments in Aboriginal services demonstrates
that when Aboriginal peoples are included in decision making, they make
very different decisions than when local government bureaucrats make decisions, which is the case with TO-main.

While visiting governance networks in Toronto, I observed, as in Vancouver,
how they facilitated keeping communication channels open regarding
available services in the community, thus allowing members to strategize
as to how to deal with changing circumstances. TO-Ab member Jennifer
Abbott articulated this perceived benefit, specifying that bringing the major
Aboriginal community service partners together on a regular basis "provides helpful information that can be used to refer existing and future clients." These regular meetings, she said, have also strengthened professional
and personal relationships and, as a result, have reduced distrust in the
community.[46]

In the previous chapter, we saw that in Vancouver, policy innovations
and enhanced system coordination emerged not only from homelessness
governance network activity but also from institutionalized relationships
among the governance networks. This has not been the case in Toronto. As
noted above, one TO-Ab member described the relationship between TO-
main and TO-Ab, at least as it relates to Aboriginal homelessness, as "next
to non-existent."[47] Another governance network member described the lack
of integrated planning, particularly that which is inclusive of Aboriginal
people, bluntly:

> It's a big problem. No, I see that it is a huge problem, and we need some-
> body with a really strong and possibly at times nasty advocacy voice, who

can keep pulling it back and saying, "We are talking about one-third of your constituency!" If you go to a shelter and ask, "What are your policies for Aboriginal people?" And they will say, "We operate colour blind here." I'm not talking about colour blind, I'm talking about the culturally appropriate services ... So, the barriers are huge.[48]

Why does this matter? Current and former members of the most inclusive governance networks in this study continually referenced how their own information and expertise gaps were filled by others at the table and how their own assumptions about problems and solutions were challenged in such a deliberative system. To many governance network members, this is not only about creating a healthy dynamic of exchange and contestation but also about constructing effective policy. One governance network member described it this way:

You get a set of relationships with an ongoing network that you don't get with just an open house type of thing or a one-time thing where you come in and talk about something. You get an ongoing lineage of policy decisions and why things came about and then when something else comes up, it's linked to all those pieces and it's integrated across sectors.[49]

The alternative of governing via traditional hierarchy, with authority flowing from elected officials through the bureaucracy and with, perhaps, some token community consultation is inadequate for a complex issue like homelessness. The City of Toronto admitted as much in a recent report on the housing and homelessness service system, acknowledging that "many stakeholders expressed the need for ongoing engagement among the City, clients, community-based service providers and staff to support ongoing service planning, partnership development and increased collaboration" (City of Toronto, 2014, p. 22). A number of bureaucrats acknowledged, without prompting, that few, if any, of their colleagues had ever been homeless or knew anyone who was homeless and thus had little basis for making claims about services or housing models that would be effective and sensitive to the target populations.[50] To be clear, bureaucrats are essential actors in governance: they bring research, policy, and risk-analysis skills that are critical to efficient and accountable public decision-making. But it is the meeting of these very different policy actors in a regularized and deliberative setting that creates the conditions to devise and implement policy that is innovative and coordinated.

Finally, a word about TO-main, the most consistently underperforming governance network, from a policy perspective, among those analyzed thus far. It is important to emphasize just how narrowly circumscribed TO-main is in terms of authority and policy planning: it is more a consultative than a governance network, unlike the others under investigation, which have delegated authority and play a major role in policy planning and decision making. It meets infrequently and exists mostly on paper, having been created by the City of Toronto only to satisfy the NHI program requirement to create a community advisory board. The City defends the constrained role of TO-main by arguing that Toronto is different from other cities: it is a very big city that manages hundreds of millions of dollars of homelessness investments annually; thus, bureaucratic frameworks to craft policy and administer programs already existed when TO-main was formed. City officials also claim that they consult with a number of sectoral "advisory groups" consisting of homelessness civil society groups, and therefore, creating TO-main to be like VAN-main would mean having a redundant layer of bureaucracy and community involvement in policy planning. Thus, in some ways, it makes perfect sense that TO-main has underperformed compared to the other homelessness governance networks, particularly VAN-main. It is a valuable comparison, however, because TO-main has precisely the same origins as VAN-main, and we are therefore presented with a natural experiment in the consequences of institutional design.

Thus, the changes made in 2014 to the Homelessness Partnering Strategy (HPS) by the Harper government, which have made it more prescriptive by giving Housing First principles primacy and neutering the acceptable activities of the local governance networks, have not really affected TO-main. The network was never involved in community development or collaboration with the City in the first place, and the City had already bought into Housing First. If anything, it appears as though the changes to the HPS align perfectly, at least philosophically, with the agenda of the City. The changes have, however, caused great turmoil in places like Calgary and, especially, Vancouver, where the community advisory boards were engaged in a more collaborative governance process, as envisioned by the NHI in 1999.

Yet City of Toronto officials claim that even though the City's policy framework aligns with the HPS's emphasis on Housing First principles, the newly prescriptive orientation from the federal government causes problems at the local level. Just when the Province of Ontario was becoming more flexible with its homelessness and affordable housing fiscal transfers to the City, the federal government put in place new highly prescriptive rules and regulations that make policy and programs very difficult to administer. According to City officials, it is not the Housing First mandate that is the problem but rather the limited time the federal government provided to shift towards the new mandate. Furthermore, and most importantly, the strict criteria that HPS imposes to demarcate what types of programs and services are eligible for funding are far outside of mainstream understanding and have caused considerable grief and instability on the ground in Toronto in terms of services.[51] These new rules put in place by the meta-governor "are not sensitive to the unique needs of Toronto," which is a notable development given that the program was originally premised on the idea of local flexibility in response to homelessness. The more flexible previous years of the federal program (2000–14) are what "allowed Toronto to do innovative work ... so these changes are very frustrating," according to a City of Toronto official who wished to remain anonymous.[52]

The existing institutional framework in Toronto that centralizes bureaucratic power and marginalizes governance networks comes at a great cost in terms of missed opportunities. Under different circumstances, the governance networks might have been able to build strong connections in the community and harness a diversity of experience to drive further innovations, as well as to raise awareness of homelessness and build momentum towards solving the problem among the broader public and elected officials. Toronto's own Jack Layton, surely referencing his own experiences working on homelessness issues at the City, claimed that "no massive central bureaucracy is going to do the job well" (Layton, 2008, p. 305). That is, internal bureaucratic coordination in Toronto has its limits in addressing homelessness: if civil society actors lack a meaningful role in policy planning and decision, community investment in the process is likely to be minimal or non-existent.

At the time of writing, there is a hopeful development in Toronto. Long criticized from all elements of the homelessness sector for being too insular and having power that is too centralized, the City of Toronto opened up space for the newly formed Toronto Alliance to End Homelessness (TAEH) to serve as the designated advisory group to the City of Toronto on all aspects of its policy response to homelessness and housing. This is a marked change, one directed by City Council, with the aim of engaging with community stakeholders in a more sustained and substantive fashion. The TAEH is a multi-stakeholder group formed in 2014 independently from a government mandate, largely in response to civil society being shut out of the City policy planning process, as documented in this chapter. TO-main was dissolved and replaced by TAEH in 2014 – an implicit acknowledgment that TO-main was not working for the community. The TAEH reached out to the City of Toronto and made a strong case for its substantive inclusion in shaping the policy response to homelessness and housing, given the collective expertise of its members. A number of City officials were dismissive of TO-main as marginal because it had a limited mandate and existed only because of the requirement of the federal government HPS program. The City, they believed, had a responsibility to look at the "system-wide, bigger picture" of the whole housing and homelessness service sector.[53] Yet as we saw in Vancouver, that city's homelessness governance networks did precisely this wider policy work all along, even though they also had the task of prioritizing and allocating Government of Canada homelessness investments.

City officials claim that the TAEH will be better positioned to look at the bigger picture of the whole system, not just HPS investments like TO-main was. Reflecting on the new relationship between the City and the TAEH, a City official claimed in 2015 that the "diverse and broad range of discussions make it such that "in terms of policy," every area is on the table – the various sectors and City begin to appreciate the interconnected nature of policy and decisions and each learn from each other."[54] Those involved with TO-main and with other governance networks that have had a limited role in the policy process at the City would claim that this is precisely why they demanded to be more involved and thus might be surprised (though pleased) to hear this new perspective from a City official. Inclusion of diverse voices is a benefit that critics claim could have been realized from the beginning if the City had been truly committed to institutionalizing a role for the service sector in the policy process.[55]

In the years after TO-emerg disbanded, the City of Toronto engaged in one-time consultations with community sector groups rather than in the type of network governance documented in these pages. This new relationship with the TAEH may mark a turning point, since the City of Toronto has made a commitment to engage "with TAEH to seek feedback and advice on the transformation of Toronto's housing and homelessness services" and to "continue to do so on an ongoing basis" (City of Toronto, 2015). Among the City of Toronto policies and programs that TAEH hopes to develop and refine are the Streets to Homes program, shelter policies and funding, new services for specific client groups (e.g., women, LGBT, Aboriginal peoples), and a more explicit harm-reduction policy framework at the City level (City of Toronto, 2015). It is too early to determine the influence of the newly established TAEH-City of Toronto relationship and the extent of the sustained commitment to engage in more substantive network governance, but it appears to be a positive development.

Homelessness has not been high on the agenda of the public or elected officials in Toronto for nearly a decade, and there are no serious and comprehensive institutions like the governance networks in Metro Vancouver to push officials in Toronto in that direction. Whereas Vancouver has a long history of collaborative network governance and Toronto has a comparatively centralized bureaucratic governance framework, Calgary, the focus of the next chapter, occupies a unique place between these two, with interesting dynamics that have emerged as a result.

5

Calgary: Corporate Network Governance

Alberta is a rich province. Possessed with an abundance of natural resources, especially oil, Alberta has been the engine of growth for the country, and Albertans have enjoyed the highest per capita GDP in Canada. It is also a province with a conservative political culture that places high value on individualism, entrepreneurship, and personal responsibility, all of which are emphasized, to various degrees, by all major political parties at the provincial level. Successive governments have trumpeted an economic agenda of low taxes and minimal government that is attractive to business, an agenda that is encapsulated by a favourite phrase of the former premier Ralph Klein – the "Alberta Advantage."

In the early 2000s, however, it became clear that not all Albertans were enjoying this much touted advantage, and some in the business community were beginning to notice – and to care. Consistent with the conservative political culture of Alberta, and in ways virtually unthinkable in other Canadian contexts, key business leaders in Calgary with ties to the oil and gas industry – most notably, Art Smith – were drawn into the homelessness issue primarily from a moral perspective. Homelessness in both Calgary and Edmonton were creeping up, from two hundred or so in the mid-1990s to thousands by 2002 (and nearly four thousand by 2015). City of Calgary planners confirmed that, on a per capita basis, Calgary had a much greater homeless rate than Vancouver, Toronto, or even New York City (Laird, 2007). The Alberta Advantage was not trickling down to everyone. Business leaders like Art Smith were incredulous that a rich province like Alberta could simultaneously be host to citizens living under such unacceptable conditions.

While these key business leaders drew much needed attention to homelessness in Calgary and, in a sense, legitimized heightened concern about the issue among Calgarians, the growing problem of homelessness was never linked explicitly to the prevailing economic paradigm of Alberta and its structural determinants; rather, it remained within the realm of unfortunate personal circumstances that required charitable contributions. This framing of the issue would soften over the years to acknowledge more serious structural drivers of homelessness, but to a certain extent, it would continue to be viewed from an individualistic perspective. For example, the much-vaunted *Calgary's 10-Year Plan to End Homelessness* (Calgary Committee to End Homelessness [CCEH], 2008) was framed principally in terms of how much ending homelessness would save the taxpayer in the long run. The unique political context of Alberta shapes the policy and governance response to homelessness in a way that, on the one hand, represents the leading edge in Canada but, on the other hand, may limit the ultimate reach of policy if the major structural drivers of homelessness are bracketed out of the conversation.

The highly institutionalized and inclusive governance networks in Calgary have produced considerable policy innovation and system coordination, particularly during periods of less constrained metagovernance. The analysis of the governance networks in Calgary provides evidence for network governance theory as presented in Chapter 2, but the uniqueness of the governance networks and the evolving metagovernance context also add nuance to the theoretical claims.

The Political Institutional Architecture

As noted in previous chapters, because homelessness has mental health, drug policy, affordable housing, poverty, criminal justice and victimization, and neighbourhood dimensions, the issue lands on the desks of bureaucrats and elected officials at all levels of government in Canada. Just as Vancouver and Toronto exhibit critical differences in their governance structures and relationships among authorities, Calgary, too, has distinct governance features that shape the development of homelessness policy.

One shared governance feature across all three cities is Government of Canada policy and programs. Like Vancouver and Toronto, Calgary was a beneficiary of a relatively strong federal government role in the provision of affordable housing until the 1990s, when the Chrétien government completed the slow withdrawal of financial transfers under the guise of reducing the deficit. It is difficult to overstate the importance and consequence of this unilateral policy decision: with the annual provision of new social housing units across the country dropping from twenty-five thousand in 1983 to zero in 1993, a homelessness crisis hit Calgary, just as it did Vancouver and Toronto.

This federal government decision affected all of the provinces in more or less the same way, but the various provincial governments reacted differently. While Alberta's orientation towards and organization of housing and homelessness shares some features with Ontario and some with British Columbia, Alberta also has distinct features all its own. The province had a similar response to that of Ontario in the aftermath of the federal government affordable housing cuts, which was to cut its own expenditures and effectively download the responsibility (read: problem) to municipalities. Recall that British Columbia and Quebec were the only provinces to attempt to replace the lost federal expenditures on affordable housing with increases in their own. While long-time Premier Ralph Klein was drawn into supporting a few ad hoc measures based on appeals from friends sympathetic to the issue of homelessness (Scott, 2012), the provincial government (until recently) was minimally involved in this issue and made it a relatively low priority, which was exemplified when, for a time, homelessness was, inexplicably, a responsibility of the Seniors ministry.

By 2008, however, the Alberta government, moving closer to the BC government's response, was using key levers of policy control and responsibility for affordable housing and homelessness, exemplified by the province-wide plan titled *A Plan for Alberta: Ending Homeless in 10 Years* (Alberta Secretariat for Action on Homelessness, 2008). In 2013, a one-of-a-kind Interagency Council on Homelessness was launched, uniting all relevant provincial government ministries associated with homelessness – including Municipal Affairs and Housing, Health, Human Services, and Justice – along with key civil society groups and local governments. Indeed, at the time of writing (2015), the Province of Alberta has the most comprehensive provincial response to homelessness in the country. Recall that in Ontario, much homelessness policy activity was, during the Harris years, downloaded to the municipal government level, where it remains; the key policy levers, therefore, are in the hands of the City of Toronto.

In some respects, at the local government level, Calgary looks more like Toronto than it does Vancouver. Since it is an amalgamated urban area that has expanded through incremental annexation of suburban municipalities over the years, it has no regional government like the one that Toronto once had and the one that currently exists in Metro Vancouver.[1] Calgary's urban area, and therefore the concentration of the homeless population, is captured under a single local government in the City of Calgary, unlike in Metro Vancouver, where twenty-one autonomous local governments must cooperate on urban issues, like homelessness, that have transborder implications. This important institutional feature would have considerable governance and policy consequence if the City of Calgary played a significant role in homelessness policy and programs, but it does not. The City's involvement in housing and homelessness is much less significant than that of Vancouver and Toronto, both of which have taken on major roles and responsibilities.

The City of Calgary has the same key homelessness-policy levers as other cities do – namely, the control over land use and development – yet it has never fully leveraged that control through inclusionary zoning policies such as we see in Vancouver and, to a lesser extent, in Toronto. The City of Calgary has not been completely absent from the housing and homelessness arena, though; in fact, it was an early organizer of homeless counts in the city, beginning in 1992, and had housing planners who participated in local planning and strategizing around affordable housing and homelessness, including involvement in *Calgary's 10-Year Plan to End Homelessness* (CCEH, 2008). But the City has never truly owned any of the activity, in part because local politicians have more or less rejected the idea that the local government is chiefly responsible for this issue and because developers have strongly resisted creating affordable housing. Instead, the City of Calgary has largely vacated homelessness-policy space, leaving it open for a unique non-state governance entity called the Calgary Homeless Foundation.

Establishing a Baseline: The 1995 Policy Context

In 1995, Calgary, like all other Canadian cities, had a policy vacuum with respect to homelessness. With the federal government having recently abandoned its commitment to affordable housing, the provincial government downloaded most of the important related policy files to the local level, and the City of Calgary had no policy plan that would enable a larger role in the homelessness issue to fill in the gaps. As in Vancouver and Toronto, the emerging homelessness crisis in Calgary prompted a systematic review of the system serving the homeless population, which revealed a system largely dependent on charitable organizations and faith-based groups providing temporary shelter. Two reviews of the system paint a disheartening picture of life for an abandoned class of Canadians but also allow us to determine the policy baseline from which to track policy changes in Calgary from 1995 to 2015. The *Calgary Homelessness Study* (Arboleda-Flórez & Holley, 1997), funded by Alberta Health, and the *Street Speaks* survey (City of Calgary, 1996), funded by the City, were designed to support the work of the newly established Ad Hoc Steering Committee on Homelessness.

These two studies were landmark research documents in the late 1990s, and their findings shocked the system. *Street Speaks* identified the needs of persons experiencing homelessness, as well as the determinants of and potential solutions to the problem. The contents of this survey not only were contrary to conventional wisdom at the time but also contradicted what service providers believed were appropriate solutions. The *Calgary Homelessness Study* was significant because it smashed persistent myths about homelessness – in particular, that homeless individuals were essentially all strung-out alcoholics or addicts. Instead, these studies revealed that nearly half of the homeless people in Calgary were employed and had been homeless for a relatively short amount of time. According to Bob Hawkesworth, who served on Calgary City Council for years, it was a finding "that really captured the public's imagination, because they could identify with people who were working, and it was appalling to think that they couldn't find housing" (Hawkesworth, 2003, p. 61).

Researchers Julio Arboleda-Flórez and Heather Holley (1997), in the *Calgary Homelessness Study*, reported a number of gaps in the homelessness service system, including a lack of sufficient emergency shelter spaces; a dearth of agencies supporting families, Aboriginal people, women, and seniors; and very little coordination among the fourteen agencies that represented the core of service provision in Calgary. Half of the service agencies at this point were faith based organizations that relied on donations and volunteers rather than government grants and trained service professionals. The study also reported some worrying trends consistent with other cities in Canada in the aftermath of federal and provincial affordable housing and social service cutbacks, including 200 percent increases in shelter utilization and more diversified demographics of the homeless (not merely single men). In addition, it showed that nearly half of emergency shelter inhabitants were employed, confirming a lack of affordable housing as a key driver of the problem.

Despite contrary perceptions from outside of the homelessness sector, Arboleda-Flórez and Holley (1997) found no duplication in services, but they did find a worrying undersupply of emergency shelters and affordable housing: 38 percent of a sample of homeless individuals surveyed said they had been turned away because of lack of space, resulting in them sleeping outside. The authors also found limited health and social services to meet the basic needs of the homeless in Calgary. They identified the key barriers to an effective response to homelessness as lack of government funds to support emergency services, provincial government shelter rules, and a lack of agency cooperation in the collection of data on those receiving services. In short, this late-1990s review of the homelessness service sector in Calgary paints a bleak picture of the time and reveals that the Alberta Advantage never quite applied to a growing slice of the population.

Creating Governance Networks

The mid-1990s was a period of turmoil in many Canadian cities, which bore the brunt of federal government – and subsequent provincial government – cuts to affordable housing investments and the continued erosion of social assistance relief for citizens. Calgary was no exception. With homelessness exploding on the streets, growing by hundreds every year, a group of civil society actors and government officials, in 1996, formed the Ad Hoc Steering Committee on Homelessness, a merger of distinct but small-scale efforts at the municipal and provincial levels. This governance network was co-chaired by two elected officials, City alderman Bob Hawkesworth and provincial government MLA Bonnie Laing. As with TO-emerg, this institutional leadership gave the committee heightened legitimacy and profile, despite the name suggesting a temporary, project-specific focus. The Ad Hoc Committee would serve as the precursor to the long-standing Community Action Committee (CAL-main), which is unparalleled in size and activity compared to any of the other governance networks investigated here. When the Ad Hoc Committee became CAL-main, the co-chairs remained the same and there was continuity among the core membership from the service community.

The political links that the co-chairs of the Ad Hoc Committee provided to the two levels of government proved essential to pulling in the respective bureaucracies and leveraging the resources and policy capacity at the beginning of the committee's tenure (Hawkesworth, 2003). In addition to its co-chairs and a diverse set of homeless service providers, the Ad Hoc Committee recruited homeless individuals as central participants in problem definition, research, and proposed solutions. Their involvement was premised on the idea that for complex social issues such as homelessness, involvement from the people most impacted by it was key to effective problem solving – a position consistent with prominent normative deliberative democracy theorists (Young, 2000). The organizers believed that linking the policy, program, and experiential dimensions of homelessness in Calgary would result in a stronger voice for the homeless and would generate community awareness as well as partnerships and coordination within the sector.

The twofold goal of the Ad Hoc Committee in this period was to study the issue from the perspective of all of the important interests in the sector and to make policy recommendations. A massive effort towards this goal took many months and involved eight working groups representing various parts of the sector. Along with a major policy conference, the work of these groups constituted the major intellectual thrust towards a Community Action Plan, which identified five strategic directions to address homelessness: housing supply, an "umbrella system" to coordinate services, community awareness, Aboriginal services, and implementation.

Implementation was perhaps the biggest question mark in all of this. The Ad Hoc Committee was just that: it was an ad hoc, side-of-the-desk activity for all members, who had regular work commitments in the sector, and the effort lacked a backbone organization. As luck would have it, an entirely distinct community organization interested in homelessness in Calgary was just being created and was looking for a mandate: the Calgary Homeless Foundation, which I will call CAL-CHF. Formed in 1998 by businessman Art Smith, who had recently learned of the extent of the homelessness crisis unfolding in Calgary, CAL-CHF originated not from the grassroots but from the halls of power and influence in Calgary. Art Smith recruited friends and contacts from the highest levels of business and government, including the premier at the time, Ralph Klein, to organize a collective response to homelessness.

Members of the Ad Hoc Committee (the earliest version of CAL-main) watched the creation of CAL-CHF and were skeptical of its goals and approach. Despite the sincerity of Art Smith, the earliest days of CAL-CHF were infused with a sense that those in the non-profit sector had failed to solve the problem of homelessness and it was time for the successful capitalists to come in and save them from themselves. CAL-CHF was composed of outsiders to the homelessness sector, and while all of those concerned about homelessness viewed the private sector as an essential partner in solving the problem, the leadership of CAL-CHF did not share the conventions of extensive community consultation and deliberative problem-definition and policy-making (Scott, 2012). While CAL-CHF has evolved consider-ably since it was formed, the bureaucratic character of CAL-CHF remains a fundamental source of tension in the relationship between CAL-CHF and CAL-main today.

The primary mandate of CAL-CHF upon its creation was to marshal private and public dollars to be devoted to the acquisition or construction of affordable housing in Calgary. It was an extraordinarily lean organiza-tion, with only one staff member in the early years, since Art Smith always intended that every dollar possible should go directly to the cause at hand, not to creating a parallel bureaucracy (Scott, 2012). As such, CAL-CHF had little capacity to generate a strategic plan, but the new Community Action Plan, devised by CAL-main, had been created with extensive community involvement and joint planning; all it needed was a vehicle to implement it. After some initial skepticism from the homelessness sector about what Art Smith was up to, executive directors of some of the major homeless service providers heard Smith's pitch and signed on. CAL-CHF therefore became the vehicle and governance institution charged with the implementation of Calgary's first Community Action Plan.

CAL-CHF was not exactly a community-based effort or a traditional governance network, despite the presence of some community voices on its board of directors. The organization needed a mechanism to link it, on an ongoing basis, to the community; at this point, the Ad Hoc Committee evolved into the more institutionalized Community Action Committee (CAL-main) and began a long and complicated relationship with CAL-CHF. Designed to be the collective voice for the community and the key source of policy and program advice to CAL-CHF, which at the time was merely an implementation agent, CAL-main also sought to preserve its autonomy from CAL-CHF. CAL-CHF would slowly evolve and grow into a major force, with private dollars and, later, provincial government homelessness dollars flowing through it. It eventually became much more than an imple-mentation agent; in fact, it evolved into a policy generator.

CAL-main also expanded to become an unparalleled collection of agen-cies and civil society representatives in the homelessness sector. Its full membership now exceeds one hundred, and it has a large executive from diverse segments of the homelessness sector. To this day, CAL-main has preserved the numerous working (or sector) groups that formed to help devise the first Community Action Plan, each of which represents a particu-lar sector and elects a chair to be its representative at CAL-main. While the sector groups have not been static since their formation, and some are more active than others, they have tended to include the following homelessness sectors: singles, families, youth, women fleeing violence, mental health and addictions, seniors, and Aboriginal peoples. These sector groups have generated sector-specific one- and three-year strategic plans and play an important role in the prioritization and allocation of funds over which CAL-main exercises control. In this regard, CAL-main was a natural choice as the community advisory board for the National Homelessness Initiative (NHI) when it was launched in 1999, and it continues to serve that function under its successor, the Homelessness Partnering Strategy (HPS). In this role, CAL-main, like VAN-main and TO-main, is tasked with devising a community plan to address homelessness and with making decisions regarding federal government investments in Calgary. Thus, despite the differences across the cities in the precise governance relationships, these three governance networks share similar purposes and tasks and can be fruitfully compared.

CAL-main and CAL-CHF would continue to exist simultaneously as collectivities with distinct mandates, while also being connected, in that CAL-main, until 2008, served as the link between the CAL-CHF board of directors and the homelessness sector and CAL-CHF serves as the financial agent for CAL-main for the purposes of the federal HPS program. CAL-main and CAL-CHF have this somewhat bizarre relationship in part because the City of Calgary avoided taking on the "community entity" role, unlike Metro Vancouver and Toronto. Since CAL-main had no institutional home in local government, the federal government forced a marriage between CAL-main and CAL-CHF, because CAL-main is, legally speaking, just a group of civil society actors, not an incorporated entity that can formally administer federal government funds.

In 2008, despite the efforts of CAL-main and CAL-CHF, homelessness remained stubbornly high, so much so that, by 2015, Calgary's homeless population had exceeded 3,500 indviduals (Passifume, 2015). CAL-CHF was, in essence, rebooted with Calgary's imported *10-Year Plan to End Homelessness*, which began an aggressive drive by CAL-CHF to take more control of efforts in the sector (CHF, 2010). I say "imported" because the idea for ten-year plans began in the United States and had a charismatic salesperson in Philip Mangano, the Homelessness Czar, as some called him, under President George W. Bush. Although these plans are meant to be community-wide efforts, in practice, they come with some predefined principles based on their use on the United States, two of which are the Housing First paradigm and a focus on the most chronically homeless. Housing First, as described previously, is a rights-based framework for addressing homelessness that starts with the premise that the first thing a homeless person needs is a home (with accompanying relevant services) and that a homeless person should not first be required to demonstrate a "readiness" for housing by dealing with issues like mental illness, addiction, trauma, or income inadequacy. Housing First principles have considerable intuitive appeal and, in fact, have been demonstrably successful for some populations, but one controversial part of Housing First is that by definition, it focuses resources on the chronically homeless, who generally constitute the most visible homeless population. Thus, Housing First is criticized by some segments of the homeless sector as a mechanism "to clean up the streets"; in addition, in a context of scarce resources, the Housing First approach necessarily diverts money from prevention, families, and other more episodic experiences of homelessness, like women fleeing violence.[2]

Calgary's 10-Year Plan to End Homelessness (CCEH, 2008) was devised and drafted not by CAL-main but by an ad hoc group called the Calgary Committee to End Homelessness (CCEH). The CCEH encompassed more than the homelessness sectors that are represented at CAL-main; the organization included business interests, private foundations, charitable organizations, and government officials. Key components of the *10-Year Plan* include eliminating chronic homelessness (via Housing First), retiring 50 percent of shelter spaces in five years, reducing the average stay in shelters to seven days (since revised to ten days), and obtaining $3.1 billion from government and private sector sources to construct affordable housing and increase rent supplements. It was primarily the CCEH members who found the Housing First paradigm most appealing, with key members of CAL-main being less convinced, although by 2008 the situation was deteriorating so rapidly in Calgary that even the skeptical hoped this would be a silver bullet. Maria Giacomin, at the time with the Calgary Urban Project Society, was skeptical of the focus on the most chronically homeless but felt that "we have to give it a try" (quoted in Scott, 2012, p. 136). On the one hand, one of the advantages of drawing on the voices and skills of those previously outside of the housing and homelessness services system is that they have fewer preconceptions about what needs to be done; on the other hand, they may come with a certain naïveté about how alternative approaches, like Housing First, may work in the context of the whole system, according to one interview respondent who wished to remain anonymous.[3] While this paradigm shift may have been controversial among some long-standing agencies, the ten-year plan process managed to rope the provincial government into a more serious engagement in housing and homelessness, with a significant short-term injection of investments into Calgary.

As with the Community Action Plan in 1998, CAL-CHF was ultimately selected as the vehicle to implement *Calgary's 10-Year Plan to End Homelessness* – again, because the City of Calgary refused to own anything related to housing and homelessness, although this time, the City had significantly more resources and staff to execute and reorient the housing and homelessness sector. Alternative vehicles to implement the plan were considered – including the City of Calgary, the provincial government, a new organization, or the newly organized CAL-CHF – but the consensus was that there needed to be a single point of accountability and ultimate responsibility. After CAL-CHF was selected to implement the plan, CAL-main was once again brought in as the central advisory body for CAL-CHF, formally serving as a subcommittee of CAL-CHF. The newly empowered CAL-CHF was initially granted considerable goodwill from those working in the homelessness sector, in part because of the significant new resources that were extracted from the provincial government in concert with the implementation of the plan. But as in the past, CAL-CHF and CAL-main exist in a complicated marriage, one that goes through happy times as well as more challenging periods. CAL-main still possesses the authority to establish priorities and make investment decisions regarding Government of Canada homelessness funds; it has always had ambitions to be more than that, but in recent years, it has been crowded out by CAL-CHF. This has brought about various revisioning exercises since 2008 aimed at carving out a clearer role for CAL-main. These matters are even more pressing today because, in 2008, CAL-CHF wrote its own organization's death notice: in 2018, CAL-CHF would dissolve, as that would be the point at which homelessness will have ended in Calgary (Scott, 2012, p. 4). At the time of writing, despite the stubborn persistence of homelessness in Calgary, the clock at CAL-CHF headquarters is still counting down.

Applying Theory to Calgary's Networks

Like the networks in Vancouver and Toronto, the key features of the two Calgary homelessness governance networks can be categorized into two groups: internal properties (their institutionalization and inclusiveness) and external properties (their metagovernance context).[4] Figure 2.4 (page 43) positions CAL-main and CAL-CHF in the network governance matrix with respect to institutionalization and inclusiveness. Compared to TO-main,

TABLE 5.1
Metagovernance contexts of Calgary governance networks

Metagovernor leadership (agency)	Institutional policy space (structure)	
	Narrow	Expansive
Cooperative	*Administrative* metagovernance (CAL-CHF, 1998–2015)	*Dynamic* metagovernance (CAL-main, 1998–2008)
Contentious	*Straitjacket* metagovernance (CAL-main, 2008–15)	*Volatile* metagovernance

CAL-main is much more institutionalized and inclusive. CAL-CHF is distinct from any other governance network in this study; like the other networks, it began as a network of community actors, but it has since moved towards a more corporate model of governance, with a powerful secretariat performing much of the most important policy analysis and program development. Still, CAL-CHF practices sufficiently collaborative governance to be analyzed as a governance network.

Like that of the networks in Vancouver and Toronto, the analysis of the Calgary homelessness governance networks must be completed by examining their metagovernance contexts, which, regardless of a network's internal properties, tends to have a mediating effect on its performance. The Calgary homelessness governance networks are placed in their respective metagovernance categories in Table 5.1.

Figure 2.6 (page 46) illustrates the different impacts of dynamic and straitjacket metagovernance contexts on policy development, and we will see that metagovernance context explains CAL-main's early policy achievements as well as its more recent listlessness.

Having described and contextualized the Calgary governance networks, we move now to the policy changes in Calgary during the period under investigation, 1995 to 2015, in order to place the Calgary homelessness governance networks within the theoretical framework outlined in Chapter 2.

Policy Innovation and System Coordination, 1995–2015

I track the policy innovation and system coordination of Calgary's networks following the same method as for Vancouver and Toronto. A comparison of the Calgary governance networks with those in Toronto shows that the former exhibit more numerous and substantive policy innovation and system coordination in the past twenty years than the latter. The policy achievements in Calgary are comparable in scale to the policy outputs of the Vancouver networks – though in some respects, they are quite different.

CAL-main

Integrated governance network theory predicts that CAL-main would generate relatively high levels of policy innovation and system coordination, since it is one of the more institutionalized and inclusive of the governance networks under investigation and it operated in a dynamic metagovernance context in its first ten years, and this prediction is generally borne out. In the period from 2008 to 2015, however, CAL-main has had limited policy influence in terms of innovation and coordination, and this is primarily due to the heavily constrained metagovernance context under which it has operated during that time. The early years of policy innovation and coordination, in which CAL-main operated under a dynamic metagovernance context, will be documented first.

CAL-main achieved profound policy innovation, in the form of new governance approaches or ways of organizing the sector, in its early years. The network's first major innovation was related to its structure as a site through which to channel sector-specific knowledge and expertise. In ways more sophisticated than any governance network examined in Vancouver and Toronto, CAL-main is more of a confederation of sector networks than a single governance network. CAL-main comprises eight long-lasting sector networks: singles, families, family violence (women), mental health, addictions, seniors, youth, and Aboriginal peoples. Each of these subsectors has its own one-year and three-year strategic plans, and each elects its own chair, who represents it to CAL-main's executive authority. While some of these subsectors have been more active than others, interview respondents almost universally suggested that collectively, these eight networks have been a powerful force inducing policy change in the sector.

Meeting records from CAL-main indicate that it was in these meetings where emerging trends on the ground were first identified and solutions contemplated, trends such as the changing demographics of the homeless population, which government did not appreciate or acknowledge; the massive growth in demand for emergency services; the surprising (to agencies) preference among homeless clients for centralized services; and the first signs of the intersectional drivers for homelessness that draw in sectors like corrections and child welfare, systems that do not conceive of themselves as part of the homelessness sector (Community Action Committee [CAC], minutes, 2003, 2004, 2006). The awareness of this intersectionality would later evolve into one of the most innovative changes emerging out of Calgary from CAL-CHF – the systems planning framework (CHF, 2012). Evidence suggests, however, that this framework originated in the early years of CAL-main as various sectors shared experiences and identified developing trends. Leslie McMechan, who is involved in the youth sector, said that in the early days "we were doing a lot of systems work too because we always felt that the problem was that the provincial government didn't acknowledge non-Child Protective Services kids," demonstrating that other sectors – in this case, the child welfare system – could be a major feeder into homelessness in ways that government would have never recognized.[5]

In terms of system coordination, CAL-main is among the most elaborate and successful of the eight governance networks studied. Not only is it larger in membership than most of the others, perhaps accounting for the less-than-active membership among some agencies, but it is structured with coordination in mind as a key principle. Because CAL-main is, in many ways, more of a confederation of eight sector networks of agencies than a single governance network (like VAN-main, for instance), it was the originator of numerous system coordination initiatives. For example, one of the first tasks of the group of agencies that would later form CAL-main was to initiate and direct the first-ever studies to get a baseline understanding of services in Calgary and how they were experienced by homeless clients. These early studies – *Street Speaks* and the *Calgary Homelessness Study* – directly shaped policy and investments in the working homeless and in homeless families because they identified emerging issues that were previously underappreciated or misunderstood by government funders (Hawkesworth, 2003).

One of the chief coordination ideas that came out of the 1998 *Calgary Homelessness Study*, which CAL-main directed, was the idea of the "umbrella system," a new way of thinking about service provision that sought to unite agencies under a common and cohesive framework that involved coordination, standards, centralized data management, and agency partnerships. This idea had the potential to shift thinking away from agency-centric service mandates towards privileging homeless individuals' perspectives and experiences. CAL-main identified a significant appetite for this approach among not only the homeless population but also some agencies. Other agencies resisted the umbrella system idea, seeing adopting common

standards or having to take direction from elsewhere as a potential infringe-
ment on their autonomy. This caused the umbrella system idea to go on ice
for a number of years. With the passage of time and some education in the
sector, agency resistance to this new conceptualization waned, and by 2008,
the newly empowered CAL-CHF was able to implement the umbrella idea
to create one of the most coordinated systems in the country. According to
one agency executive director in Calgary, the forcing of the service-sector
components together "under an umbrella, if you will, has been positive in
standardizing and raising the bar around standards. It's been good in terms
of elevating the recognition that people need to have training and qualifica-
tions and experience and education to do this work well."[6]

While the idea of a formal umbrella system remained controversial and
thus would sit on the shelf for a number of years after it was first floated
by CAL-main, many agency representatives suggested that CAL-main itself
had value in terms of system coordination, replicating the findings from the
more effective of the Vancouver and Toronto governance networks. One
interviewee claimed that CAL-main provided a critical opportunity to learn
"a little bit about other people's programs" and to "refer people back and
forth."[7] Another respondent, Sue Fortune of Pathways to Housing, com-
menting on the impact of CAL-main on system coordination, said, "I think
we need to work together and understand the other agencies that are offering housing, because sometimes transferring of folks is necessary."[8] And
yet another CAL-main member, Nic Calder of the John Howard Society,
while grumbling about the time investment associated with the network,
still maintained its importance in terms of coordination: "We actually get
really helpful information that helps us to shift our programming in a certain direction, or information about what another agency is doing that we
could maybe adopt or kind of tweak and change and fit into our context.
And I think it really does help us achieve all of our goals."[9] In the absence of
institutionalized governance networks, this dynamic is less apparent, as the
case of Toronto illustrates.

Two additional concrete examples of system coordination organized and
driven by CAL-main are the Community Forum, which occurs twice a year
and affords agencies the opportunity to take stock of what is emerging on
the ground to consolidate a vision in terms of appropriate response, and the
biannual Leadership Forum, a smaller gathering of key decision-makers in
Calgary to contemplate higher-order policy and funding issues. According
to participants, these are key venues to "explore intersections between sectors" and engage in a "dialogue with other systems" (e.g., corrections, child

welfare, mental health) that contribute to homelessness by virtue of their policies (CAC, 2013, p. 6). It is at CAL-main meetings and at these forums where key policy-makers and funders in Calgary have learned of policies and programs that were not working as intended and needed to be refined.

According to meeting records, among the examples of policy and program problems identified at CAL-main are transit policies for homeless youth and housing for seniors. CAL-main has also been a key source of resistance to what it has called a "one size fits all" approach, which many in the service community believe Housing First represents (CAC, 2012, 2014a, 2014b; CAC, minutes, 2013). CAL-main has been partially successful in pulling CAL-CHF away from the one rationality, Housing First, that appeared to form the basis for all of its work. It is becoming evident that the Housing First approach may not be effective for meeting the diversity of needs among the homeless population, even if the broader philosophy is generally accepted. Thus, CAL-main, by virtue of its sector diversity and dynamism, has managed to successfully convince key decision-makers of a more comprehensive response to homelessness, much as VAN-main and VAN-emerg have influenced key provincial policy-makers in BC Housing.

CAL-main preceded the 1999 launch of the National Homelessness Initiative (NHI) but was drawn into the program to perform the function of the federally mandated community advisory board. While CAL-CHF also existed at this time, CAL-main was more of a community-oriented network that could perfectly fulfill the NHI requirements; CAL-CHF was focused on capital investments in affordable housing, which was (and still is) expressly prohibited as a priority under NHI rules. Thus, CAL-main focused on the program and service investments in Calgary, funded through the NHI, whereas CAL-CHF remained focused on capital investments in building or acquiring affordable-housing units, primarily through private sector funding, complemented, in later years, by provincial funding (CAC, minutes, 2003).

The main task of CAL-main, as mandated by the NHI, is to prioritize and allocate approximately $6 million annually in homelessness programs. CAL-main represents the most elaborate community deliberative process of decision making on homelessness programs among the networks compared in Canada. The network's collaborative granting process (CGP) is an extraordinary effort that can take as long as one year, from devising requests for program proposals to final decisions. The CGP begins with the distribution of program proposals received from community agencies to the relevant sector within CAL-main – that is, to one of the network's eight institutionalized subsector networks, which evaluate, deliberate on, and rank the proposals. The subsector recommendations are then sent to the Sector Council of CAL-main (made up of the chairs of all eight subsectors), which accepts or refines the recommendations and then sends them to the larger CAL-main table. Finally, the CAL-main decisions for program funding are sent to the (Calgary) Funders' Table, which consists of the leadership of CAL-CHF, CAL-main, Alberta Gaming, Family and Community Support Services (Alberta government), and community foundations like United Way (CAC, minutes, 2003). (The Funders' Table was replicated in Vancouver as the Metro Vancouver Investors' Table, discussed in Chapter 3.) This process, which may seem overly elaborate for $6 million, in fact enjoys considerable support among participants, who continually reflect on it as one of the best examples of their work in terms of process and outcomes.

According to one member involved in the CGP, the Funders' Table, "to the best of my knowledge, is a unique concept, maybe in North America, maybe in Canada ... where a number of different people with ability to fund these proposals get together and try to coordinate their priorities and their funding resources" (quoted in Hawkesworth, 2003, p. 79). The idea is to try to fuse ground-level agency perspectives into policy and program funding decisions with a higher-level strategic approach by the funders, who can see macro-level needs across the city. One advantage of a broader Funders' Table is that if a program proposal does not meet the strategic priorities of one funder, it may fit those of another, and the funders, working collectively, can better see how programs fit together as a whole.[10]

When interviewed, those who have participated in the CGP generally referenced the positive value of an institutionalized space in which ground-level agencies are granted authority to collectively shape the service sector; this aligns with similar findings in Vancouver and Toronto. The CGP is a process through which "many difficult decisions were made as part of the deliberation process" and "the funding recommendations are reflective of the objectives the sectors would like to achieve" (CAC, minutes, 2004, p. 2). Internal reviews of the CGP are conducted regularly, and while modifications have been made over the years to be more efficient while retaining an inclusive decision-making space (e.g., removing the Sector Council middle step), the reviews concluded that "overall the results of this work are excellent" (CAC, minutes, 2004, p. 3). In fact, while CAL-main members are quick to critique what the network does not do well or how it does not live up to its potential, internal surveys of members reveal that most feel that what CAL-main does best is marshal an exceptional amount of knowledge and expertise and keep major funders attuned to what is happening on the ground (CAC, membership engagement survey, 2011). We know from the more in-depth analysis of this type of collaborative decision-making at VAN-main that decision-making conducted in this fashion rather than in the traditional bureaucratic manner results in systematic differences in the policy priorities and programs selected.

For the first ten years of the National Homelessness Initiative, the Government of Canada gave wide latitude to governance networks like CAL-main, which encouraged some experimental efforts, programs, and service models. One feature of CAL-main decision making regarding funding that is different from government-driven processes is that the network makes provisions to allow for what are called "out-of-cycle" program funding applications, an acknowledgment that community service needs do not always align with government funding and accounting cycles. This was evidenced in meeting records, although some CAL-main members began to worry that allowing for out-of-cycle applications was causing the network to drift from its "emergency" or "very special case" framework, and CAL-main eventually reined in – but did not eliminate – the opportunities for this type of application. Changing dynamics on the street or in response to policy or program changes at other levels of government (e.g. emergency shelter closures, rapidly rising demand for services among youth, or weather-related forces) mean that homeless service providers often need to respond quickly. CAL-main, given its agency-based membership, is well aware of such pressures and recognizes that the traditional once-per-year funding cycles of governments are a major barrier. Consequently, it was keen to shift from and accommodate a limited amount of out-of-cycle program funding.

According to one former CAL-main member, Robert Parry, who reflected rather critically on CAL-main, the CGP is one of the best outputs of the governance network. If there were no community-oriented effort towards policy planning and decision making on funding, "the decisions would be horrible," he said, adding that "the federal government has no idea" what works and what does not.[11] Leslie McMechan, a CAL-main member who has been involved in a number of CGP processes, recalls that CAL-main once had "a lot of leeway" in terms of investments, but this changed in 2014 with the metagovernance changes to the federal HPS program. She described the program as having "changed now, completely," and the federal approach as very rigid: "This is the box and we are not going outside the box."[12]

CAL-CHF

While all of the governance networks under investigation are different from one another to varying degrees, CAL-CHF is unique among the eight networks in that it is a formally incorporated charitable foundation with key elements of a collaborative ethic. It has also been delegated more authority from government to address homelessness than any of the governance networks examined in this book (and probably more than any across the whole country), especially after 2008, when it was selected by the Province of Alberta and the City of Calgary to implement *Calgary's 10-Year Plan to End Homelessness* (CCEH, 2008). Yet even from its creation in 1998, CAL-CHF has been responsible for considerable policy innovation and system coordination, despite its initial limited mandate – to raise money from the private sector for the construction of affordable housing and to serve as the vehicle for the implementation of the first Community Action Plan in 1998. This mandate slowly expanded such that by 2015, CAL-CHF was indisputably the unrivalled authority for homelessness policy and programs in Calgary.

The early years of the CHF were focused primarily on fundraising through the private sector; it received no money from the provincial or municipal governments for affordable housing.[13] The provincial government, like most others in Canada, had just withdrawn from social housing provision, partly in response to the federal government withdrawal, and thus was not exactly prepared to re-enter the policy field that it had just vacated a few years earlier. Over the years, CAL-CHF has slowly leveraged private dollars to acquire and maintain affordable housing units, and by 2015, the organization owned thirty buildings with over five hundred units in total, and another eight new apartment buildings were under development (CHF, annual report, 2014). Although the Province of Alberta recommitted to a role in affordable housing in 2008, in conjunction with Calgary's *10-Year Plan*, and provided substantial funds to help CAL-CHF acquire these properties, it remained a priority of CAL-CHF, as a founding partner of the 2012 RESOLVE campaign, to seek out private sector funds to fund the construction or acquisition of affordable housing units. RESOLVE, a partnership of nine agencies with the goal of raising $120 million, had raised $16 million by early 2015.

One of the earliest policy innovations to emerge from CAL-CHF was a damage-deposit loan program. CAL-CHF learned from the 1998 *Calgary Homelessness Study*, directed by CAL-main, that nearly half of all homeless people in Calgary were employed but were trapped in homelessness because they could not afford the damage deposit required to secure a housing unit. This finding went against all conventional wisdom inside government about the primary features of the homeless population: namely, that all homeless people were lazy, unemployed drug addicts. Service agencies and advocates for the homeless knew this to be true, but they needed non-government-controlled governance networks like CAL-main and CAL-CHF to demonstrate this to government and thus force its hand, which is exactly what happened. The idea of loaning funds for damage deposits was popular among CAL-CHF board members, many of whom came from the business community and, perhaps not surprisingly, adhered to the personal responsibility theory of homelessness (Scott, 2012). Art Smith, the businessman who initiated CAL-CHF, secured financial support from private sector friends to launch the damage-deposit loan program, the rapid uptake for which signalled that it was meeting a key need in Calgary. In 2004, CAL-CHF transferred the program to an organization called Momentum, because administering this program was preventing CAL-CHF from obtaining charitable status, which was viewed as necessary to more effectively raise private sector funds for affordable housing.[14]

Upon the 1999 announcement of the Government of Canada's National Homelessness Initiative (NHI), under which CAL-main was named the community advisory board and thus tasked with deciding how to prioritize and allocate federal dollars, CAL-CHF was selected as the "community entity" (the role played by Metro Vancouver and the City of Toronto) for the purposes of the program, essentially making it an administrative agent for the Government of Canada. CAL-main existed before CAL-CHF was formed but was a bit suspicious of its growing role, especially since the CAL-CHF board comprised mainly business people from outside the sector. But each network agreed to work collaboratively because of the mutual need for both networks to be successful in their own mandates (e.g., CAL-CHF is part of the Collaborative Granting Process as a funder); CAL-main focused on homelessness programs, and CAL-CHF focused on capital investments in affordable housing (CAC, minutes, 2003). In the early 2000s, CAL-CHF began to acquire affordable housing buildings with the funds acquired from the private sector and with occasional City of Calgary financial or in-kind support on particular projects.

CAL-CHF members, aware of their lack of direct access to policy levers – that is, of not having institutional space or authority to make policy decisions, even in an advisory role – engaged in considerable sophisticated lobbying and education of senior decision-makers, primarily in the provincial government. CAL-CHF benefited from having high-profile public relations experts as members of the board, who were assembled in a Government Relations Committee to "compile a database of politicians and civil servants and other 'influencers' who can be turned into 'champions'" devoted to ending homelessness in Calgary (CAC, minutes, 2004). This was, however, a long-term strategy, so CAL-CHF, in the mid-2000s, did not produce the type of policy innovation and sectoral coordination that many had hoped it might. The former CEO of CAL-CHF, John Currie, noted that CAL-CHF, during its first eight years, had experienced success in terms of providing temporary housing but not long-term housing (Laird, 2007). Yet the behind-the-scenes education and advocacy by CAL-CHF later paid big dividends, when CAL-CHF relaunched in 2008 with considerable buy-in from the highest levels of the provincial government.

In response to rapidly rising homelessness from 2000 to 2007 – from thirteen hundred to thirty-five hundred homeless estimated by the point-in-time homeless count (Scott, 2012) – CAL-CHF and others in the homelessness sector were mobilized to rethink how they were doing things in terms of policy and programs; they were convinced that something had to be done to goad the province to the table. To this end, members of CAL-CHF and CAL-main, as well as others outside of the homelessness sector, came together to devise *Calgary's 10-Year Plan to End Homelessness*. The plan's goal was that by 2018, no one would be homeless for longer than seven days. CAL-CHF, with considerable membership from the private sector, believed that the message that would most effectively convince Albertans to try to end homelessness was that it would be less expensive to address homelessness aggressively than to continue to manage it via emergency shelters and, less visibly, through hospitals and jails. One of the major innovations brought to Calgary as part of the *10-Year Plan*, which CAL-CHF is charged with executing, is the principle of Housing First, described earlier. The Province of Alberta rallied strongly behind Housing First and provided additional funds to CAL-CHF for the purpose of implementing this approach. CAL-CHF prioritized the chronically homeless for Housing First programs, which, in essence, responded to public concerns about growing street homelessness.

Housing First is popular among those who advocate a "right" to housing, as well as among more conservative elements of society because it tends to result in erasing the most visible manifestations of homelessness in business districts. And it was a remarkable success for the prioritized population: in a sample of 270 people housed for twelve months, 92 percent of clients retained their housing and also improved their physical and mental health conditions, resulting in reductions in the use of hospitals, emergency rooms, and ambulances and in interactions with police (CHF, annual report, 2012). A national Housing First experiment by the Canadian Mental Health Association produced similar results for the chronically homeless, but it was successful in part because of the substantial resources ($100 million) devoted to the study (Doberstein & Smith, 2015). Although the Government of Canada endorses Housing First, it does not supply funds towards housing construction, and in contexts where resources are scarce, funds tend to be diverted away from other populations that may not be best served by Housing First, including youth, Aboriginal people, and families (CAC, 2014b). These three populations represent the chief areas of growth in homelessness in Calgary since 2008 (CHF, 2014), and thus, Housing First remains a controversial policy approach among some in the homelessness sector.

A policy direction advanced by CAL-CHF that represents both innovation and system coordination is what is known as the "systems planning" agenda. Recall that in 1998, CAL-main floated the idea of an umbrella model whereby data, service standards, and coordination would fit within a cohesive whole but faced resistance on implementation as agencies feared a reduction of autonomy. According to Bob Hawkesworth, who was involved in the formation of the umbrella model conceptualization, "agencies worried that the Calgary Homeless Foundation [CAL-CHF] or government might use funding of an umbrella model as a means to dictate policy and operational considerations" (Hawkesworth, 2003, p. 107).

The model remained controversial in some sectors in 2008, but there was a growing sense that big change was needed, and it was time for a governance body like CAL-CHF to push this through the remaining pockets of resistance in the service community. The first critical step to devising a more sophisticated map of the service system in Calgary was the implementation of the Homeless Management Information System (HMIS) in 2011. Despite the long-established piecemeal efforts of some individual agencies to make better use of data about their clients, there was much that decision makers did not know about the homeless population and their interactions with the housing and service system. According to Alina Turner, formerly of CAL-CHF, moving towards HMIS would provide the opportunity to do the following:

- gather system-wide, standardized data on individuals experiencing homelessness, including how long they had been without a home, their demographic characteristics, and their needs

- obtain a better understanding of the experiences of homeless individuals by tracking the services they received
- improve co-ordination between agencies, resulting in better referrals and a reduction in administration
- improve decision making on program design and policy proposals. (Scott, 2012, p. 180)

CAL-CHF was able to incentivize service agencies to join the standardized data regime by virtue of its status as one of their funders, first as a pilot exercise with a small number of agencies to demonstrate that this was not about colonization but about more effective operational framework. CAL-CHF thus exercised its spending power to generate some alignment in the sector, which most service agencies agreed was necessary to avoid individuals slipping through the cracks. As this spread across service agencies in Calgary in 2011–12, the rich data coming in allowed CAL-CHF to begin to think about how to design a more sophisticated "system of care" characterized by coordinated services, housing, and programs (Scott, 2012). This led to the development of the CAL-CHF System Planning Framework, which focused on identifying system gaps and priorities for investment; leveraging data for performance measurement; establishing standards of care; and moving towards common intake, assessment, and referrals (CHF, annual report, 2012). Critical to the evolution into a system of care is the agreement of agencies and funders on collective screening, referral, prioritization, and intake processes, so that wherever a client presents in the system, all paths leads to housing and to needed supports. Thus, a central goal of CAL-CHF in the second phase of implementing the *10-Year Plan* was to develop a consistent process of moving homeless clients through the system in a fair, effective, and efficient way.

The sense from many in the service sector is that some of these reforms – particularly standardized data collection, standards of care, and coordinated assessment and access – are beginning to transform what was once a fairly siloed homeless-serving sector to a more coordinated, efficient, and effective sector. And while these reforms involved the service sector in planning around implementation, top-down directives from CAL-CHF were essential in spurring the critical shifts towards data standardization and sharing, as well as systems planning. Although some stakeholders are critical of the sometimes heavy-handed approach of CAL-CHF, others suggest that some of the major changes that were necessary for the sector to be more effective required a coercive hand.[15] CAL-CHF leadership is certainly aware of the critique in the community of their approach, with former CEO Tim Richter admitting, "We shocked the system with the pace. It was pretty relentless. We pressed people to act quickly, hoping to imbue the sector with some urgency" (quoted in Scott, 2012, p. 187).

As a central part of the strategy around systems planning, CAL-CHF devised and implemented a system of coordinated access and assessment (CAA) in late 2013. The purpose of CAA is "to facilitate a standardized process of assessment and centralized point of entry to the Housing First programs to address homelessness in Calgary," and CAA is designed as a triaging model, to meet the needs of the most vulnerable first, and a diversion mechanism, to reduce unnecessary new entries into the homelessness system (CHF, 2013). The CAA system aims to solve a number of problems in the housing and homelessness service sector, the first being the difficulty of measuring how clients are being served across the various housing programs in the city without a mechanism to track their experience. Without tracking data, there was limited accountability among agencies for the programs they offer. The second problem that CAA aims to ameliorate is the temptation among agencies to "skim the cream" – to select for their programs clients who are low acuity (i.e., less vulnerable and thus easier to serve), leaving the most chronically homeless underserved. The third major problem before the creation of CAA was related to each agency having its own assessment procedure and independent wait-list, which is not only inefficient for both the client and agency but also limits an agency's information on what housing programs and services clients have used in the past and were, perhaps, not appropriate for their situation. CAA thus attempts to standardize data collection for those seeking housing to better match acuity and needs to specific housing programs, thus helping people move successfully and efficiently through the system (CHF, 2013).

CAA has been implemented in Calgary under the leadership of CAL-CHF, which, by virtue of its funder status, is able to shift the behaviour of agencies that receive its funds for Housing First programs. All CAL-CHF-funded agencies that offer housing must participate in CAA as part of their service contract, and while there was consultation on implementation, the decision to move towards CAA was controversial among some segments, in part because it demands a huge effort from agencies and its success depends entirely on actual housing units being available.[16] That said, a system of coordinated access and assessment was an objective specified in the original *10-Year Plan* published in 2008, beginning with agencies shifting to the Homeless Management Information System (HMIS) in 2011, with the clearly defined goal of leveraging HMIS to move towards coordinated intake and assessment, which was a key community-derived priority (CHF, annual report, 2011).

CAA hinges on the use of standardized means to assess the acuity of clients seeking housing, and for this, CAL-CHF demands that agencies use a standard assessment tool to collect self-reported information on clients regarding their needs and vulnerabilities – the same tool that is in use in Toronto. The standard assessment tool is "to ensure fairness in placements with the focus on serving those with the most acute needs first and to accurately match the client to resources" (CHF, 2013). A client must complete an assessment in order to be entered into placement consideration by one of the four placement committees of CAA – high acuity, moderate acuity, youth, and family – which meet weekly to place clients in available housing programs. The placement committees are co-chaired by a CAA coordinator funded by CAL-CHF and a CAL-CHF representative and are principally constituted by the relevant housing agencies funded by CAL-CHF, who collectively decide who, among the client list, will be matched to available and appropriate housing units and program spots. Thus, even at the program level, mini-governance networks collectively problem-solve and deliberate over the appropriate placement of clients in housing programs.

The benefit of CAA, according to one respondent, is clear: "All the players trying to end homelessness who offer housing sit at the same table and look at this database and work together."[17] Placement committees not only place clients in appropriate housing, but also, through their weekly meetings, are able to maintain a real-time database of the status of the clients waiting for housing and to explore, on an ongoing basis, the opportunities outside of the CAA system for housing and services. Observing the placement committees in action confirmed that agencies are open to resource exchange and partnerships to fit a client's needs, demonstrating an impressive problem-solving dynamic in the context of extraordinarily scarce resources. For example, a housing vacancy at one organization was not quite suitable for a high acuity (e.g., chronically homeless) client under discussion, so another organization agreed to provide relevant support services to make the placement happen and thus to increase the likelihood of the client's success.

Calgary is one of the first major cities in Canada to institutionalize a comprehensive, coordinated system of assessment and access to housing, although it is the last among cities in Alberta, in part because of its larger scale and complexity. When interviewed, most agencies involved reported efficiency gains with respect to assessment and spoke positively about the more objective and accountable method of placing clients into housing. As of spring 2014, more than eight hundred assessments of individuals seeking housing had been completed, with an average of about thirty new assessments completed per week, indicating strong interest in CAA among service users (CHF, annual report, 2014). Despite these ostensible successes, some in the community are still critical of CAA, saying that it merely generates a single, long list of those waiting for housing, which is ineffective without any major new investments in actual housing units. In the four placement committee meetings I observed, there were fewer than five openings for *very* long lists of clients in need, and in one of the meetings, there were no housing openings at all. In these cases, the sophistication of the CAA process is undermined by the lack of capacity in the housing system. Yet another respondent said, "At first I was really against coordinated access and assessment. Now I find it's nice in the sense that when somebody's homeless you don't have to call ten different programs to try to get them on a wait list. So there's a lot less of that, making calls and checking in all the time."[18]

While there are those outside of the CAA process who remain very critical of its implementation, as well as some involved with CAA who have a certain amount of ambivalence, a more significant number believe that it is a revolutionary step towards more effectively addressing homelessness in Calgary, even if there have been hiccups along the way towards implementation. CAL-CHF was not surprised that CAA implementation was met, almost instantly, with a lack of affordable and supportive housing vacancies and with resistance from some community partners. In early CAA planning documents, CHF officials claimed they were clear that "this will not solve the bottleneck issue: more need for housing than there is space. However, this will help to manage waitlists, triage as best we can, identify gaps, information to advocate for more funding, lack of housing in the city."[19] At the very least, most involved with CAA would agree with the sentiment offered by one respondent:

I think it opened up conversations, discussions, partnerships. We're working together. We need to work together and understand the other agencies that are offering housing ... because there are a lot of people who don't really fit anywhere. We all know their name because they've cycled through all our programs. I think it [does] do a better job of identifying gaps in services to the homeless population.[20]

To another respondent, "the fact that those agencies all sit in the same room together is quite remarkable, and you don't actually realize that until you go somewhere else [referring to the weekly placement committee meetings]."[21] Despite all of the challenges and critiques, one housing agency leader suggested that "this should be good for our clients, so let's do what we can."[22] It is important to note that the information collected on clients isn't just used for placement. It is used to understand – in a quantifiable, non-anecdotal way – where the gaps in the system are, information that can be used to demonstrate investment need to senior levels of government.

On a broader level, CAL-CHF recognizes that while system coordination within the homelessness sector is absolutely necessary, it may not result in substantive change unless other "feeder" sectors of homelessness are brought into the conversation. In this regard, CAL-CHF is considerably further ahead than the Vancouver and Toronto governance networks in drawing in policy actors at the highest levels from mental health, corrections, and child welfare in order to stop the flow of entries into homelessness as a result of policy failures in other issue areas. Before CAL-CHF started collecting systematic data on clients and their histories, it was widely known anecdotally that the failures of other policy sectors was a key contributor to the growing homeless population. Correctional facilities, mental health institutions, and child and family services were effectively discharging individuals into homelessness. One respondent closely involved in systems planning with CAL-CHF recalls, "A couple of years into the plan, we realized, 'Oh, my God, all of these other systems are involved in it too.'"[23] Yet CAL-CHF and the homelessness sector partners have little to no influence on these massive institutions of care, mainly at the provincial level, which are difficult to engage into accountability and responsibility for homelessness.

Yet the picture emerging from the data being tracked across the city suggested that such institutions and their policy failures were overwhelming the homeless-serving agencies, and that if left unchecked, these failures would overwhelm any gains made *within* the sector in terms of coordination and integration. A key area of focus in the second phase of implementing the *10-Year Plan*, therefore, is the engagement of social service funders and mainstream systems outside of homelessness – chiefly health, corrections, and child and family services – to try to iron out major disjunctures at the nexus between the various systems (CHF, annual report, 2012). CAL-CHF has had some notable successes in drawing the Calgary Police Service, City bylaw enforcement officials, and Alberta Health Services into its Systems Planning Advisory Committee (SPAC), which resulted in positive changes to policy, particularly with respect to police and bylaw enforcement. Indeed, one enforcement official said, "I don't have keys to housing. I now have a lot of friends that do, so, basically, it's a collaboration and integration of services."[24] But the SPAC never became a venue for the big conversations about how corrections, mental health, and child welfare systems and policies need to be reformed and better aligned. Asked whether some of the efforts by CAL-CHF leaders to engage with leaders in some of these funnelling systems have managed to create change, one respondent said, "It is pretty minimal at this point."[25]

At the leadership level, however, CAL-CHF continues to make efforts to reach out to counterparts in the other relevant systems, encouraging them to appreciate that while policy failure may not show up in their own system, it may manifest in another system – the end-of-the-line system, which tends to be the homelessness sector. One example of an institutionalized mechanism for broader systems planning around homelessness is the Alberta Interagency Council on Homelessness (discussed in more detail below). With a few exceptions, noted below, most respondents acknowledged that the broader systems planning agenda is a worthwhile endeavour. One argued that "our clients dip into justice, hospital, housing and treatment. We all have to work together ... [to] streamline it, and the client is the one who gets the best service."[26]

Part of the challenge for those in the homeless-serving sector is making the case to the other feeder systems that, as one interviewee put it, "we are there dealing with the same people around similar issues, so how can we collaborate and communicate better and work alongside each other instead of against each other?"[27] The Calgary Discharge Planning Committee of CAL-CHF, with membership from corrections and health, is attempting to grapple with these connections to larger systems, but it is not clear to those involved that the major policy change required will find its origin there.[28]

Another respondent echoed this sentiment, claiming that "the social services world always has to do band-aid solutions and quick fixes to make up for other systems and their dysfunction."[29] Many in the social services sector are sympathetic to this argument but are skeptical about an easy solution, because any effective solutions will involve fundamental reconceptualizations of mental health, corrections, child welfare, social assistance rates, affordable housing, and even poverty. Affordable housing is undoubtedly the most significant barrier in the system, but it is not a conversation that the City of Calgary, the Province of Alberta, or the Government of Canada appear willing to seriously entertain with sufficient long-term financial support. And according to some respondents, this is where the original framing from CAL-CHF in business-friendly terms – that they were tackling homelessness principally to reduce the long-term burden on taxpayers – undermines a larger conversation about systemic inequalities and injustices in modern Canadian society. As one critical respondent said, "It was all about cutting the cost to the rest of us, saving the mainstream money from these people who abuse our systems. So that's a problem because that premise set us on a path."[30] As a result, according to another interviewee, "nobody talks about the real systemic piece of why this is all happening."[31]

Policy Change Derived from Other Sources

As was made clear in previous chapters, policy innovation and system coordination also comes from non-network players like mayors, city councillors, and premiers. One feature outside of the governance networks that makes Calgary different from Vancouver and Toronto is the City's current relative absence in generating a policy response to homelessness. In the early days of the homelessness crisis, the City was the only institutional player in the game. In fact, it engaged in some pioneering work, including conducting, in 1992, what many believe to be the first homeless count in a Canadian city (although it was not nearly as comprehensive as the pioneering VAN-main 2002 count, a major innovation now replicated virtually everywhere in the country). The City was also instrumental in funding early studies conducted by CAL-main and was always present in the development of the successive homelessness plans beginning in 1998. But it was never the lead organization or the one ultimately responsible for implementing plans, policies, and programs. The City is not totally absent today: it runs the Calgary Housing Company, has housing and social planners who are tapped into discussions and efforts in Calgary, and provides contributions to particular projects and programs on a small scale. Otherwise, though, it is not a major player in the field. This may be due, in part, to the emergence of CAL-CHF as the principal local governance body tasked with ending homelessness, but local political leaders remain divorced from the major debates in the field, including those over which the municipal government has complete control, such as inclusionary zoning and land-use policies that can incentivize the creation of affordable housing units.

Alongside an absent City of Calgary was an absent Province of Alberta for many years. Apart from Premier Klein providing some ad hoc resources in the late 1990s and early 2000s, the Province of Alberta took a hands-off approach until the tenure of Premier Stelmach, who responded to CAL-CHF's pleas to get the province back in the game. Under Stelmach in 2007,

Alberta became the first province to initiate a province-wide ten-year plan, *A Plan for Alberta: Ending Homeless in 10 Years* (Alberta Secretariat for Action on Homelessness, 2008), providing $231 million to advance the plan. The plan was developed by the Alberta Secretariat for Action on Homelessness, which would later evolve, under Premier Redford, into the Alberta Interagency Council on Homelessness, formed in 2012 with the aim of identifying barriers to achieving the ten-year plan and exploring what systemic changes were required to address housing and homelessness in Alberta. It was designed to bring community input and expertise to the highest levels of government at the provincial level.

The Interagency Council, an example of collaboration at the provincial level that has no current peer in Canada, serves as an institutionalized mechanism for broader systems planning. It recognizes that ending homelessness "requires comprehensive solutions that cut across multiple service systems and better integration with on-the-ground community organizations" (Alberta Interagency Council on Homelessness, 2012, p. 2). The council includes representatives at the assistant deputy minister level from the homelessness-adjacent policy fields of health, corrections, and child welfare, and part of its mandate is to review funding processes and models. One close observer of the Interagency Council is hopeful, because "everybody's there at the same table, hearing the frustrations of their colleagues, whether it's a public health institution, correctional institution, or government body. And then it's shared problem solving."[32] While the council is a positive step in the right direction, the sense from some in the community is that many of the difficult lifts in terms of system reform have not been forthcoming from the Interagency Council. As one prominent member of the service community, Linda McLean, said, "We've done the systems planning, we understand the gaps ... but if the money doesn't shift with that, then it's irrelevant – we can 'systems plan' until we're blue in the face."[33] It is too early to tell whether the Interagency Council will be able to shift the resources necessary and generate the cross-sectoral policy alignment and coordination needed to make big inroads in addressing the more systemic drivers of homelessness.

While CAL-CHF and CAL-main remain the major governance bodies at the local level that shape housing and homelessness policy and programs in Calgary, other examples of innovative efforts have come from outside their mandate. One such example is SORCe: Safe Communities Opportunity and Resource Centre, launched in June 2013. In response to an expansive, though largely uncoordinated, set of homeless-serving agencies in Calgary, in 2012, leaders of organizations and agencies dealing with the homeless began to brainstorm how the system could be better coordinated at the organizational level. Although coordinated access and assessment (CAA) was coordinating housing programs, there was no mechanism to coordinate the activity of all the other agencies who provide an array of services such as drop-in centres, employment services, detox programs, counselling, and the like. What emerged from these discussions was the recognition that "an over-arching mechanism was needed to coordinate the efforts of all the agencies. This grassroots, community, collaborative approach to mobilizing existing resources and relationships was SORCe" (Safe Communities and Opportunities Resource Centre, 2014, p. 3).

SORCe serves as a centralized referral point to programs and services offered in the community and is located in Calgary's downtown core. While it operates a centralized site of referral, it is the collaborative product of grassroots organizing among agencies rather than a top-down forced marriage by a senior government or CAL-CHF. SORCe is unique because it has no external funding; its institutional space, located in a prime real estate area, is donated by the Calgary Police Service (CPS) out of its own budget and is staffed, remarkably, by a rotating set of staff from fourteen homeless-serving agencies. The conception of SORCe was, perhaps surprisingly, driven by the CPS – in particular, Inspector Curtis Olson and Police Chief Rick Hanson. CPS officers and City bylaw enforcers grew increasingly frustrated by the ineffectiveness of dealing with the homeless population via ticketing and enforcement and wanted to be able to "take them and introduce them to people that might be able to help them."[34] A number of interviewees praised former Police Chief Rick Hanson, citing major shifts in the past four years in the CPS's interactions with homeless individuals. One police officer remarked that "he does not want his officers dealing with people who are sick, who have addictions and mental health and need to be connected with resources and supports and not arrested and cycling in and out of jail, which is fantastic."[35] While some officers still prefer traditional enforcement and are not interested in playing a brokerage role, the thinking of Chief Hanson and Inspector Olson has filtered down to the ground level. For example, instead of issuing a ticket to an individual for failing to pay the transit fare, police officers may talk with the person, learn that he or she has just been evicted and has nowhere to go, and bring him or her down to SORCe for connections to services.

The philosophy behind SORCe represents a conceptual shift from program-centred to a client-centred thinking, which means, according to one interviewee, that "individuals seeking services are not 'your client' and 'my client'" but "everybody's client," and the goal is to find "the best fit" for each individual.[36] The idea is to provide a single point of access for individuals in need, and SORCe is staffed by individuals who are specially trained with knowledge of the service landscape so they can make appropriate referrals that will result in a simpler experience for the client and faster access to services. The first step for most individuals upon their arrival at SORCe is an initial assessment of need, which may proceed to a formal assessment, through coordinated access and assessment, towards receiving housing funded by CAL-CHF. Also, an individual may receive targeted referrals to non-CAL-CHF housing opportunities, mental health and addiction treatment, employment and training, and transportation, as required. In some cases, SORCe staff are able begin service enrolment immediately and provide transport, rather than rely on a cold referral and hope the client goes to the agency sometime in the future.[37]

While still in its early days, SORCe represents an innovative, grassroots effort to collaborate at the organizational level to generate more system cohesion and coordination. Some, however, are skeptical of its operationalization and effectiveness, including some who are involved with it. It has no external funding, and its hours of operation are limited to regular working hours, Monday to Friday, which, while convenient for staff, may not align with the service needs and patterns of homeless individuals.[38] Also, SORCe primarily serves to coordinate existing services, which means that it is inherently limited by the capacity of the system, and it has no independent mechanism through which to initiate broader change.

Theoretical Implications

This analysis of the governance networks in Calgary provides findings that generally conform to the theoretical model described in Chapter 2, which predicts that highly institutionalized and inclusive governance networks will generate or contribute to superior policy innovation and system coordination, depending, in part, on the metagovernance context. The Calgary networks, especially CAL-CHF, are highly institutionalized and inclusive, and numerous examples of policy innovation and system coordination have flowed directly from their activities.

Some of the most innovative policies and clearest examples of system coordination in the country have emerged from the two governance networks in Calgary. In its first ten years, from 1998 to 2008, CAL-main was a leading force in generating innovative policy ideas like the umbrella system, which would later form the basis for CAL-CHF's coordinated access and assessment process, and the systems planning framework, which is at the leading edge in Canada in drawing in relevant sectors like mental health, corrections and child welfare and encouraging them to take more responsibility for policy failures that contribute to homelessness. CAL-main also developed the most elaborate form of collaborative decision-making on homelessness programs documented among the governance networks in all three cities, which continues to this day. CAL-CHF has likewise emerged as a policy leader on homelessness, owing, in large part, to its strong leadership but also to its unique status as a community-based collaborative governance body that institutionalizes community expertise and cooperation to address homelessness. Key examples include the development of standardized shelter data collection and coordinated access and assessment into housing programs, both of which could be developed and implemented only with community participation and engagement.

The empirical analysis in Calgary also confirms that, as theorized, the metagovernance context has a powerful mediating influence on the performance of the governance networks. This is most clearly demonstrated by CAL-main, which operated under a dynamic metagovernance context from 1998 to 2008 and produced considerable innovations and effective policy coordination. Yet because of a number of factors, including governance tension with CAL-CHF and narrower mandates from the Government of Canada, CAL-main's capacity to produce innovative policy and to contribute to policy coordination has been seriously curtailed since 2008, consistent with metagovernance theory advanced in this study.

As in Vancouver, one finding not predicted by integrated governance network theory is how important the relationships among governance networks are to their performance and sustainability. CAL-main and CAL-CHF are more intertwined than any set of governance networks examined in Vancouver and Toronto, and this close relationship provides both advantages and disadvantages. CAL-main existed before CAL-CHF was formed, but since CAL-main is more of a confederation of sector networks, without a backbone organization, CAL-CHF has emerged as the major player in Calgary, with corresponding resentment among elements of CAL-main membership. Yet CAL-main retains a key role in the prioritization and allocation of Government of Canada funds, represents the main connection to the community, and possesses a legitimacy on policy and program matters that CAL-CHF has struggled, at times, to gain. The two networks became even more closely intertwined in 2009, when CAL-main members reported that this consolidation of involvement with CAL-CHF caused more tension, since it pulled CAL-main closer to the policy mandates set by CAL-CHF, despite intense disagreement within the broader social service community on the appropriate path forward, particularly with regard to the use of Housing First as the primary approach in dealing with homelessness.

During periods of productive collaboration between CAL-main and CAL-CHF, these networks have generated among the most innovative policies and programs in Canada, yet there have also been a number of periods of unrest when CAL-main, a community-centred governance network, has felt coopted or boxed in by CAL-CHF, as is the case at the time of writing (2015). CAL-main members feel that they are the governance network with the most legitimacy, given their inclusivity and history, yet they report that even though they are formally tasked with advising CAL-CHF on policy and programs, they have minimal influence on policy and program choices. This is critical, because CAL-CHF controls key policy levers and much of the money, since significant provincial money towards housing and homelessness flows through CAL-CHF. While key staff members of CAL-CHF claim that CAL-main retains an advisory role, other staff claim that, in reality, CAL-main has limited influence on CAL-CHF policy. New leadership at CAL-CHF, as of 2014, has given hope to many CAL-main members that the networks may be entering another period of productive collaboration. But while previous periods of internetwork fighting and frustration were, in part, overcome by a community liaison person, who acted as a link between CAL-main and CAL-CHF, this position was defunded in 2014; because of this loss, the current period of turmoil may continue longer than both groups might wish.

As we conclude the third comparative case study of homelessness policy development, it is important to reflect on the theoretical implications of the key findings from all three cases. In essence, we have discovered what some scholars have referred to as a "collaborative advantage" – a way of working together that produces an end result, in policy terms, that could not be achieved by an organization or a government department acting alone. A central objective of this book is to investigate homelessness in Canadian cities through the lens of integrated governance network theory, and more specifically, to more clearly articulate how governance network institutionalization and inclusiveness influence policy innovation and system coordination. Thus far, I have provided evidence that a correlation exists between governance network properties and policy outputs in three Canadian cities, but building on governance network theory requires us to move beyond correlation and work towards explanation. That is, *why*, and under what contexts, do governance network institutionalization and inclusiveness influence policy innovation and system coordination? Why did we see the production of a collaborative advantage in some contexts and not in others? These questions provide the focus for the next chapter.

6

Building a Collaborative Advantage

A great many people interviewed over the course of my research for this book agreed with the idea, articulated by one respondent, that the better we understand the people around us and "how they experience the world, what their histories are, the better we understand the context we are living in," and this enhanced mutual understanding makes for "better decisions."[1] But almost in the same breath, the very same people would tell me that being a part of a homelessness governance network is a taxing and sometimes frustrating effort, because of not only the lack of resources available to solve the problem but also the sheer difficulty of brokering the issues and competing demands in the sector. These challenges rouse passion among all involved, and thus, governance network deliberations and policy planning can be fraught at times. But few respondents indicated that, ultimately, it is not worth the effort. In fact, when individuals were asked whether they would prefer that the government strip down all of this collaborative network governance and simply hand over homelessness policy and governance to the bureaucracy under the guidance of elected officials, eyes would invariably widen in horror.

Thus, most of those interviewed, including local government bureaucrats, relayed seemingly contradictory messages: governing via networks is hard and fraught at times but is absolutely necessary to resolve a complex issue like homelessness. There are so many moving parts and related sectors that contribute to homelessness that it is essential to have not only interagency collaboration within the sector but also intersectoral networks (e.g., homelessness, housing, mental health, corrections, child welfare, etc.); otherwise, innovative solutions in one area will merely plug a single hole and the problem will simply become more intense elsewhere. There is broad agreement, then, that some form of network governance or collaborative governance is vital to address urban homelessness effectively, in part because it leads to achievements that would not be possible in a siloed organizational context. In essence, network governance has the potential to produce what Chris Huxham (1993) calls a "collaborative advantage."

That governance networks can produce superior policy innovation and system coordination to that produced by traditional bureaucratic policy planning and decision-making is a central contention of integrated governance network theory, but it is also key to the field of collaborative public management. Network governance represents what scholars Siv Vangen and Chris Huxham (2010, p. 163) call a "synergy that can be created through joint-working." Yet they explain that the collaborative advantage is not commonly evidenced in practice because of the difficulties of managing the complexity and competing interests of institutions and actors, challenges that can lead instead to "collaborative inertia." In this chapter, I discuss the conditions that generate a collaborative advantage in governance networks, as well as those that contribute to collaborative inertia. Integrated governance network theory specifies the causal mechanisms that link governance network properties to public policy development, and it can be applied across various policy domains in Canada and beyond.

Causal Mechanisms

Scholarly use of the concept of "causal mechanisms" is diverse and, at times, contradictory. To many, these mechanisms are non-observable processes (Bhaskar, 1979; Bunge, 1997; George & Bennett, 2005), but to others, they are only observable, involving movement "down" from correlation to causation (Kittel, 2006; Mahoney, 2001). To some scholars, causal mechanisms are deterministic (Little, 1991), but to others, they are probabilistic (Elster, 1999). For the purposes of building and refining theory, I define causal mechanisms simply as the pathway or process by which an effect is produced (Gerring, 2008).

It is critical to note that causal mechanisms are not *intervening* variables; rather, they are relational concepts to help clarify a theory. Not every social scientific theory yields an implicit and singular mechanism – in fact, most do not. For example, in democratic peace theory, the correlation between democracy and peace may be well established (although increasingly under dispute [Rosato, 2003]), yet there is intense disagreement on *why* democracy discourages conflict among nations. Therefore, the most path-breaking and valuable scholarship on governance network theory, like that on democratic peace, is specifying *how* things happen through causal mechanisms.

Sociologist Jennifer Earl (2008) specifies three critical criteria that must be met to produce a credible "mechanismic" account: the evidence must show (1) that variation exists among the variables of theoretical interest, (2) that a mechanism was responsible for altering the relationship between variables under investigation, and (3) that the mechanism has portability in similar contexts. On the first criterion, Chapters 3, 4, and 5 document the variation in the independent variables (institutionalization and inclusiveness of the network) and variation in the dependent variables of interest (policy innovation and system coordination). This chapter specifies the operative causal mechanisms in this context (criterion two) and makes a case for their more general application in governance networks (criterion three). Two key causal mechanisms emerge inductively from the empirical research (in particular, from extended participant observation within the networks): brokerage and persuasion. These mechanisms help explain the relationship discovered between governance network properties, on the one hand, and policy innovation and system coordination, on the other.

Brokerage, as a causal mechanism produced from governance network activity, provides the first part of the explanation for why governance networks matter to policy innovation and system coordination. Brokerage can be defined as the forging of social connections among previously unlinked persons and sites (Burt, 2005). Noted German philosopher Jürgen Habermas (1991) contends that exposure to dissimilar views in the public sphere will encourage intrapersonal reflection. According to political scientist Seyla Benhabib (1992, p. 140), interactions with those with differing views is "essential for us to comprehend and to come to appreciate the perspectives of others." Brokerage relations lower the costs of communication and coordination among unconnected social sites, transforming relationships by establishing social, political, and economic ties (Lichbach, 2008). Brokerage as a causal mechanism, therefore, may deactivate the previously sharp boundaries between policy actors, whether from government or civil society, and allows actors to leave their various silos in order to interpenetrate and, thus, may lead to greater understanding of different facets of the policy problem.

Persuasion, as a causal mechanism that emerges from network activity, provides the other part of the explanation for why networks matter for policy innovation and system coordination. This is consistent with deliberative democracy theory, which rests on a premise of the transformation of preferences among actors along the path to consensus (Young, 2000). Scholars suggest that governance network activity has policy consequences because various actors are exposed to different experiences, new research, and other jurisdictions' efforts and will promote them within the network (Mintrom, 1997). This theoretical foundation connects with policy-learning scholarship, which has identified the potential of such a confrontation of ideas and perspectives in institutions of collaborative decision-making to contribute to a productive learning process among diverse policy actors (Lindquist, 1992).

My basic causal mechanism argument in integrated governance network theory is this: brokerage and persuasion are emergent and dynamic properties of more institutionalized and more inclusive networks, and it is these properties that drive policy innovation and system coordination. Whereas the three chapters focusing on Vancouver, Toronto, and Calgary demonstrate that certain properties of governance networks correlate with higher levels of policy innovation and coordination, the causal mechanisms of brokerage and persuasion help to explain why this correlation exists.

The Interaction of Cause and Context

While causal mechanisms can help to explain the relationship between sets of variables, they are not deterministic. Mechanisms alone do not cause outcomes; rather, causation "resides in the interaction between the [causal] mechanism and the context in which it operates" (Falleti & Lynch, 2009, p. 1145). Empirically backed accounts of the operation of causal mechanisms thus require an articulation of the political context, "since what the outcome of their operation turns out to be depends quite a lot on the relevant context" (Bengtsson & Ruonavaara, 2011, p. 405). Thus, it is the interaction between mechanism(s) and context that influences the outcome.

The most important features of the political context as it relates to the activity of governance networks are the conditions of metagovernance, the "governance of governance," or how government crafts and manages less hierarchical public decision-making: in the case of homelessness, this means decision making by governance networks that involve state and civil society actors jointly devising and implementing public policies and programs.

Several key lessons emerge from metagovernance theory, confirmed by the empirical features of metagovernance documented in the preceding chapters, that help us understand how certain dimensions of metagovernance produce the context under which the specified causal mechanisms operate (or do not operate) to generate the policy outputs investigated.

Recall that two key elements of metagovernance are the institutional policy space granted to the governance network – from narrow to expansive – and the metagovernor leadership dynamics – from cooperative to contentious. These two metagovernance features form the relevant metagovernance context under which the causal mechanisms of brokerage and persuasion are operable and thus generate policy innovation and coordination. Table 6.1 places the eight governance networks into four theoretical categories within integrated governance network theory that capture the metagovernance contexts, which, in turn, interact with the causal mechanisms discussed in this chapter. The evidence from the preceding three chapters suggests that the metagovernor leadership dynamics can have a profound effect on the stability and productivity of a governance network, irrespective of the internal features of the network design.

The theoretical categories of metagovernance constitute the relevant contextual differences under which the causal mechanisms, which emerge as a result of governance network activity, gain operability in terms of producing policy innovation and system coordination. That is, all highly institutionalized and inclusive governance networks will produce the causal

TABLE 6.1

Categories of metagovernance context relevant to the operability of causal mechanisms

Metagovernor leadership	Institutional policy space	
	Narrow	Expansive
Cooperative	*Administrative* metagovernance e.g., TO-main, VAN-Ab (2003–present)	*Dynamic* metagovernance e.g., VAN-main (2000–14), VAN-emerg, TO-emerg – Layton, CAL-CHF, CAL-main (1998–2008)
Contentious	*Straitjacket* metagovernance e.g., TO-Ab, VAN-Ab (2000–03), VAN-main (2014–present), CAL-main (2008–present)	*Volatile* metagovernance e.g., TO-emerg – Pitfield

FIGURE 6.1 Conceptual map of causal mechanisms linking metagovernance
networks to policy outputs

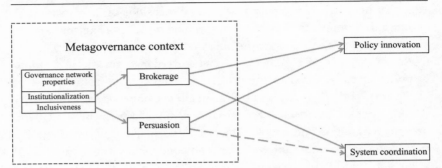

mechanisms of brokerage and persuasion, but the impact on policy of these
emergent dynamics will depend on the metagovernance context of the governance network. The next section demonstrates, using empirical data and
analysis from the eight governance network cases, that a governance network may produce brokerage or persuasion but will not drive policy innovation and coordination if it exists in a straitjacket or volatile metagovernance
context.

Figure 6.1 presents the full integrated governance network theoretical
model, specifying the governance network properties, the causal mechanisms of brokerage and persuasion, the metagovernance context as a mediating force, and the relationship of these three factors to policy development.
The governance network is depicted as having two features, institutionalization and inclusiveness, which are, respectively, the driving properties of
governance networks that produce the causal mechanisms of brokerage and
persuasion. As noted above, more institutionalized governance networks will
result in strong brokerage, and more inclusive governance networks will offer opportunities for persuasion. The production of the causal mechanisms,
however, occurs in a particular metagovernance context, which acts a filter
influencing whether the causal mechanisms will have policy consequence.

Figure 6.1 depicts precisely how the two causal mechanisms jointly produce the effect in terms of policy outputs. Policy innovation is the result of
the joint production of brokerage and persuasion: that is, both are needed
to produce strong policy innovation. System coordination is primarily produced by brokerage, and persuasion functions as an enhancing mechanism, which is represented with a dashed arrow. The following paragraphs

leverage empirical data and analysis from participant observation and interviews from all eight governance networks to demonstrate the value of this theoretical model and the relationship between the causal mechanisms and the metagovernance context that can produce a collaborative advantage from network governance.

This study was designed to engage in a comparative analysis of three Canadian cities in terms of homelessness governance and policy over a period of twenty years, but it was also structured to compare equivalent governance networks in each city. In essence, I analyzed a natural experiment in governance, given that the equivalent governance networks in each city (e.g., VAN-main, TO-main, and CAL-main) were all created at the same time and for the same purpose but took different structural forms and have evolved in very different ways. We are able to leverage this level of control to test precise theoretical claims in ways that would be less compelling without such controls.

Theoretical Claims and Mainstream Networks

We begin our discussion of theoretical claims as they relate to the government networks in the three cities with VAN-main, TO-main, and CAL-main. Figure 6.2 presents these three networks in terms of their production of causal mechanisms and their metagovernance contexts in 2005, a date chosen simply for illustrative purposes. VAN-main is the most institutionalized and inclusive governance network of the three and, as will be demonstrated shortly, produces the most brokerage and persuasion, as depicted by the relative thickness of the arrows connecting the properties of the governance network to the causal mechanisms. The metagovernance context mediates how powerfully the causal mechanisms will act on the dimensions of policy. VAN-main's context is characterized by cooperative metagovernor leadership dynamics and a relatively open policy space, since it is not heavily constrained by its managing metagovernor, Metro Vancouver; thus, it operates in a dynamic metagovernance context. As a result, the causal mechanisms of brokerage and persuasion contribute to high policy innovation and coordination. TO-main, by contrast, is the least institutionalized and least inclusive governance network, so brokerage and persuasion have less opportunity to emerge (depicted by small arrows); furthermore, the administrative metagovernance context at the City of Toronto restricts TO-main's activity to a narrow policy role. Therefore, the causal mechanisms, already weak, are effectively blocked from operating by the administrative

FIGURE 6.2 Comparative analysis of VAN-main, TO-main, and CAL-main by operative causal mechanisms and metagovernance context in 2005

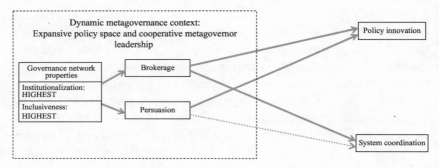

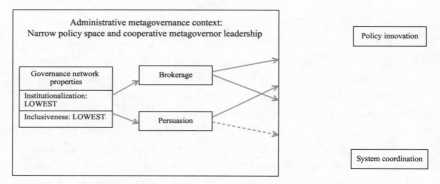

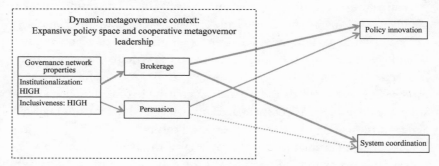

metagovernance context, and policy innovation and coordination are seriously inhibited. CAL-main, in 2005, was more similar to VAN-main than to TO-main, being situated in a dynamic metagovernance context that allowed the governance network the latitude and policy space in which to experiment and coordinate efforts without too many bureaucratic rules or roadblocks. Therefore, at this point in time, CAL-main was responsible for major innovations and system coordination efforts, in part because the metagovernance context was one that contributed to, rather than inhibited, policy innovation and system coordination.

The metagovernance context changed dramatically in 2014 for all of the HPS-associated homelessness governance networks. What was formerly a relatively flexible metagovernance context became one more characterized by straitjacket metagovernance. As noted in previous chapters, in 2014, the Harper government dramatically changed the scope of the HPS program from one that, for the most part, allowed the local homelessness governance networks to set policy priorities and make investments according to their needs and specific context to one that is more prescriptive on policy and restrictive on the activity of the governance networks. For many governance networks like VAN-main and CAL-main, fulfilling the requirements of the HPS program was just one of their functions, and as we have seen in the previous chapters, it carved out additional space and activity associated with addressing homelessness, including systems planning, shelter coordination, community development, and local advocacy efforts to raise awareness. These activities are now outside the scope of the HPS program, and VAN-main is no longer permitted to fund them or direct its administrative support from the Metro Vancouver government to work on these issues, which has compromised a great number of the policy and program gains documented in previous chapters.

Figure 6.3 below shows how the new metagovernance context for VAN-main and CAL-main has essentially cut off their potential for policy innovation and system coordination.[2] Now that the policy directives are considerably more prescriptive (towards Housing First), VAN-main members increasingly see less value in their involvement; because many options and activities are no longer possibilities, their work is no longer based on a genuine process of deliberation and problem solving. The policy space has been dramatically shrunk, exclusively because of changes to metagovernance, not the internal features of the governance network. The same dynamic has played out in CAL-main, causing great concern among those who have been part of its collaborative governance efforts over the years. This very

FIGURE 6.3   Comparative analysis of VAN-main and CAL-main by operative causal mechanisms and metagovernance context after 2014

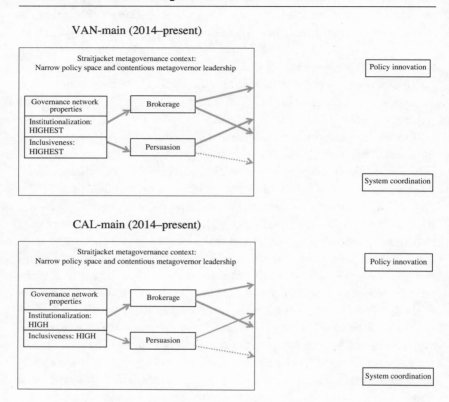

VAN-main (2014–present)

CAL-main (2014–present)

clearly illustrates the explanatory power of metagovernance in shaping the performance and outcomes of network governance.

Theoretical Claims and Aboriginal Networks

Figure 6.4 provides further evidence of the substantial power of metagovernance to contribute to policy innovation and coordination when appropriately designed but also to seriously disrupt policy development when restrictive or imbalanced. A look at VAN-Ab during two distinct periods – from 2000 to 2003 and from 2003 to the present – highlights how critical the metagovernance context is to the operability of the causal mechanisms. During the first period, the Government of Canada metagovernor placed VAN-Ab in an inappropriate decision-making box, which tied its hands

FIGURE 6.4 Comparative analysis of VAN-Ab, 2000–03, and VAN-Ab, 2003–15, by operative causal mechanisms and metagovernance context

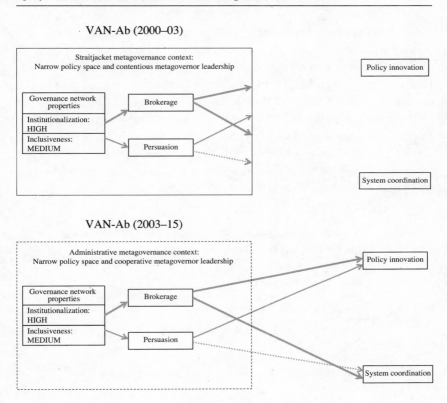

and directly resulted in failed policy planning and implementation. Basic rules and operating procedures set forth by the metagovernor had large consequences. For example, the local Aboriginal governance networks were only able to set policy and allocate funds to homelessness programs with a labour-market dimension and were restricted from allocating money to capital projects (e.g., building supportive housing). Within this restrictive context, the causal mechanisms produced by the institutionalization and inclusiveness of the governance network, despite their strength, were rendered inoperable and were thus unable to contribute to policy innovation and coordination.

To the credit of the metagovernor, when Government of Canada bureaucrats learned of the dysfunction they had created within the Aboriginal homelessness governance networks, they changed the rules to be similar to those for the mainstream governance networks like VAN-main (Smith, 2004). The changes were fully implemented in 2003 and continued thereafter, which freed up VAN-Ab (and other Aboriginal homelessness governance networks across the country) to set policy and allocate funds in a less restrictive metagovernance context, as depicted in Figure 6.4.

Returning to the comparative analysis of similar governance networks, Figure 6.5 presents VAN-Ab and TO-Ab after the federal metagovernance changes in 2003 in terms of the causal mechanisms and the metagovernance context. Note that VAN-Ab and TO-Ab are similar in strength to the causal mechanisms produced because of the internal features of the networks. VAN-Ab is as institutionalized, though more inclusive, than TO-Ab, resulting in permeable boundaries between network actors (i.e. brokerage) and more persuasion potential in VAN-Ab than TO-Ab. In addition, the

FIGURE 6.5   Comparative analysis of VAN-Ab and TO-Ab by operative causal mechanisms and metagovernance context

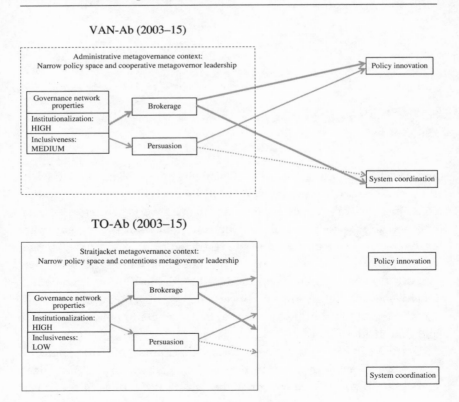

metagovernance context for TO-Ab is more constraining than that for VAN-Ab, primarily because neither the City of Toronto nor TO-main collaborate, formally or informally, with TO-Ab on policy planning or funding allocations. The metagovernance thus renders inoperable the brokerage produced by TO-Ab that would otherwise contribute to system coordination. Conversely, VAN-Ab and VAN-main have institutionalized relationships of policy planning and allocations, constructed by the managing metagovernors, which is particularly important to promote system coordination in Metro Vancouver.

Theoretical Claims and Emergency Networks

The final comparison is presented below in Figure 6.6, which depicts the causal mechanisms and metagovernance context of VAN-emerg, TO-emerg, and CAL-CHF – the three governance networks created from the bottom up, largely by civil society actors who were primarily concerned, initially at least, with emergency or short-term responses to homelessness. (Note that while CAL-CHF was not emergency focused, it was created by civil society actors, not via a mandate from government.) VAN-emerg is a highly inclusive and moderately institutionalized network that exists within a dynamic metagovernance context. Likewise, CAL-CHF is unique among the homelessness governance networks investigated in that it is an incorporated charitable organization with extensive community membership and it has been drawn into a central policy-making role by government over its lifetime. Despite essentially being delegated the authority to devise and implement homelessness and housing policy in Calgary by the federal, provincial, and municipal governments, CAL-CHF has been afforded considerable policy space from its metagovernors and thus operates within a dynamic metagovernance context. By contrast, TO-emerg was granted expansive institutional policy space but was subjected at times to very contentious metagovernor leadership dynamics characteristic of a volatile metagovernance context; these dynamics, while allowing TO-emerg to contribute to spurts of policy innovation, created internal struggles that hampered policy coordination across the sector in Toronto.

The case of TO-emerg is particularly demonstrative of how governance networks may – but do not necessarily – produce brokerage relations that dismantle social boundaries and foster mutual learning and consensus building. Over time at TO-emerg, boundaries hardened and the politics became contentious rather than consensus oriented. This is, in fact, consistent

FIGURE 6.6 Comparative analysis of VAN-emerg, TO-emerg, and CAL-CHF by operative causal mechanisms and metagovernance context

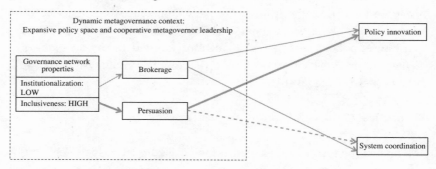

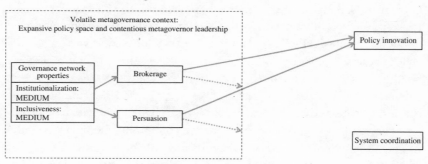

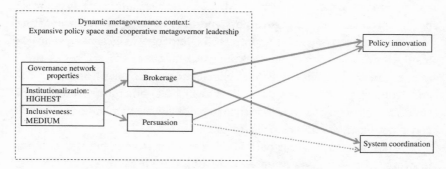

with political scientist Diana Mutz's (2002, p. 120) experimental data showing that exposure to differing perspectives on issues may harden those views if the individuals involved have low "perspective-taking ability" – meaning a personal capacity to entertain others' points of view. In contrast to the other seven governance networks, the civil society members of TO-emerg tended to be more radical, with ties to activism and advocacy rather than service provision, and their orientation was not always accustomed to compromise.

In summary, the comparisons above show that the properties of the governance network – specifically, institutionalization and inclusiveness – independently determine the strength of the causal mechanisms of brokerage and persuasion, respectively, in integrated governance network theory. Clearly, though, the operability of the causal mechanisms in driving change in policy outputs is contingent on the metagovernance context: that is, a constrained and contentious metagovernance context can render strong causal mechanisms inoperable. The following sections draw on extensive participant observation data and interviews with actors in all eight governance networks to illustrate specifically how the production of the causal mechanisms of persuasion and brokerage tend to generate the policy innovation and system coordination documented in the three cities, but they do so only if the metagovernance context is one that is conducive to collaborative network governance.

Network Governance and Policy Innovation

Brokerage and persuasion, the pre-eminent causal mechanisms linking governance networks to policy innovation and coordination, are clearly evident in the most institutionalized and inclusive governance networks (e.g., VAN-main, CAL-CHF, and VAN-emerg) and absent in the least institutionalized and inclusive governance networks (e.g., TO-main and TO-emerg). Several empirical examples, informed by interviews and participant observations, provide evidence to bolster these theoretical claims.

VAN-main, VAN-emerg, CAL-CHF, and CAL-main are highly institutionalized governance networks that provide meaningful opportunities for diverse government and civil society actors to engage in regular exchanges, both instrumental and strategic. In terms of instrumental exchanges, civil society actors have used these venues to share informational and service-based resources skilfully. For civil society actors coming from the shelter, housing, mental health, addictions, and youth sectors, the institutionalized "round table" at each meeting of the networks provides a valuable opportunity for silos to be broken down to reveal gaps in services and policy blind spots. One example from a VAN-emerg member illustrates the brokerage resulting from network activity. Judy Graves, prominent Vancouver homeless advocate and a member of VAN-emerg, related the story of VAN-emerg renting a bus to take shelter providers on a tour of other shelters, because shelter providers rarely have the opportunity to see other shelters in operation and so had "developed a horrible mythology about everybody else. Yeah, 'this shelter is crap, he turns everybody away,' or 'their shelter is crap, they turn nobody away.'" As a result of this tour, providers developed "a huge appreciation for one another's work."[3] Over time, this contributed to a real policy innovation among shelter providers such that they now engage in healthy competition to be the "lowest barrier" shelter for clients.[4]

Institutionalized governance networks not only benefit civil society actors in instrumental ways through brokerage, but they also help government actors who hold additional decision-making power outside of the governance network mandate. For example, BC Housing, the provincial government agency that dominates the housing and homelessness policy fields and expenditures in the Metro Vancouver region, is an active and vital member of both VAN-main and VAN-emerg. Karen O'Shannacery of the Lookout Emergency Aid Society expressed her belief that BC Housing's active membership at VAN-emerg was necessary for the Crown agency "to understand the pressures that the shelters were undergoing because they had no other way of getting that rich information."[5] A governance network that institutionalizes relationships between civil society and government thus has mutually productive brokerage dynamics. "We are in the field," said O'Shannacery. "We know what's happening, we can bring a different viewpoint."[6] Government members can speak to new programs, service closures, and policy changes at the political level, and can help civil society actors navigate the bureaucracies at multiple levels of government. For Celine Maboules, a City of Vancouver bureaucrat previously involved in VAN-main, it was "great to have that mix of government and then community folks to really talk about what the reality is out there ... and it has helped to educate us on some of the issues and some of the challenges that are happening in other municipalities."[7] Alice Sundberg, former chair of VAN-main, likewise stated, "We all learn from each other, which is the other beauty of the way the policy is actually developed is that it is done in an eclectic environment, with different ideas and perspectives coming in that we have to sift through."[8]

Beyond affecting the instrumental day-to-day provision of services, the brokerage mechanism also has strategic policy consequence, driving policy innovation. There are a number of examples of policy innovations, particularly from VAN-main and VAN-emerg, in which members themselves point to the relational aspects of the governance network as causal determinants. For example, the provincial policy framework for homeless shelters was transformed from one with archaic rules on eligibility of access to shelters and maximum length of stay to one of the most permissive and lowest-barrier shelter systems in the country; both shelter providers and BC Housing respondents identified the relationships and activities of VAN-emerg as critical in driving these policy innovations.[9] In fact, according to a former BC Housing official, Michael Anhorn, the joint activities of VAN-emerg, as an early advocate for low-barrier shelters, and VAN-main, as an early funder of such shelters, "took away the risk and shaped BC Housing's thinking" in terms of policy.[10] A long-term VAN-emerg member, reflecting on the subsequent high-level and innovative policy changes by BC Housing for the shelter system, said, "I don't think that would have ever happened if BC Housing had not been listening to the ongoing dialogue in this group."[11]

We see similar dynamics in Calgary emerging from the activities of CAL-CHF and CAL-main. As demonstrated in the previous chapter, CAL-CHF has been a key driver of policy innovation in Calgary, including coordinated access and assessment, systems planning, and housing program pilots. These innovations emerged from a practice at CAL-CHF, described by a network member, in which leadership asked members, "If you can have anything you wanted for this client, what would it be? Forget about money. Forget what we have, we don't have. And people sort of put out their wish list and some good ideas came out of that and matched up with the gaps."[12] In CAL-main, another respondent confirmed the power of institutionalized and regular occasions to problem-solve via governance networks: "Now we're all sitting at the table, and we just have the ability to work together because we're all in the same room. I think before [CAL-main] we were all trying to kind of come up with some of our solutions. We just didn't know the right people to contact all the time."[13]

Brokerage thus emerges from institutionalized and inclusive governance networks, developing as a result of regular and ongoing interactions and exchanges. Policy actors from across sectors with little previous contact or knowledge of each other's activities come together to exchange resources and information. This alone, however, does not drive policy innovation. Persuasion is the complementary causal mechanism that, in conjunction with brokerage, contributes to innovative policy development when diverse actors engage in deliberation and alter the perspectives of policy actors and decision makers. Among the most institutionalized and inclusive governance networks, members were clear that governance network activity was critical to understanding the sector, identifying emerging issues, and recognizing the intersections among social and economic dynamics.

For example, unsurprisingly, civil society actors often have their own biases (usually aligned with those of their sector) with respect to the appropriate solutions to homelessness, but several VAN-main and VAN-emerg members candidly revealed that governance network engagement had had a powerful impact on them, reorienting their perspectives on homelessness issues, a clear indication that brokerage and persuasion mechanisms were at work. In another example, one of the recent co-chairs of VAN-main, Alice Sundberg, who has had many years in a leadership role in the affordable housing sector, confessed that she "came in with an attitude that it was really obvious to me what the real problem was and how to solve it," like others who initially adhere to a singular solution like employment, shelter, or mental health services. "Obviously I was wrong," she admitted, "because I thought that was all there was to it. I learned how complex it is."[14] This type of conversion among network members is what contributes to policy innovation, because their understandings of the status quo are challenged. This was echoed by respondents from CAL-CHF, one of whom said, "This matters on a policy level, but also on a service level. We sit together and try to have a conversation about what does this individual need to be successful? How can we try something new and creative?"[15]

It is important to note that not all good ideas emerge from civil society and not all status quo or retrograde ideas are protected from change by government bureaucrats. In fact, although it was CAL-CHF leaders who pushed the idea of greater use of standardized data to track interventions on an initially very resistant service sector, it was brokerage and persuasion at both CAL-CHF and CAL-main that helped facilitate the acceptance of this approach. A member of the CAL-CHF administrative secretariat explained this evolution:

> There was so much resistance from the community because the idea of data was never at the forefront, and particularly from the perspective of social workers, which you understand because you're always in crisis mode and there's no time and we can't collect all this information. So there's a huge learning curve in even implementing that system, getting people trained, and understanding the implications for FOIP [Freedom of Information and Privacy] and the value data can bring to generating more effective

interventions. And by pumping that data back into the community so that they can see the richness of it and how much learning potential there is in it.[16]

The perspectives of youth and Aboriginal people are universally viewed as particularly valuable across the governance networks, given their vulnerabilities and disproportionate share among the homeless population. Respondents associated with VAN-main were clear that their efforts to include youth and Aboriginal perspectives were not simply to check off a demographic box to satisfy some vague desire for inclusion; rather, they served the practical purposes of informing decision making and driving change. The vast majority of bureaucrats have lives divorced from the experience of homeless youth and Aboriginal people, and many of them readily acknowledge that they need people closer to these experiences to be part of the policy-making process. One former bureaucratic manager of VAN-main remarked on community actors: "I think they just have more direct contact with the issue, and City staff ... don't have the same level of contact with the issue."[17]

The relationship between the inclusion of diverse voices and policy development – through the causal mechanism of persuasion – can be illustrated with an example from VAN-main's experience with youth. In its first five years, VAN-main created and supported a Youth Working Group (YWG) consisting of youth with lived experience of homelessness to help the larger network advance policy in this area. Although it was difficult to maintain membership and regular attendance, many VAN-main members reflected positively on the substantive impact these youth had on persuading the broader membership to engage in certain areas and abandon others. A bureaucrat formerly involved with VAN-main remarked that the YWG "really opened eyes to people about what it was like to be a youth on the street ... I mean first of all most of us sitting around the table were not homeless as youth." He went on to elaborate: "We heard specific examples of what did work for individuals, which sometimes was very helpful and especially when it was contrary to the evidence" produced in bureaucracies.[18] The YWG was afforded substantial power, to the point, according to Kingsley Okyere, former Metro Vancouver Homelessness Secretariat manager, that the governance network "basically made decisions guided by those points and the questions that they raised."[19]

When asked whether different decisions would be made if government alone made decisions on policy priorities and allocations in this field rather than the network of government and civil society actors, both government and civil society members of VAN-main almost unanimously declared, immediately and decisively, "Yes." In fact, it was bureaucrats who were most emphatic that different decisions would be made, perhaps because they also participate in City-internal decision-making processes regarding homelessness and housing funding. Why would there be a difference? It is not merely the diversity of policy actors but also the deliberative activity that is central to network governance. When VAN-main makes decisions as a network about proposed programs, the membership "comes in with their own scores and then you talk about it and it's a great way to learn new things," remarked a City of Vancouver bureaucrat formerly involved in VAN-main.[20] This is consistent with the empirical counterfactual analysis of real decision data presented briefly in Chapter 3. A senior BC Housing official was clear that if government controlled the process, "there would be different decisions made, and my worry would be they would be made in isolation from the reality of what is happening on the ground."[21] Officials at the City of Toronto, however, were much more circumspect about this question, perhaps because they do not involve TO-main members in decision making with respect to funding allocation, which is controlled by City of Toronto bureaucrats.[22]

The governance networks with the most innovative policy are those that are the most institutionalized and inclusive, because these were the ones that produce the emergent dynamics of brokerage and persuasion. VAN-main and VAN-emerg meet regularly and are populated by very diverse voices that have a privileged role in deliberation and decision making. Conversely, the least innovative homelessness governance networks are those that are less institutionalized and less inclusive. A governance network like TO-main is weakly institutionalized and constrained by the metagovernor such that there is limited evidence of brokerage relations and few opportunities for meaningful learning and deliberation captured by the persuasion mechanism. Two TO-main members who wished to remain anonymous spoke of this governance network as being a mere shell, largely created to satisfy the federal mandate to create a community advisory board, while all policy priorities and allocations were driven by the City bureaucracy and formally approved by Toronto City Council.

One TO-main member claimed that the network meets about once per year to inform members what the City has been doing, with network members having no meaningful opportunity to deliberate or plot innovations: "I thought maybe it would be a little more open for discussion."[23] When contacted to participate in this research, two other TO-main members had forgotten they were part of the governance network, which certainly signals a lack of brokerage relations developing from the activity of TO-main. Another TO-main member said that with such infrequent meetings, the network is simply "not able to be as effective."[24] Thus, what is clear from TO-main meeting minutes and from speaking with current and former TO-main members is that the network is so weakly institutionalized that there are few opportunities to engage in the resource exchange, learning, and deliberative action that would allow it to drive policy innovation.

Network Governance and System Coordination

The most institutionalized and inclusive governance networks are associated with more coordinated and cohesive policy and programs. The brokerage that results from active and integrated governance networks is chiefly responsible for the system coordination that is achieved, with persuasion acting as a secondary mechanism that enhances the effect of that coordination. Governance networks provide a regular and less hierarchical venue (than standard political-administrative decision making) for government and civil society to develop constructive exchanges and can help resolve existing tensions that contribute to isolation in the sector. Policy silos in homelessness are particularly inefficient and ineffective because of the complexity of this social, economic, and often personal problem; vulnerable citizens can too easily slip through the cracks and lose whatever progress they have made when the policy actors in the sector are compartmentalized in their own specialties (Golden, 1999). Governance networks that are most institutionalized (e.g., VAN-main, CAL-CHF, and CAL-main) are those that contribute most substantively to system coordination, principally because of the brokerage relations that are developed. Conversely, those that are least institutionalized (e.g., TO-main) produce weak system coordination, explained by the absence of strong brokerage among government and civil society actors.

At a basic level, an institutionalized network of diverse policy actors provides a regular venue for government and civil society brokerage relations to take shape and manifest themselves in improved system coordination. Since their origins, VAN-main, VAN-emerg, and VAN-Ab have sent envoys to each other, thus developing institutionalized relationships of exchange in terms of both information and resources. These strong brokerage relations are observed in joint activities of VAN-main and VAN-emerg, like housing policy forums, Homelessness Action Week, and jointly sponsored pilot programs, as well as in resource exchange and partnerships in smaller initiatives at each governance network. For current and former members of these highly institutionalized governance networks, it is the establishment of relationships (brokerage) that explains these collaborative efforts that produce system coordination. According to one former VAN-main bureaucratic manager,

> It is really easy for people to get separated, and [service providers] have got such a big job and so few resources that you can really kind of get your head stuck in the sand. So RSCH [VAN-main] has really provided a venue for that kind of sharing of information and I think without RSCH [VAN-main] you wouldn't have had a kind of coordination.[25]

CAL-main and CAL-CHF display a similar degree of internetwork pollination, suggesting that key policy gains and coordination efforts would not succeed without such engagement and collaboration. Members of CAL-main and CAL-CHF share similar stories of brokerage relations, citing several reasons or motivations for their sustained involvement. Leslie McMechan, member of CAL-main, elaborated on these reasons:

> One of them is to throw our perspective into the mix. Some of it is about asking questions and bringing awareness to issues that our agency faces and adding that to the group. Another part is getting information – attending all of those meetings, we actually get really helpful information that helps us to shift our programming in a certain direction, or information about what another agency is doing that we could maybe adopt or kind of tweak and change and fit into our context. And it really does help us achieve our goals.[26]

Though some CAL-main members, former and current, reflect on the exhaustion and, at times, divisive atmosphere of network governance work, others the importance of this work to address the complex problems of homelessness. One in particular said, "This is the thing I think Calgary does the best. We all try to work together and we keep the lines of communication open. And I think we understand that – and I certainly understand – that it isn't about me. This is about the [homeless] person."[27] Echoing respondents in Vancouver, CAL-main members reflected that network governance has helped them to "learn how to organize ourselves to understand whose role was what" and helped to create a culture such that "we all understand that there is a greater purpose and greater success rate if we collaborate."[28]

The brokerage relations also stimulate an engaged and productive civil society sector that coordinates itself at a level below official government policy, the best example of which is from VAN-emerg. On member related that in the mid-1990s in Metro Vancouver, "there were numerous shelters and they are all working in isolation [with] various shelter requirements. We didn't even know how many shelters beds that actually existed around the region. We didn't know the rules and regulations; we didn't even know the hours that shelters were operating."[29] One of the earliest tasks of VAN-emerg, in order to achieve some system coordination, was thus to get a baseline understanding of service provision and learn about all of the shelter actors in the region. Tangible evidence of brokerage is detectable in comments of shelter providers: "It's sharing – not just official, executive director to executive director," said one provider. "Staff [at different shelters] at night are talking to each other. It's more of a community dealing with the issue ... Knowing what others are doing helps us" (cited in GVSS, 2007a). Regarding increased collaboration and sharing of resources among shelter providers, one provider commented: "It's easier to share resources or ask for help when we all know and trust each other."[30]

One final pattern in institutionalized governance networks, showing that brokerage directly contributes to enhanced system coordination, is that strong brokerage relations can help resolve existing tensions in the sector. In the shelter sector, the governance network activity of VAN-emerg has helped soften – though not eliminate – some of the competition and jealousy among shelter providers. Establishing relationships among shelter leaders at the governance network, followed by the aforementioned tour of the shelters for VAN-emerg members, largely stopped "the infighting."[31] System coordination is achieved because these brokerage relations help shelter providers "figure out what their colleagues are doing, what works for their agency and [what] doesn't."[32] They can then adopt strategies that have worked for other agencies. Brokerage relations also allow members from different agencies to put faces to names, and, as one network member said, "that can't be underestimated."[33] There are examples of this in the Toronto case as well, particularly in the Aboriginal network. One long-time TO-Ab member, Frances Sanderson, recalled that prior to governance network institutionalization, "we didn't know how to take each other ... We were cautiously supportive of each other," but over time, "we sort of meshed together as a group. And I think that's been one of the positive things that has come from [the governance network]."[34]

This was echoed by CAL-CHF member Sue Fortune, who commented that in the network's early days, members "were a little more defensive." But in time, a shift occurred as people realized that "we're in this together. We're not you, me, and them. We're under one big umbrella."[35] A particularly active service provider involved with CAL-CHF emphasized the importance of working together: "I love collaborating. I think we need to work together and understand the other agencies that are offering housing ... and I think CHF activity did do a better job of identifying gaps in services to the homeless population here."[36] Yet another CAL-CHF associate said, "There's always stresses and strains when you go into some sort of coordinated system. I think the logic is that this should be good for our clients, so let's do what we can."[37] In other words, collaboration is not easy or without conflict, but it is essential to success in the sector.

The tension inherent in such collaborative policy-making is most clear when examining the interactions between VAN-main and VAN-Ab over time, which illustrate the power of brokerage relations that can emerge out of institutionalized network governance. The relationship between Aboriginal policy actors and government necessarily begins with the historical legacy of colonialism, some level of resentment from Aboriginal peoples, and, typically, some ignorance among non-Aboriginal government officials and civil society actors. This is all to say that considerable hurdles need to be cleared before productive relations can be developed. Within this context, the institutionalized and inclusive governance networks of VAN-main and VAN-Ab have provided a venue to engage in mutual learning and relationship building that can build towards policy coordination. One key VAN-main member reflected that a few years ago, "the relationship was frayed a little bit, likely due to a lot of misunderstanding over some minor issues. Sometimes it doesn't take much. These are tough issues that we are dealing with and there are two different streams, different views about how things should be approached and sometimes there is no meeting of minds."[38] At the time of writing, the relationship between VAN-main and VAN-Ab is cooperative. "We've made a conscious effort to engage them in conversations," said a VAN-main member about VAN-Ab. "We go to their meetings more often; we give presentations regarding the decisions RSCH [VAN-main] has made or some of the plans for the future."[39]

Consistent with the theoretical model presented in Chapter 2, we see productive brokerage relations emerging in VAN-main and CAL-main; some challenges associated with all of the Aboriginal homelessness governance networks, given the legacy of their interactions with governance bodies in Canada; and very little brokerage production in TO-main. A CAL-main respondent reflected that social service agencies' engaging in collaborative planning and implementation "is quite remarkable, and you don't actually realize that until you go somewhere else."[40] An example of that "somewhere else" is TO-main. TO-main is the least institutionalized and least inclusive of the eight governance networks under investigation, and the evidence suggests that it produces the weakest brokerage and persuasion dynamics. These weakly formed causal mechanisms are unable to contribute substantially to policy coordination, principally because the metagovernance context imposed by the City of Toronto bureaucracy seriously constrains the activity of TO-main, which meets infrquently and a very narrow mandate. In contrast to the nexus of VAN-main, VAN-Ab, and VAN-emerg, and to a lesser extent that of CAL-main and CAL-CHF, only marginal relations have been established among the governance networks in Toronto during the period of study. Interviews and an examination of the meeting notes of TO-main and TO-emerg revealed that the closest these two networks got to establishing a relationship was when TO-emerg was asked to comment on the draft 2003 Community Plan (ACHSIP, minutes, 2003). There were no envoys and no joint meetings, and little evidence was found of system coordination between these networks.

Some system coordination, however, does exist within the City of Toronto bureaucracy, because it is the centralized planning authority for homelessness policy development in Toronto. But this does not mean that the sector and civil society is coordinated; in fact, the evidence from the governance networks suggests otherwise. As mentioned in previous chapters, in 2014, the City of Toronto embarked on a major reorganization of its housing and homelessness policy framework, with vague references to building more substantive networks in the sector and with the explicit acknowledgment of a lack of existing coordination of efforts across the city. Thus, while the City of Toronto is able to coordinate government investments because it manages federal, provincial, and municipal homelessness programs, there is a lost opportunity to harness the governance networks to organize the sector and civil society actors to produce the innovations and sector coordination seen in Metro Vancouver and Calgary.

Networks as Sites for Brokerage and Persuasion

Beyond the immediate value of the theoretical model to explain the variation in homelessness policy development and implementation in Vancouver, Toronto, and Calgary from 1995 to 2015, what do these conclusions offer to integrated network governance theory? The causal mechanisms specified from the empirical examination of these eight cases may be portable to governance network arrangements in other sectors and policy domains and other levels of government. Thus, the emergent properties of highly institutionalized and inclusive governance networks – brokerage and persuasion, respectively – are likely to be produced in other network governance arrangements and to have a measurable effect on policy innovation and system coordination. However, as mentioned above, these causal mechanisms are not deterministic but depend critically on the metagovernance context of the governance network.

Through the analysis of the eight homelessness governance networks, I have argued that brokerage and persuasion are the emergent dynamics of institutionalized and inclusive governance networks and that these mechanisms, in conjunction with the metagovernance context, co-produce policy innovation and coordination. The critical point is that although causal mechanisms are produced by the activities of the governance network, it is in conjunction with the metagovernance context that such dynamics shape policy outputs. The production of the causal mechanisms from governance network activity provides insight into how a collaborative advantage can be produced from network governance; a collaborative advantage will only occur if the metagovernance apparatus is sufficiently flexible and the diversity of interests are managed effectively and channelled towards productive exchanges and policy learning.

Something special can emerge out of network governance that would not be produced in the absence of such governance institutions. This is the definition of a collaborative advantage, and while it is by no means easy to achieve, it is demonstrably present from the policy outputs of VAN-main and CAL-main, at least prior to 2014, when a metagovernance context afforded the policy space and latitude to innovate and coordinate. While all of the governance networks across the three cities demonstrate this theoretical argument, TO-emerg in particular provides compelling evidence that an otherwise institutionalized and inclusive governance network, if mismanaged, can be fatally undermined.

The changes made in 2014 to the Homelessness Partnering Strategy by the Government of Canada – the ultimate metagovernor in this context – threaten the productive operation of several of the governance networks examined in this book. A program once heralded as a flexible federal initiative that sought to produce a national response to homelessness while respecting local autonomy and the unique needs and goals of particular localities has recently been reconfigured to place the local homelessness governance networks into a much narrower box, with much stricter rules and regulations from the metagovernor on policy priorities and governance structures, thus threatening their potential to achieve policy innovation and coordination. Despite ostensibly good intentions to try to focus the investments at the local level, the metagovernance restrictions are completely contrary to trends in the homelessness sector towards more collaboration, community development, and systems planning, which new rules and restrictions discourage and, in some cases, explicitly prohibit. Such changes and their implications for homelessness governance in Canada, as well as for network governance in other policy domains, is the focus of the final chapter.

7

Towards a Solution

Three years before his death in 2011, Jack Layton released a revised and updated edition of his 2000 book, retitled *Homelessness: How to End the National Crisis*, a signal that the issue that defined his tenure as a Toronto city councillor remained central to him in his pursuit of the office of prime minister. To him and many others in the homelessness policy community, few actions short of a dramatic policy change from the federal government, including substantial affordable housing and homelessness investments, would turn the tide on this seemingly intractable policy problem. And this remains fundamentally true today.

Yet this book demonstrates that some major cities – in particular, the homelessness governance networks in them – have produced varying degrees of policy innovation and system coordination over the past twenty years. Indeed, when reflecting on his time in politics and his advocacy for policy change, Jack Layton also claimed that one of the most important lessons he learned "is that energy and ideas spring from the community ... not from mandarins in Ottawa" (Layton, 2008, p. xxviii). This view is not at all controversial within the homelessness policy community or in the normative social science literature, especially among deliberative democracy, network governance, and critical policy studies scholars. Thus, a high premium is placed on the community as an agent of change and policy ideas and as a force that should be brought into the policy process to challenge technocrats and elected officials "to help raise awareness and to suggest creative strategies and solutions" (Layton, 2008, 301).

Institutionalized inclusion, via governance networks, of the voices of those most affected by policy is consistent with the plurality of conceptions of legitimate political authority in Canada and elsewhere, which includes state-centred, expert, private (market), and popular authority (Skogstad, 2003). The question considered in this book is whether civil society actors – in this case, homelessness service providers, affordable housing providers and advocates, mental health professionals, and charitable organizations – bring something special (and positive) to the policy process, something that cannot be obtained via traditional hierarchical bureaucracies. While each of the eight governance networks under investigation is different, the clear answer that emerges is yes – provided they can be designed and managed effectively by metagovernors to extract the dynamism from their activity and to facilitate productive deliberations and relations with structures and rules without stifling that activity.

Governing by Networks in the Homelessness Sector

This book examines homelessness policy development in Vancouver, Toronto, and Calgary during the period from 1995 to 2015, specifically investigating the claim that the properties and dynamics of the governance networks that exist in each city explain why the policies and programs in Vancouver and Calgary are generally more innovative and coordinated than those in Toronto. While there are examples of innovative policies and programs in Toronto, a comprehensive look at the policy landscape over time reveals a relationship between network governance patterns and policy outputs.

In 1995, prior to the creation of any of the eight governance networks, the policy contexts in Vancouver, Toronto, and Calgary shared many similarities: no formal homelessness plans, a concentration of services in the downtown core, an emergency bias to policy, a lack of coordination of services, and little to no data of the homeless population that could be used to engage in long-term planning. Yet at the time of writing in 2015, while all three cities have much more sophisticated plans and strategies to address homelessness, Vancouver and Calgary differ from Toronto in important ways in terms of policy innovation and system coordination – two key features of policy that are related to an effective policy response to homelessness. This study demonstrates that the more institutionalized and inclusive homelessness governance networks in Vancouver and Calgary help to explain this variation. The analysis of analogous governance networks across the three cities, which exhibit variation in terms of institutionalization and inclusiveness, demonstrates that the structure and dynamics of governance networks are largely responsible for the presence (and absence) of policy innovations and system coordination in Vancouver, Toronto, and Calgary. That VAN-main and CAL-main adopted a more networked approach and TO-main a more municipalized, bureaucratic approach – despite their shared origins within the federal NHI program – allowed for fruitful comparative analysis of their policy outputs over an extended period.

The study also examined policy development through the alternative theoretical lenses of local institutional structures, the social construction of ideas, and the leadership of policy actors. A number of important policy innovations were the result of elected official leadership and some system coordination emerged from local political-administrative (non-governance network) institutions. Clearly, elected official leadership is a critical source of policy change and momentum: Toronto Mayor Mel Lastman, in the late 1990s, launched the Mayor's Task Force to investigate and respond to the homelessness crisis; Toronto city councillor Jack Layton, as leader of TO-emerg, initiated policy change; and Mayor Gregor Robertson, in Vancouver, set ending homelessness as a high personal priority. These examples, however, do not contradict the claim that governance networks matter, since there are multiple pathways to policy development in complex and multi-level policy domains – it is not a zero-sum scenario. Still, more numerous and, arguably, more substantive innovative and coordinated policy frameworks can be linked directly to institutionalized and inclusive governance networks over the extended period of inquiry.

While this book documents significant examples of policy innovation and system coordination in Vancouver, Calgary, and Toronto over the past twenty years, the truth remains that these gains remain partially undermined by a federal government that refuses to acknowledge a meaningful role in the provision of affordable housing. In addition, in 2014, the Harper government introduced dramatic changes to the metagovernance context of the networks studied, thus threatening many of positive policy developments identified in this book.

The Government of Canada used to play a major role in the provision of affordable housing in Canada, and it was its hasty exit from this area in the 1990s that many credit with the spike in homelessness across all Canadian cities shortly thereafter. Following this crisis, created in large part by the Government of Canada, the federal government tiptoed back into affordable housing with the Affordable Housing Initiative, a program that extended from 2001 to 2011, entering into bilateral agreements with all provinces to provide a relatively modest $124 million in annual contributions to affordable housing projects. The program, now called the Investment in Affordable Housing, was doubled under Harper in 2011 to provide $250 million annually until 2019, although this is still orders of magnitude less than what is required to address the problem.[1]

The federal Homelessness Partnering Strategy (HPS) is not an affordable housing program; local investments typically include homelessness services such as drop-in centres, addictions programs, and other supportive measures. In fact, metagovernance rules dictate that cities are not permitted to use HPS funds towards the construction of affordable housing, which the federal government (going back to Chrétien) maintains is the primary responsibility of the provincial governments; HPS funds must not be used by cities to make up for inadequate provincial government spending on affordable housing. In 2014, the HPS was renewed by the Harper government until 2019, though at a further reduced annual investment of $119 million (from $135 million).[2]

In this broader context, it is important to reflect on recent changes emanating from the Government of Canada, the ultimate metagovernor for most of the homelessness governance networks examined in this study. These changes further reinforce the claims derived from integrated governance network theory that the metagovernance of networks powerfully shape their performance. Until 2014, the Government of Canada had considerable flexibility, from a governance and policy perspective, built into the HPS program – first created as the NHI in 1999. Even the "requirements" were flexible. For example, the federal government did not dictate who within the community, civil society, or local government needed to be involved in the governance network, and it accepted the unique policy priorities for funding identified in each community plan. Apart from a restriction on funding affordable housing, the local governance network had wide latitude to produce a policy and program package that it felt was most appropriate to its circumstances and needs.

This changed quite dramatically in 2014, when the Harper government made major changes to the HPS program, including regulating more strictly the acceptable activities of the governance networks and, for the first time in the history of the program, making explicit demands on how the local governance networks invested their homelessness funds. The federal government now mandates that 65 percent of all funding be applied to Housing First programs. While this approach has considerable merit, it tends to privilege those who are chronically homeless, which constitutes a small portion of the homeless population (even if these individuals consume a disproportionate share of services). The critique of Housing First from the policy community is not that it is a wrong-headed policy per se but that it is one model that is being advanced as a cure-all for homelessness in Canada.

Another restriction introduced by the Government of Canada on the policy choices of the local homelessness governance networks is the elimination of health-related services and supports as initiatives that local decision-makers can prioritize and fund. For example, local governance networks are not permitted to prioritize or fund any program that has a harm-reduction approach to homelessness. This is stunningly inconsistent with the federal government's emphasis on Housing First, which emerges out of harm-reduction thinking. Equally disruptive to local governance network policy planning is a new restriction on any activities that are associated with raising awareness of the issue of homelessness, advocacy, networking across the sector, and community development (to raise capacity within the sector to respond to homelessness).

Such changes dramatically reshape the federal government's role in the HPS, which was initially designed precisely to raise capacity for the local area to respond to homelessness, not to be a glorified administrative arm of the Government of Canada in each locality. These fairly dramatic reforms were not expected from the Harper government, which, upon coming to power in 2006, heralded an "open federalism" approach that would seek to respect the powers of other levels of government and would not dictate policy at the local level outside of its constitutional sphere of jurisdiction (Doberstein, 2011). By dramatically reforming what was previously a laudable flexible program in terms of governance and policy, one that largely deferred to the priorities and activities that emerge from a community process, to a program that is severely restricted in terms of shaping policy, the Government of Canada has reshaped, for the worse, the metagovernance of all the associated homelessness governance networks. Perhaps the central finding of this cross-city comparison of homelessness governance networks is that inappropriate or overly heavy-handed metagovernance can seriously inhibit the dynamism, innovation, and coordination that has characterized the previously high-performing governance networks. Simply put, these recent metagovernance changes threaten many of the important policy gains presented in this book.

Considerable resistance to these changes emerged from governance network members in Vancouver, Toronto, and Calgary. The most common critique from across the country was that the new rules were imposed by the federal government without any appreciation of or flexibility for local circumstances. For example, CAL-main membership wrote a stinging letter, attached to their Community Plan to be sent to the federal minister for approval, which, in part, said that they are

> concerned that the new HPS Housing First Model will exacerbate the problem of homelessness in Calgary. The approach being taken in applying the 65% - 35% formula could put at least 600 individuals and families at risk. Economically, a reduced return on investment for any existing or new "Housing First" program is highly likely as many in the homeless population will not benefit from the Housing First approach due to their specific characteristics and circumstances. All types of housing and support programs (not just Housing First) are needed. We conclude that best practices within the local context should be the basis of all government-funded programs. We identify a number of different populations that cannot be served well under the Government of Canada's Homeless Partnering Strategy's restrictive "Housing First" definition. (Community Action Commitee [CAC], 2014b, p. 23)

This type of direct, written, and public rebuke of Government of Canada policy from local governance networks is quite unusual and reflects a deep frustration with how this initiative has been turned on its head from the previous iterations that, as we have demonstrated, contributed to much success at the local level. CAL-main membership went on to write that the disproportionate emphasis and forced prioritization of Housing First does little to help youth, women and families fleeing violence, and Aboriginal people, all of whom need other service models. Even worse, the Housing First emphasis creates bizarre incentives: people, in effect, need to be chronically homeless to be served under this model. The letter from CAL-main to the government goes on:

> The common theme of the above examples is that effective, made-in-Calgary solutions cannot be employed under our 65% Housing First funding. The CACHH [CAL-main] supports the Housing First philosophy

and principles, we recommend dropping the restrictive HPS definitions imposed around "chronic and episodic," and we recommend instead supporting homeless programs and services that demonstrate best practices in a local context. The current framework that focuses 65% of the HPS investment on chronically and episodically homeless individuals severely limits the ability of Calgary's well evolved homeless serving system to do evidence based work. (CAC, 2014b, pp. 27–28)

Similar resistance over these recent changes in metagovernance occurred not only in Vancouver and Toronto but also in cities not investigated in this book. In Montreal, for example, governance network members were so hostile to the new changes, which they argued inhibit Montreal from being able to respond to the unique needs of the community, that they engaged in a public battle with the Government of Canada. Pierre Gaudreau, coordinator of Réseau d'aide aux personnes seules et itinérantes de Montréal, contended that "the federal government wants to orient its funding in the fight against homelessness toward one type of intervention ... What is asked by the government of Quebec, by the city of Montreal and by community organizations is that the federal government retains a model that (funds) different interventions and different projects" (Montreal Gazette, 2014).

Tim Richter, the president of the Canadian Alliance to End Homelessness and a strong advocate of the Housing First philosophy, also warned the Government of Canada about such dramatic changes to HPS and the effect on local level policy planning and coordination: "It's also important to remember that Housing First is a critical component of ending homelessness, but it is not a silver bullet. There are many other critical elements that need to support community plans and Housing First programs in order to reduce and end homelessness" (Parliament of Canada, 2013). The concern among many civil society and government actors at the local level is precisely that one rationality or service model dominates in a very complex policy field that involves a population comprising individuals and families with diverse experiences and reasons for becoming homeless. This is especially important since recent evidence coming from the United States on Housing First approaches is not as positive or universally effective as it once was thought to be (Groton, 2013; Núñez, 2013; Schiff & Schiff, 2014; Stanhope & Dunn, 2011), yet the Government of Canada is forcing local governance networks to adopt this model, disrupting and indeed forcing them to abandon many service models and approaches that have been successful but do not conform to the government's preferred model.

It is not that Housing First as a philosophy is wrong-headed or that the approach is fundamentally flawed; in fact, it is a social justice victory that government has implicitly acknowledged the right to housing. Rather, it is an effective response for a relatively small portion of homeless individuals – namely, the chronically homelessness, and specifically those with mental illness and/or substance abuse problems. Many in the community acknowledge the importance of addressing the needs of this constituency, but they also contend that the really big concerns today are families that are poor, possibly even working, and are simply unable to afford housing but have no mental health or addictions issues. Ralph da Costa Núñez, president and CEO of the Institute for Children, Poverty, and Homelessness (based in New York City), believes that there should be a Housing First approach "for families and individuals who just need housing. But there also needs to be a Housing Second option for folks who need education or other job training and placement assistance. Lastly, there needs to be a Housing Third option for individuals and families with problems that compound their job and/or housing situation" (LaMarche, 2014).

Housing First does not serve the people mentioned by Nunez, and they are a massive and growing segment of the homeless population. The strongest critics of Housing First, which was first advanced by the Bush Administration in the United States, see it as a way to clean up the downtown cores of cities for business and tourism interests and argue that it circumscribes a very narrow population of those "deserving" of benefits like subsidized housing and services – the mentally ill and chronically homeless – while leaving out almost everyone else, most of whom are simply poor. This is now being realized in Canada: because of the federal government emphasis on Housing First, local governance networks can only really prioritize the most chronically homeless.

In earlier chapters, I differentiated four types of metagovernance and demonstrated how metagovernance mediates the relationship between network properties and policy outputs like innovation and coordination. The 2014 changes to the HPS affect all of the governance networks in Canada, essentially placing them all into a straitjacket metagovernance context; this particular type of metagovernance seriously impinges on network activity that may produce policy innovation and coordination. The new restrictions of policy and governance in the federal HPS program are suffocating the network governance principles on which this program was created and which have been demonstrated to contribute to important policy innovation and coordination of homelessness response.

Theoretical Framework Revisited

This study is guided by concepts from the network governance, metagovernance, and deliberative democracy literatures, which together form an integrated governance network theory. Homelessness is often studied as an exclusively urban issue, but this study shows that policy actors at all levels of government – both inside and outside of the governance networks – have powerfully shaped homelessness policy in Canada over the last two decades. The metagovernance framework captures how the multi-level nature of governance in Canada may set unique governance and policy trajectories in jurisdictions, depending on how institutions are structured. Embedded in the overarching metagovernance framework is network governance theory, which serves as the principal guiding theoretical lens for this study, the most important aspect of which is to conceptualize governance networks in terms of both structural and relational dimensions as key determinants of policy development. The design and membership of governance network, as well as the linkages within them, play important roles in shaping the development of policy. Finally, embedded conceptually within network governance theory is deliberative democracy theory, serving as a guide to the micro-level dimensions of governance network activity. Concepts articulated in deliberative democracy theory help to address a key weakness in network governance theory: the underconceptualization and measurement of the practice of governance network activity.

What are the implications of the findings, both anticipated and unexpected, in relation to integrated governance network theory? What does it tell us about public policy? The findings not only lend evidence to the key claim of network governance theory – that network institutionalization and inclusivity matter to the development and implementation of policy at the extremes of the institutionalization and inclusiveness dimensions of governance network structure – but also add much needed nuance to the role of metagovernance in mediating the policy outputs of network governance.

Thinking about governance networks as "deliberative systems" has been characterized by governance theorist John Dryzek (2010) as an important next frontier in deliberative democratic scholarship, and this study is an early response to this call. Governance networks are examples of deliberative democracy in practice; they provide the opportunity to put some meat on the bones of the deliberative democracy concepts of inclusion, representation, persuasion, and consensus decision-making. These concepts help refine traditional network governance theory, which has struggled with conceptualizing and testing the linkages between the practice of governance networks and public policy. The empirical work in this study – especially the observation, for an extended period of time, of several of the governance networks at work – reveals and gives depth to the causal mechanisms at work in such real-world deliberative contexts. Linking these causal mechanisms, brokerage and persuasion, to network governance concepts of institutionalization and inclusivity and to the metagovernance context, all of which have potential to drive policy innovation and system coordination, is the most important theoretical contribution of this research. (See Figure 6.1, page 166, for an illustration of this model.)

But why is it that only some governance networks generate innovative and coordinated policy? I have shown that two causal processes are principally at work: brokerage relations and persuasion. Governance networks provide a key venue for the development and nurturing of brokerage relations, thus making more permeable the previously sharp boundaries between policy actors. Highly institutionalized and inclusive governance networks provide regular venues for social boundaries among disparate policy actors in government and civil society to be dismantled as these actors develop relationships of exchange and trust and draw on diverse perspectives in the policy-making process. In theoretical terms, these findings conform to political philosopher Charles Tilly's (2003, p. 219) suggestion that the institutionalized forging together of diverse policy actors leads to incremental boundary change and expansion, "creating shared representations" of the boundary that previously divided them. The evidence in these pages suggests that the brokerage that emerges in such governance networks indeed alters relations among policy actors, allowing collective action to spread along the newly created network pathway, as theorized by political sociologist Doug McAdam and colleagues (2001).

The second causal process linking governance networks to the dimensions of policy is persuasion. Key institutional features of governance networks are deliberation and an ethic of information exchange, horizontal relations, and argumentation that is distinct from the rules, procedures, and hierarchy that are characteristic of bureaucracies. The comparative historical policy analysis in this study identifies numerous concrete instances in which decisions made in highly institutionalized and inclusive governance networks would not have been made if authority had rested solely within the bureaucracy. Persuasion as a causal mechanism therefore captures the process by which policy actors are exposed to distinct perspectives and arguments about policy problems and solutions, perspectives and arguments that are subject to confrontation and challenge in a non-hierarchical decision-making setting. Evidence from the eight networks examined bolsters the claim that confrontation among diverse actors in a network "can be a potentially productive learning process" (Lindquist, 1992, p. 148). The positive findings in VAN-main and CAL-main, as well as the negative findings in TO-emerg, likewise lend further evidence to political scientist Diana Mutz's (2002, p. 120) finding that one's "perspective-taking ability" (i.e., the capacity to entertain others' points of view) will shape whether the effects of exposure to differing views leads to a softening or hardening of boundaries or views on issues.

While brokerage and persuasion are the causal mechanisms that emerge from highly institutionalized and inclusive governance networks, their effect on policy is powerfully mediated by the metagovernance context: a strongly constrained or inappropriately structured metagovernance context can hamper the effects of the causal mechanisms on policy development and implementation.

None of this is to suggest that network governance is easy to administer or free from conflict, or that it magically produces consensus on policy that is both innovative and well coordinated. In fact, none of those features are characteristic of network governance in the eight governance networks studied here, which have all exerted considerable effort to manage relationships and maintain energy and enthusiasm and have often gone through periods of frustration and fractured decision-making. Indeed, the networks that have faced fewer such challenges (e.g., TO-main) have not been tasked with real decision-making or influence. When real choices need to be made through deliberative efforts in governance networks, these challenges are present but not insurmountable. In fact, this cross-city analysis has shown that with effective network management and metagovernance, the dynamism of governance networks can be harnessed to drive policy innovation and system coordination in ways that are much less likely to occur over the long run in highly bureaucratic and hierarchical institutions.

Network governance and deliberative democracy, in their respective literatures, are typically framed in democratic terms, with the benefits of increased representation as a normative objective. Yet the narrative emerging from this study is really a story about expertise and policy learning to create more effective policy. This comparative longitudinal analysis demonstrates that for too long, homelessness policy made in the towers of bureaucracies has been developed and implemented in contradiction to realities on the ground and at times divorced from effectiveness. Anti-panhandling and anti-squeegee laws may satisfy a political constituency, but they certainly do not represent a meaningful or effective homelessness or poverty policy; in fact, they only serve to further alienate and marginalize struggling Canadians. Strict social assistance eligibility and outlays that fail to cover housing costs – let alone food, clothes, and other expenses – can actually trap Canadians in vulnerable conditions rather than give them a helping hand. And spending many millions per year to get homeless individuals off the street is significantly less efficient than preventing homelessness altogether with a sensible and coordinated social and economic safety net.

That integrated network governance has been shown to drive policy innovation and coordination should not be extrapolated too far. To be clear, governance networks alone will not solve the homelessness crisis in Canada. Substantial public sector investment is required to correct for the market failures and societal and personal forces that cause homelessness in this country and elsewhere. In times of austerity, government spending on homelessness and housing is often the easiest to cut, given the political marginalization and diffuse distribution of very low-income and needy Canadians. Yet governance networks can create a counterbalance to the inadequacies of the traditional liberal democratic institutions, which privilege certain constituencies over others. Governance networks not only infuse alternative perspectives into the policy process but can also, as we have seen, generate issue momentum and political will to create lasting change towards ending homelessness. Network governance is more demanding of bureaucracies and civil society, is often frustrating for those involved, and requires careful design and management, but it is clear that traditional institutions of policy-making alone are simply not up to the task of ending homelessness.

The theoretical implications of the findings in this study thus also support the emerging metagovernance literature. This study draws on the metagovernance concept to show that how a governance network is created, the tasks with which it is charged, and the entity to whom it is accountable places it in a particular space in the policy process. Indeed, the metagovernance context of a governance network can tell us something about the possibilities and limitations of the governance network in the policy process – and thus its potential to drive policy innovation and coordination. This study suggests that metagovernor leadership style has an important effect on the stability of the governance network and thus on its ability to shape policy development. Equally important, the governance network mandate sets critical limits on its activities; the amount of policy space, as a factor affecting a network's ability to shape policy, is independent of the features of the network itself, such as the diversity of the membership or the internal decision-making processes.

There is no ideal model of metagovernance to be applied in all governance contexts, but the categorization of metagovernance into four specifies some features that can disrupt that activity of governance networks. For example, what I have called volatile metagovernance – in which the governance network is given a very loose mandate and metagovernor-network relations are contentious – is a very unstable context. Contentious metagovernor-network relations probably need to be placed in a more controlled policy space to have productive and stable governance patterns. As evidenced from TO-emerg, elected officials may not serve as the most effective metagovernors because of their inherently politicized nature and their relatively ephemeral presence in the policy system. Metagovernance is thus not only a new task for government but is also a difficult task that is prone to failure. Metagovernance that is too restrictive and hierarchical can give rise to resistance and conflict among network actors, stifle policy innovation, and reduce the willingness of network actors to invest their energy and time in joint problem-solving (Damgaard, 2006), whereas metagovernance that is too flexible can lead to governance chaos and even governance failure (Doberstein & Millar, 2014; Torfing, 2012).

Expanded Application of Network Governance Theory

While this book focuses exclusively on homelessness policy-making, many policy domains in Canada are characterized by network governance; thus, these findings and integrated governance network theory can relate to policy and governance contexts beyond the issue of homelessness. Network governance – that is, governance that includes non-state actors in policy planning and public decision-making – appears in diverse policy areas such as immigrant settlement, economic development, urban Aboriginal policy, and even health care, in Canada and elsewhere. This new pattern of governance is at once *the product* of shifts towards new public management (NPM) principles that seek to reduce the lead role of the bureaucracy in managing public problems and a *reaction against* NPM's market-based principles; in many cases, these principles have proven to be incompatible with the demands of modern governance, which is complex, multi-level, and consultative (Conteh & Roberge, 2013). Therefore, we need to know how to effectively manage complex governance institutions like these, which are premised on harnessing the dynamism of civil society towards more innovative and effective policy but are notoriously difficult to manage and sometimes fail (Torfing, 2012).

A brief look at a few areas other than homelessness can illustrate how the findings of this study, however narrow they may seem, are relevant to a great many and diverse issue areas in modern governance in Canada and elsewhere. For example, the observation that the metagovernance context of governance networks is essential to productive and stable policy-making is particularly relevant to urban Aboriginal self-governance in Canada. Urban Aboriginal governance has emerged as an important new frontier in the study of federalism, multi-level governance, and urban politics in Canada (Peters, 2011; Peters & Andersen, 2013). Whereas the study of Aboriginal self-government with territorially linked land bases (typically in rural areas) has been the preoccupation of most scholars of Aboriginal politics in Canada, the urban context is a site of Aboriginal governance experimentation and expansion. The court decision in *Canada v. Misquadis* (2003) made it clear that urban Aboriginal communities possess a limited right to self-determination and, specifically, a right to deliver services based on their indigenous identity. Since half of all Aboriginal people in Canada live in urban areas, this is a decision with significant implications for our continually evolving federalism and multi-level institutional framework, yet it has not received due attention from scholars (Belanger, Awosoga, & Head, 2013).

Aboriginal governance in Canadian cities is best characterized today as ad hoc and program-specific public administration rather than as political self-government. The governance institutions are principally service oriented (e.g., labour market, housing, and homelessness) and are justified on the basis of responding to a policy problem, not a political problem. They resemble the "community of interest" model derived in the Royal Commission on Aboriginal Peoples as a model for urban Aboriginal governance in Canada, a form of self-governance that is based on voluntary citizenship and is limited to sector-specific service provision (Frideres, 2008). Self-government for Aboriginal peoples in urban contexts may never look like Treaty self-government, for numerous legal and practical reasons; instead, it will probably resemble more of a "co-production" of policy as it relates to the needs and development of urban Aboriginals. So as was asked at the beginning of this book, we can ask, Do urban Aboriginal self-governance institutions matter to policy and programs? That is, is there evidence that they generate and implement policy and programs that would not otherwise be pursued by municipal bureaucracies who consult the Aboriginal community on relevant issues like homelessness, housing, employment skills and training, and public health? Like homelessness governance networks, urban Aboriginal governance networks consist of mainly civil society actors from Aboriginal organizations and are placed in an arena of policy-making that is strongly shaped by the state as a metagovernor. In fact, the Aboriginal experience with metagovernance is especially important to consider, given the long history of state management of their affairs.

Another area that is ripe for comparative assessment and analysis is public health care delivery in Ontario. In 2008, the Province of Ontario introduced thirteen local health integration networks (LHINs) to manage non-hospital health care spending in the province. These governance networks consist of representatives from the civil society, professional, and government sectors and are mandated with jointly devising and implementing policy and programs. The thirteen LHINs, covering the entire province of Ontario, are not simply advisory networks but have real decision-making authority with respect to funding and coordinating services, authority delegated from the Minister of Health and Long-Term Care. In fact, the LHINs, collectively, allocate $20 billion. The networks have a complex and lengthy Memorandum of Understanding with the ministry, and thus, important dimensions of metagovernance constrain the nature of their decision making. Although LHINs are controversial for a number of reasons, they do not suffer from a lack of sustained engagement from citizens and health administrators, precisely because they have an empowered institutional structure (Ontario Ministry of Health and Long-Term Care, 2008).

The final example of potential cross-pollination of the theoretical framework advanced in this study is in relation to the so-called Quebec model of governance. Quebec has a long history of network governance, and jointly negotiated policy-making traditions are an important part of the political culture in the province, which is reflected in the considerable attention that scholars have given to Quebec model (Dufour, 2004; Fontan et al., 2009; Hamel & Jouve, 2006; Klein, Tremblay, & Fontan, 2014; Mendell & Neamtan, 2010; Noël, 2002). In the economic policy sphere, for example, the Quebec government created *les corporations de développement économique communautaire* (CDECs), local governance networks that are intended to address local economic development and neighbourhood revitalization. The Quebec model of governance, however, has undergone significant changes in the last decade, principally because of metagovernance decisions made by the provincial government since Premier Jean Charest. In short, the provincial government limited the representation of individual members of the local population, froze sectoral representation (from business, institutions, community groups), and enhanced municipal and provincial elected official representation on CDECs such that they constitute the majority (Fontan et al., 2009). These actions, of course, reduced the power of the local community to shape the direction of CDECs and turned the networks into extensions of government. The policy result was immediate – a shift from local economic development focused on revitalization, empowerment, and social justice to development focused on entrepreneurship and employability, consistent with the provincial government's neoliberal orientation (Fontan et al., 2009). The CDECs have thus been transformed from locally driven and representative governance networks, each negotiating and implementing local priorities, to a transmission belt for provincial government policy. The CDECs in Quebec, as well as other examples of network governance in the province, could be fruitfully analyzed and explained using the theoretical framework of metagovernance and network governance articulated in this book. Additionally, analyzing these different cases of network governance in Canada could help to refine the theoretical framework advanced in this book.

Questions for Future Research

While this research establishes clear linkages between governance networks and policy development and conceptualizes the macro-forces (metagovernance) and micro-forces (emergent causal mechanisms of deliberative systems) at work, several unanswered questions remain that warrant further research. First, for the purposes of advancing an integrated governance network theory, it is necessary to test the causal claims articulated and confirmed in this study in other jurisdictions and policy domains, and I have provided some issue areas above that are likely to be most fruitful for comparative analysis. Homelessness governance networks tackle a complex policy problem affecting a very marginalized population. In this context, governance networks are arguably appropriate from practical-administrative and normative-democratic perspectives. It is not as obvious that governance networks are appropriate in nuclear policy, financial regulation, or military procurement, for example. Thinking about these issues in normative terms is important when considering whether these governance networks can and should be scaled up beyond the local level, where we typically find them.

Second, a question not directly addressed in this study relates to measuring the democratic virtues and vices of governance networks. How do we determine whether network governance arrangements enhance democracy? Some scholars and observers take this for granted, but governance theorist Dryzek (2010) reminds us that "a network may be deliberative without necessarily being especially democratic" (p. 125). Indeed, a central critique of network governance arrangements is their potential to be undemocratic and unaccountable, since they tend to include unelected civil society actors in decision-making that affects society as a whole (Esmark, 2007; Papadopoulos, 2007). Establishing clear links between the structure and dynamics of governance networks and policy development has implications for public policy and administration scholarship, particularly with respect to accountability and fiscal federalism. We may value diverse perspectives in policy-making – especially if they drive policy innovation, as demonstrated in this study – but is it legitimate for civil society actors to have such a privileged role in decision making?

The broad narrative emerging out of this study of governance networks is one of an interactive relationship between civil society members and bureaucrats that harnesses the expertise and knowledge of community and local government actors, while generally making decisions within the comfort level of bureaucrats responding to various political constraints. This is consistent with the work of political scientist Grace Skogstad (2003), who specifies that this is the path to take to resolve contemporary governance challenges and political authority. For governance network critics, the findings should make clear that we should not be afraid that these governance networks are not sufficiently supervised or steered by government. And for network governance proponents, the evidence simultaneously demonstrates the value of having diverse perspectives in a less hierarchical decision-making structure. Networks clearly matter to policy development and decision making.

The exploration of the metagovernance dimension in integrated governance network theory provides a credible, though incomplete, response to the critique of lack of accountability in network governance, since it shows that networks are typically steered and supervised by bureaucrats and their elected masters, thus completing the accountability circle. Yet this response is limited by its focus on top-down, output mechanisms of accountability and democratic legitimacy, leaving bottom-up, input mechanisms like representativeness, trust, and credibility among network actors undertheorized and without adequate operationalization (Kohler-Koch, 2010). Future research to operationalize input legitimacy concepts would be helpful to develop more complete conceptualizations of accountability in new governance arrangements and, in particular, to answer the question of how metagovernors create the conditions that harness the potential innovative capacity of joint problem-solving among government and civil society, balancing it against demands of democratic accountability.

Finally, while all but two of the governance networks featured in this study are currently active, there are significant theoretical and empirical gaps in understanding network governance failure, in contrast to highlighting their virtues with respect to policy innovation and coordination. Because of the limited scope of this study, the (existential) governance failure of TO-emerg has not been explored in detail. A key difference of TO-emerg in relation to the other governance networks studied is its elected official leadership. While it is plausible that the politicized nature of this position contributed to its failure, there is not enough comparative evidence to confirm this. Governance failure happens not just existentially but also in situations characterized by conflict, resource hoarding, and closure to some groups. To governance network scholars like Sørensen and Torfing (2007c, p. 110), governance network failure can be seen as a result of the failure "to balance openness and closure, consensus and conflict, and efficiency and legitimacy," and some imbalances can be "fatal." These elements must be tackled for integrated governance network theory to be refined.

A Final Thought

While this book focuses on homelessness policy development in Canada and on informing and refining integrated governance network theory, it is more fundamentally a narrative about the direction in which modern public administration and governance is evolving – that is, towards a governance framework that draws in civil society actors more than has been previously acknowledged in Canadian public administration studies. There is also a new role for the public service that increasingly involves managing relationships and facilitating deliberative problem solving rather than formulating expertise and analysis within the confines of bureaucratic hallways. Despite all of the international literature detailing the changing nature of the state and the increasing role of civil society actors in the policy process, particularly from European scholars, there have been minimal empirical and theoretical contributions with respect to network governance and its impact on public policy in the Canadian context.

Network governance asks us to rethink the roles of bureaucrats, civil society actors, and, indeed, elected masters in the policy process, just as new public management once asked us to revisit the privileged role of the bureaucracy in the implementation of policy. Whereas new public management was never able to answer the call to solve complex policy problems – instead, zealously focusing on finding efficiencies – network governance offers a pathway to satisfy emerging expectations of a more open and problem-solving-oriented policy process; it does this without threatening the foundations of liberal democracy in terms of the supremacy of elected officials and their ultimate accountability to citizens. Evidence is being accumulated from around the world – including in this book – that civil society and bureaucratic actors in institutionalized governance networks can bring diverse knowledge and perspectives to a policy issue and that deliberations can be a genuine site of persuasion and transformation among actors, resulting in more innovative and coordinated – and indeed, more effective – policies and programs that address some of the most important issues that government confronts. This all hinges on the state, as a metagovernor of network governance, rethinking how it facilitates and manages such modern governance patterns: the lessons provided in this book suggest that a metagovernor can either channel the dynamism of state and civil society actors to make inroads on some of our most egregious problems or stifle that dynamism, preserving the status quo. Sometimes, the more difficult option is the only one that will work.

Notes

Chapter 1: The Homelessness Puzzle in Canada

1 Calgary does not collect this information in a comparable way in their point-in-time counts.
2 Common individual-level behavioural explanations surrounding drug and alcohol addictions are in fact *consequences* of extreme poverty and a failure of government policy (particularly mental health services) to prevent people from slipping through the cracks, and are *not themselves the explanations* for the growth of homelessness in Canada.
3 Metro Vancouver is studied rather than only the City of Vancouver for two reasons. First, to ensure comparable (though not equal) scale of analysis, since the City of Calgary and the current City of Toronto are amalgamated cities. Second, this is the scale at which the federal government homelessness funding is managed in Vancouver.
4 For the sake of easy comparison among the eight networks examined, I have changed the acronyms typically used in the community for the governance networks. The Greater Vancouver RSCH, for instance, is referred to as VAN-main.
5 The Aboriginal population in Calgary experiences a disproportionate share of homelessness, and, like Vancouver and Toronto, Calgary does have an Aboriginal homelessness governance network. I decided, however, to exclude the Calgary Aboriginal Steering Committee on Housing and Homelessness from this study, since I could obtain neither sufficient documentation of its activities over the years nor cooperation from its leadership. The committee's leadership rebuffed multiple attempts and strategies to secure appropriate and mututally agreed upon methods of inquiry.

Chapter 2: Integrated Network Governance

1 I draw upon the policy and governance network literature more substantively than the others because network scholars have devoted more attention to explicitly linking network structure to policy development in explanatory theoretical terms.

2 This research strand led to the development of a number of typologies of policy networks (Atkinson & Coleman, 1992; Coleman & Skogstad, 1990; Marsh & Rhodes, 1992; Van Waarden, 1992), applied as analytical tools for examining exchange relations among state and non-state actors, with a working assumption that these patterns are consequential to policy outcomes, particularly the likelihood of policy change.

3 Likewise, Canadian political scientists William Coleman, Grace Skogstad, and Michael Atkinson (1996) investigated how the policy network, combined with the character of policy feedback, influences whether paradigm shifts occur as rapid and politically explosive (as per Peter Hall, 1993) or as a slow and tightly managed process. They found that corporatist policy networks are associated with an iterative, deliberative, problem-solving trajectory to paradigm change whereas state-directed or pressure-pluralist networks are more likely to be associated with politically explosive, rapid policy change.

4 Carleton University researchers Katherine Graham and Susan Phillips (1998) also presented an edited volume of participatory urban governance in Canada, concluding that substantive citizen engagement in policy-making can make a policy difference. Who is invited to participate and how that participation is structured are critical variables in producing positive and effective participatory processes.

5 Habermas (1991) likewise contends that exposure to dissimilar views in the public sphere will encourage intrapersonal reflection.

6 Tilly (2003, p. 219), however, suggests that "conversation" as a causal mechanism can lead to incremental boundary change in the case of routine interaction, such that a new "zone of shared representation" is generated.

7 There are certainly other dimensions of policy that could be examined, ranging from macro-level dimensions like total homelessness expenditures to narrower ones like the number of outreach workers per capita, but policy innovation and system coordination capture the most relevant dimensions in the homelessness policy community.

8 An example of two homelessness-related policies working at cross purposes would be an aggressive outreach program to link street homeless persons to services and a bylaw that criminalizes sleeping in public squares and parks. They work at cross purposes because the bylaw will drive the street homeless into the shadows (places they will not be discovered) and thus further away from accessing services.

9 The exception is TO-emerg, which ceased to exist in 2006, so that year is used for TO-emerg.

10 We must be mindful, however, of the possibility that high institutionalization could also lead to bureaucratization, lack of imagination, and risk aversion.

Chapter 3: Vancouver

1 Quebec and British Columbia were the only provinces to respond in this fashion, and Ontario, as will be described in Chapter 4, led by Mike Harris, cancelled all planned contributions to affordable housing.

2 VAN-emerg also obtains funds to assist with its planning and coordinating functions from local governments in Metro Vancouver, charitable foundations like the Vancouver Foundation, United Way, and the Central City Mission Foundation.

3 Contribution agreements are legal documents that set out the terms and expectations between the Crown and the receiving agency or party for the use of state funds for a defined purpose. As the typical purveyor of funds, the Crown has leverage to shape the behaviour of agencies.

4 Michael Anhorn, personal interview, January 24, 2012; Judy Graves, personal interview, January 10, 2012.

5 The shared-delivery model, for legal reasons, was viewed as more appropriate because VAN-main is a coalition of local government officials and community representatives to which it is difficult to ascribe legal and financial liability. In 2000, the Metro Vancouver regional government was not prepared to take on the role as the legal "community entity," so HRSDC performed this function for VAN-main under the program. (In 2011, Metro Vancouver became the community entity for the HPS program.)

6 The UAS was created in 1998 to bring together the various federal government departments with urban Aboriginal mandates to ensure that their programs more effectively serve the target population, but it was similarly structured in terms of requiring the collaboration of local civil society actors to draft strategies and policy priorities jointly (HRSDC, 2003).

7 Celine Maboules, personal interview, January 6, 2012.

8 Confidential interview, 2011; Alice Sundberg, personal interview, October 13, 2011; Karen O'Shannacery, personal interview, October 12, 2011; Celine Maboules, personal interview, January 6, 2012.

9 Peter Greenwell, personal interview, January 23, 2012.

10 Kingsley Okyere, personal interview, October 11, 2011.

11 Karen O'Shannacery, personal interview, October 12, 2011.

12 Michael Anhorn, personal interview, January 24, 2012.

13 Kingsely Okyere, personal interview, October 11, 2011.

14 It is widely accepted that while these counts systematically underestimate the homeless population, they nonetheless help decision makers understand key trend lines and demographic information about the target population.

15 Michael Anhorn, personal interview, January 24, 2012.

16 This has since been replicated in Toronto and other Canadian cities.

17 Confidential interview, 2015.

18 Michelle Ninow, personal interview, January 4, 2012. I interpret these claims to be credible because they were made by bureaucrats who participate in the analogous decision processes at their home government.

19 Michael Anhorn, personal interview, January 24, 2012.

20 Ibid.

21 Ibid.

22 Celine Maboules, personal interview, January 6, 2012.

23 Kingsley Okyere, personal interview, October 11, 2011.

24 Celine Maboules, personal interview, January 6, 2012.

25 Alice Sundberg, personal interview, October 13, 2011; Kingsley Okyere, personal interview, October 11, 2011.
26 Annie Maboules, personal interview, January 24, 2012.
27 Celine Maboules, personal interview, January 6, 2012.
28 Karen O'Shannacery, personal interview, October 12, 2011.
29 Kingsley Okyere, personal interview, October 11, 2011.
30 Patrick Stewart, personal interview, January 12, 2012.
31 Ibid.
32 Ibid.
33 Paulette Seymour, personal interview, September 10, 2012.
34 Judy Graves, personal interview, January 10, 2012.
35 Michael Anhorn personal interview, January 24, 2012. More recently, VAN-emerg explored the need for extreme (hot) weather spaces, not so much for sleeping at night but for refuge during the day, and although this is not on the agenda of BC Housing, the Crown agency remained "open to the conversation" (GVSS, 2007a).
36 Cathy Crowe and Beric German, personal interview, April 10, 2012; Alicia Odette, personal interview, April 25, 2012.
37 Michael Anhorn, personal interview, January 24, 2012; Karen O'Shannacery, personal interview, October 12, 2011.
38 Judy Graves, personal interview, January 10, 2012
39 Ibid.; Michael Anhorn, personal interview, January 24, 2012.
40 Karen O'Shannacery, personal interview, October 12, 2011.
41 Thus, from an administrative standpoint, an agreement by the three levels of government to share information and resources and jointly negotiate and implement strategic policy was viewed as the only way to make progress with respect to the problems facing the area (Carrigg, 2009).
42 Michael Anhorn personal interview, January 24, 2012.
43 Alice Sundberg personal interview, October 13, 2011.
44 Michelle Ninow, personal interview, January 4, 2012; Karen O'Shannacery, personal interview, October 12, 2011.
45 Dan Garrison, personal interview, January 6, 2012.

Chapter 4: Toronto

1 Additionally, there was a network of churches and other faith groups providing overnight shelter, drop-in services, and meals for homeless and socially isolated people in the cold winter months. There were also outreach services to connect homeless persons to social services, some of which were provided by funded organizations and others volunteer-based.
2 Metro Toronto would later be abolished when its constituent municipalities were amalgamated into the new City of Toronto in 1998.
3 Cathy Crowe and Beric German, personal interview, April 10, 2012.
4 Barbara Emmanuel, personal interview, May 8, 2012.

5 Richard Barry, personal interview, April 4, 2012; Barbara Emmanuel, personal interview, May 8, 2012.
6 Amber Kellen, personal interview, April 23, 2012; Cathy Crowe and Beric German,
   personal interview, April 10, 2012; Richard Barry, personal interview, April 4, 2012.
7 Richard Barry, personal interview, April 4, 2012.
8 Ibid.
9 Ibid.
10 Amber Kellen, personal interview, April 23, 2012; Cathy Crowe and Beric German,
   personal interview, April 10, 2012; confidential interview, 2011.
11 Recall that the other option to local communities was a "shared-delivery" model,
   whereby the local governance network would be accountable to the federal government rather than to a municipal administration or other entity. This is an important distinction in the cases examined here because of the different paths chosen by
   Vancouver, Toronto, and Calgary, where the "community entities" are, respectively,
   the Metro Vancouver regional government, the municipal government, and a private homelessness foundation. Precisely where the NHI/HPS is placed locally has
   implications for metagovernance and the policy space available to the governance
   network.
12 Confidential interview, 2012.
13 Cathy Crowe and Beric German, personal interview, April 10, 2012.
14 There were no allegations or evidence of biased decision-making or corruption
   under the previous regime; rather, the process was said to be insufficiently publicized and transparent, and all relevant Aboriginal community organizations agreed
   that they should introduce more diversity into the decision making (Jennifer Abbott,
   personal interview, July 15, 2012; Frances Sanderson, personal interview, May 28,
   2012; confidential interview, 2012).
15 Confidential interview, 2012.
16 Jennifer Abbott, personal interview, July 15, 2012; Frances Sanderson, personal
   interview, May 28, 2012.
17 Frances Sanderson, personal interview, May 28, 2012.
18 Ibid.
19 Jennifer Abbott, personal interview, July 15, 2012; Frances Sanderson, personal
   interview, May 28, 2012; Steve Teekens, personal interview, June 25, 2012.
20 Frances Sanderson, personal interview, May 28, 2012.
21 TTC driver discretion to allow a homeless person to ride for free was explicitly taken
   away in 1997, and it was not a sustainable solution, at any rate.
22 Richard Barry, personal interview, April 4, 2012.
23 Confidential interview, 2015.
24 Frances Sanderson, personal interview, May 28, 2012.
25 Frances Sanderson, personal interview, May 28, 2012; Steve Teekens, personal interview, June 25, 2012; Randy Pitt, personal interview, November 6, 2012.
26 Steve Teekens, personal interview, June 25, 2012.
27 Ibid.

28 Interestingly, in recent years TO-Ab has brought in outside non-Aboriginal assistance to systematically evaluate the Aboriginal services it funds, since the group is so small and some members are in receipt of the funds on which they make decisions.
29 Frances Sanderson, personal interview, May 28, 2012.
30 Confidential interview, 2011.
31 Confidential interview, 2012.
32 Cathy Crowe and Beric German, personal interview, April 10, 2012.
33 Ibid.
34 Confidential interview, 2015.
35 Confidential interview, 2012; Confidential interview, 2011.
36 Confidential interview, 2015.
37 Ibid.
38 Confidential interview, 2012.
39 Cathy Crowe and Beric German, personal interview, April 10, 2012; confidential interview, 2011.
40 Confidential interview, 2015.
41 Confidential interview, 2012.
42 Confidential interview, 2015.
43 Confidential interview, 2011.
44 Michael Anhorn, personal interview, January 24, 2012; Karen O'Shannacery, personal interview, October 12, 2011.
45 City officials and Aboriginal community members disagree on why there is no TO-Ab representation on TO-main. A city official claims that TO-Ab members have been invited but declined, but TO-Ab members deny this and indicate a strong desire to be involved in City decision-making regarding Aboriginal homelessness programs.
46 Jennifer Abbott, personal interview, July 15, 2012.
47 Confidential interview, 2012.
48 Confidential interview, 2012.
49 Diana Hurford, personal interview, January 20, 2012.
50 Michael Anhorn, personal interview, January 24, 2012; Dan Garrison, personal interview, January 6, 2012.
51 Confidential interview, 2015.
52 Ibid.
53 Confidential interview, 2015.
54 Ibid.
55 Confidential interview, 2015.

Chapter 5: Calgary

1 There is, however, voluntary cooperation among municipalities in the Calgary region, called the Calgary Regional Partnership, to implement a Calgary Metropolitan Plan, but it is not focused on housing or homelessness.
2 Confidential interview, 2014.
3 Confidential interview, 2014.
4 It should be noted here that Calgary, like Vancouver and Toronto, has an Aboriginal homelessness governance network. The Calgary Aboriginal Steering Committee on

Housing and Homelessness, however, is not included in this study because of insufficient records and other documentation of its activities over the years and because its leadership declined participation in this study.

5 Leslie McMechan, personal interview, January 20, 2015.
6 Ibid.
7 Confidential interview, 2014.
8 Sue Fortune, personal interview, April 23, 2014.
9 Nic Calder, personal interview, April 25, 2014.
10 Confidential interview, 2015.
11 Robert Parry, personal interview, January 19, 2015.
12 Leslie McMechan, personal interview, January 20, 2015.
13 The provincial government, however, provided critical start-up funds and in-kind support for administration and office space, the City of Calgary provided a full-time social planner in-kind to support the upstart group, and the federal government seconded a staff member as well (Scott, 2012).
14 Astonishingly, the reasoning was that if clients could pay back the damage deposit, then they weren't impoverished, and thus CAL-CHF cannot be a charity.
15 Confidential interview, 2014.
16 Ibid.
17 Ibid.
18 Ibid.
19 Ibid.
20 Ibid.
21 Ibid.
22 Confidential interview, 2015.
23 Sue Fortune, personal interview, April 23, 2014.
24 Jody St. Pierre, personal interview, April 25, 2014.
25 Confidential interview, 2014. The SPAC was much more effective at guiding the internal coordination around coordinated assessment and access, and while engagement from community stakeholders was high in the beginning, it dwindled after CAA unrolled, such that in early 2014, the SPAC was put on hold to revision its role.
26 Confidential interview, 2014.
27 Sue Fortune, personal interview, April 23, 2014.
28 Confidential interview, 2014.
29 Linda McLean, personal interview, April 25, 2014.
30 Ibid.
31 Confidential interview, 2014.
32 Ibid.
33 Linda McLean, personal interview, April 25, 2014.
34 Jody St. Pierre, personal interview, April 25, 2014.
35 Ibid.
36 Confidential interview, 2014.
37 The Calgary Public Library has also partnered with SORCe to create a new "restricted" library card that can be used for those without a fixed address, allowing such individuals access to computers, as well as to training programs and workshops

that the library offers free of charge, like resume writing, interviewing skills, and budgeting (confidential interview, 2014).

38 Confidential interview, 2014.

Chapter 6: Building a Collaborative Advantage

1 Michael Anhorn, personal interview, January 24, 2012.
2 TO-main is not as affected by these metagovernance changes from the federal government because they were always kept in a narrow policy space by their local metagovernors at the City of Toronto, unlike VAN-main and CAL-main.
3 Judy Graves, personal interview, January 10, 2012.
4 Ibid.
5 Karen O'Shannacery, personal interview, October 12, 2011.
6 Ibid.
7 Celine Mauboules, personal interview, January 6, 2012.
8 Alice Sundberg, personal interview, October 13, 2011.
9 Judy Graves, personal interview, January 10, 2012; Michael Anhorn, personal interview, January 24, 2012.
10 Michael Anhorn, personal interview, January 24, 2012.
11 Judy Graves, personal interview, January 10, 2012.
12 Confidential interview, 2014.
13 Ibid.
14 Alice Sundberg, personal interview, October 13, 2011.
15 Sue Fortune, personal interview, April 25, 2014.
16 Confidential interview, 2014.
17 Michelle Ninow, personal interview, January 4, 2012.
18 Michael Anhorn, personal interview, January 24, 2012.
19 Kingsley Okyere, personal interview, October 11, 2011.
20 Celine Maboules, personal interview, January 6, 2012.
21 Michael Anhorn, personal interview, January 24, 2012.
22 Confidential interview, 2012.
23 Confidential interview, 2011.
24 Ibid.
25 Michelle Ninow, personal interview, January 4, 2012.
26 Leslie McMechan, personal interview, January 20, 2015.
27 Jody St. Pierre, personal interview, April 25, 2014.
28 Confidential interviews, 2014.
29 Karen O'Shannacery, personal interview, October 12, 2011.
30 Ibid.
31 Judy Graves, personal interview, January 10, 2012.
32 Michael Anhorn, personal interview, January 24, 2012.
33 Ibid.
34 Frances Sanderson, personal interview, May 28, 2012.
35 Sue Fortune, personal interview, April 23, 2014.
36 Ibid.
37 Confidential interview, 2014.

38 Kingsley Okyere, personal interview, October 11, 2011.
39 Ibid.
40 Confidential interview, 2015.

Chapter 7: Towards a Solution

 1 To put this in context, the provincial government's independent contribution to affordable housing in British Columbia in 2013 was $421 million (BC Housing, annual report, 2014). Experts and advocates argue that the expanded IAH under Harper is not even half of what is required of the federal government in order to adequately address Canada's vast affordability deficit (Shapcott, 2014).
 2 In the first budget of the Justin Trudeau government, announced in March 2016, the HPS program will receive a further injection of $122 million over two years, beginning in 2016–17, though with no substantive changes to the program structure (Government of Canada, 2016, p. 101).

References

Minutes, Annual Reports, and Terms of Reference

Aboriginal Homelessness Steering Committee (Vancouver) (AHSC), Minutes, 2002, 2010, 2011

Advisory Committee on Homeless and Socially Isolated Persons (Toronto) (ACHSIP), Minutes, 1996, 1997, 1998, 1998, 2000, 2002, 2003, 2006

BC Housing, Annual Reports, 1997, 2010, 2012, 2014

Calgary Homeless Foundation (CHF), Annual Reports, 2011, 2012, 2014

Community Action Committee (Calgary) (CAC), Minutes, 2003, 2004, 2006, 2011, 2013

Community Reference Group (Toronto) (CRG), Terms of Reference, 2003

Greater Vancouver Regional Steering Committee on Homelessness (RSCH), Minutes, 2002, 2003, 2006, 2012

Greater Vancouver Shelter Strategy (GVSS), Minutes, 2003, 2004, 2005, 2006, 2007, 2009, 2010, 2011 (Terms of Reference)

Urban Aboriginal Homelessness Review Committee (Toronto) (UAHRC), Minutes, 2009, 2010 (Terms of Reference)

Other Sources

Abramovich, A. (2012). No safe place to go: LGBTQ youth homelessness in Canada – Reviewing the literature. *Canadian Journal of Family and Youth, 4*(1), 29–51.

–. (2013). No fixed address: Young, queer, and restless. In S. Gaetz, B. O'Grady, K. Buccieri, J. Karabanow, & A. Marsolais (Eds.), *Youth homelessness in Canada: Implications for policy and practice* (1st ed.) (pp. 387–404). Toronto: Canadian Homelessness Research Network.

Adam, S., & Kriesi, H. (2007). The network approach. In P. Sabatier (Ed.), *Theories of the policy process* (pp. 189–220). Boulder, CO: Westview Press.

Agranoff, R. (2006). Inside collaborative networks: Ten lessons for public managers. *Public Administration Review, 66*(s1), 56–65. http://dx.doi.org/10.1111/j.1540-6210.2006.00666.x

–. (2007). *Managing within networks: Adding value to public organizations.* Washington, DC: Georgetown University Press.

–. (2012). *Collaborating to manage: A primer for the public sector.* Washington, DC: Georgetown University Press.

Agranoff, R., & McGuire, M. (2003). *Collaborative public management: New strategies for local governments.* Washington, DC: Georgetown University Press.

Alberta Interagency Council on Homelessness. (2012). *Alberta Interagency Council on Homelessness: Roles and mandate.*

Alberta Secretariat for Action on Homelessness. (2008). *A plan for Alberta: Ending homelessness in 10 years.* Edmonton: Government of Alberta, ASAH.

Arboleda-Flórez, J., & Holley, H.L. (1997). *Calgary homelessness study: Final report.* Edmonton: Alberta Health.

Atkinson, N., & Coleman, W. (1989). Strong states and weak states: Sectoral policy networks in advanced capitalist economies. *British Journal of Political Science, 19*(1), 47–67. http://dx.doi.org/10.1017/S0007123400005317.

–. (1992). Policy networks, policy communities and the problem of governance. *Governance: An International Journal of Policy and Administration, 5*(2), 154–80. http://dx.doi.org/10.1111/j.1468-0491.1992.tb00034.x.

Aucoin, P. (1997). The design of public organizations for the 21st century: Why bureaucracy will survive in public management. *Canadian Public Administration, 40*(2), 290–306. http://dx.doi.org/10.1111/j.1754-7121.1997.tb01511.x

Bache, I., & Flinders, M. (2004). *Multi-level governance.* New York: Oxford University Press. http://dx.doi.org/10.1093/0199259259.001.0001.

Bakvis, H., & Juillet, L. (2004). The strategic management of horizontal issues: Lessons in interdepartmental coordination in the Canadian government. Paper presented at the 20th Anniversary of International Political Science Association Research Committee on the Structure and Organization of Government, Conference on Smart Practices Toward Innovation in Public Management, Vancouver, BC, June 16–17.

Bardach, E. (1998). *Getting agencies to work together: The practice and theory of managerial craftsmanship.* Washington, DC: Brookings Institution Press.

BC Auditor General. (2009). *Homelessness: Clear focus needed.* Victoria, BC: Office of the Auditor General of British Columbia.

BC Housing. (2006). Housing matters BC: A housing strategy for British Columbia. Victoria, BC: Government of British Columbia.

Belanger, Y.D., Awosoga, O., & Head, G.W. (2013). Homelessness, urban Aboriginal people, and the need for a national enumeration. *Aboriginal Policy Studies, 2*(2), 4–33.

Bell, S., & Hindmoor, A. (2009). *Rethinking governance: The centralities of the state in modern society.* New York: Cambridge University Press. http://dx.doi.org/10.1017/CBO9780511814617

Bengtsson, B., & Ruonavaara, H. (2011). Comparative process tracing in housing studies. *International Journal of Housing Policy, 11*(4), 395–414.

Benhabib, S. (1992). *Situating the self: Gender, community, and postmodernism in contemporary ethics.* New York: Routledge.

Benz, A., & Papadopoulos, Y. (2006). Introduction: Governance and democracy – Concepts and key issues. In A. Benz & Y. Papadopoulos (Eds.), *Governance and democracy: Comparing national, European and international experiences* (pp. 1–16). London: Routledge.

Bevir, M., & Richards, D. (2009). Decentring policy networks: A theoretical agenda. *Public Administration, 87*(1), 3–14. http://dx.doi.org/10.1111/j.1467-9299.2008.01736.x

Bhaskar, R. (1979). *The possibility of naturalism: A philosophical critique of the contemporary human sciences.* Atlantic Highlands, NJ: Humanities Press.

Blau, J. (1992). *The visible poor: Homelessness in the United States.* New York: Oxford University Press.

Borins, S. (2008). *Innovations in government: Research, recognition, replication.* Washington, DC: Brookings Institution Press.

Börzel, T. (1998). Organizing Babylon: On the different conceptions of policy networks. *Public Administration, 76*(2), 253–73. http://dx.doi.org/10.1111/1467-9299.00100

–. (2011). Networks: Reified metaphor or governance panacea? *Public Administration, 89*(1), 49–63. http://dx.doi.org/10.1111/j.1467-9299.2011.01916.x.

Bradford, N. (2004). Place matters and multi-level governance: Perspectives on a new urban policy paradigm. *Policy Options, 25*(2), 39–44.

–. (2008). Rescaling for a generation? Canada's urban development agreements. Paper presented to the annual meeting of the Canadian Political Science Association, Vancouver, BC, June 4–6.

–. (2014). The federal "communities agenda": Metagovernance for place-based policy in Canada. In C. Andrew & K.A.H. Graham (Eds.), *Canada in cities: The politics and policy of federal-local governance* (pp. 10–38). Montreal and Kingston: McGill-Queen's University Press.

Brown, M., & Rispoli, L. (2014). *Metropolitan gross domestic product: Experimental estimates, 2001 to 2009.* Ottawa: Statistics Canada.

Bunge, M. (1997). Mechanism and explanation. *Philosophy of the Social Sciences, 27*(4), 410–65. http://dx.doi.org/10.1177/004839319702700402

Burt, R.S. (2005). *Brokerage and closure: An introduction to social capital.* Oxford: Oxford University Press.

Calgary Committee to End Homelessness. (2008). *Calgary's 10-year plan to end homelessness.* Calgary: Calgary Committee to End Homelessness.

Calgary Homeless Foundation. (2010). *Ending homelessness: CHF report to the community 2010.* Calgary: Calgary Homeless Foundation.

–. (2012). *Systems planning framework.* Calgary: Calgary Homeless Foundation.

–. (2013). *Coordinated access and assessment: Door agency agreement.* Calgary: Calgary Homeless Foundation.

–. (2014). *Point-in-time count report.* Calgary: Calgary Homeless Foundation.

Canada Mortgage and Housing Corporation. (2011) *Rental market report: Vancouver and Abbotsford CMAs.* Housing Market Information.

Carrigg, D. (2009). How to get value for money? Lots of cash, lots of helpers, but no one in charge of bigger picture, observers say. *The Province,* February 17.

Carroll, Jack. (1998). *Report of the Provincial Task Force on Homelessness.* Ministry of Community Services, Government of Ontario. http://www.ontla.on.ca/library/repository/mon/10000/204285.pdf

Carter, T. (1997). Current practices for procuring affordable housing: The Canadian context. *Housing Policy Debate, 8*(3), pp. 593–631.

–. (2001). Canadian housing policy in transition: Challenges and opportunities. Paper presented at National Housing Conference, Australia Housing and Urban Research Institute, Melbourne, October 25.

Carter, T., & Polevychok, C. (2004). *Housing is good social policy.* Research report F-50. Canadian Policy Research Networks.

Chambers, S. (2003). Deliberative democratic theory. *American Review of Political Science, 6*(1), 307–26. http://dx.doi.org/10.1146/annurev.polisci.6.121901.085538

Church, E. (2014). Transit tops Toronto issues in poll that put Tory ahead in mayoral race. *Globe and Mail,* July 7. http://www.theglobeandmail.com/news/toronto/poll-has-john-tory-leading-in-torontos-mayoral-race/article19501401/

City of Calgary. (1996). *The street speaks: A Survey of, by, and for low income and homeless Calgarians on homelessness in Calgary.* Calgary: City of Calgary.

City of Toronto. (2000). *SCPI community plan for homelessness in Toronto.* Toronto: Shelter, Supports and Housing Administration.

–. (2003a). *SCPI community plan for homelessness in Toronto.* Toronto: Shelter, Supports and Housing Administration.

–. (2003b). *The Toronto report card on housing and homelessness.* Toronto: Community and Neighbourhood Services.

–. (2009a). Toronto housing charter: Opportunity for all. Policy statement, City of Toronto, August 5.

–. (2009b). *Toronto Community Housing Corporation, 2009–11: Community management plan.* Office of the City Manager, May 13.

–. (2010). *2011 funding allocations from the provincial Consolidated Homelessness Prevention Program.* Shelter, Support and Housing Administration, June 14.

–. (2012). *City budget 2012: Shelter, support and housing operating budget.* Toronto: City of Toronto.

–. (2013). *Affordable housing office work plan highlights 2013.* Affordable Housing Committee Meeting presentation, January 29.

–. (2014). *Housing stability service planning framework, 2014–2019.* Toronto: Shelter, Support and Housing Administration.

–. (2015). *Progress report on implementation of 2014–2019 Housing Stability Service Planning Framework.* Shelter, Support and Housing Administration, City of Toronto, March 9.

City of Toronto Street Needs Assessment. (2009). *Street Needs Assessment results.* Toronto: Shelter, Support and Housing Administration.

–. (2013). *Street Needs Assessment results.* Toronto: Shelter, Support and Housing Administration.

City of Vancouver. (2001). *A framework for action: A four pillar approach to drug problems in Vancouver* (Rev.). City of Vancouver Drug Policy Coordinator, April 24.

–. (2005). *Homeless action plan.* City of Vancouver Housing Centre, June.

–. (2009a). Interim housing plan to reduce homelessness: Strategic partnership proposal city-province-private sector. Presentation to City Council, April 7.

–. (2009b). *Report back on the Homeless Emergency Action Team (HEAT).* Manager of Social Development, April 27.

–. (2010a). *Affordable housing policy in new neighbourhoods: Housing initiatives from the City of Vancouver.* Housing policy brochure. http://vancouver.ca/people-programs/housing-and-homelessness.aspx

–. (2010b). *Short-term incentives for rental program (STIR): Program highlights.* Development Services, January 20.

–. (2012). *Vancouver's housing and homelessness strategy, 2012–2021: A home for everyone.* http://vancouver.ca/files/cov/Housing-and-Homeless-Strategy-2012-2021pdf.pdf

Coleman, W., Skogstad, G., & Atkinson, M. (1996). Paradigm shifts and policy networks: Cumulative change in agriculture. *Journal of Public Policy, 16*(3), 273–301. http://dx.doi.org/10.1017/S0143814X00007777

Community Action Committee, Calgary. (2012). *CACHH social policy framework consultation.* Retrieved from administrative secretariat, Calgary.

–. (2013). *Report from the CACHH Community Forum.* Retrieved from administrative secretariat.

–. (2014a). *Report from the CACHH Community Forum.* Retrieved from administrative secretariat.

–. (2014b). *Homelessness partnering strategy, 2014–2019: Community plan.* Retrieved from administrative secretariat.

Community Reference Group. (2002). Building on successes: The community plan for the Supporting Communities Partnership Initiative (SCPI) in Toronto 2003 to 2006. Shelter, Supports and Housing Administration, City of Toronto.

–. (2007). City of Toronto Homelessness Partnership Initiative Community Plan, 2007–2009. Shelter, Supports and Housing Administration, City of Toronto. http://homelesshub.ca/sites/default/files/15g4etvo.pdf

Considine, M., Lewis, J., & Alexander, D. (2009). *Networks, innovation, and public policy.* New York: Palgrave Macmillan. http://dx.doi.org/10.1057/9780230595040

Conteh, C., & Roberge, I. (2013). *Canadian public administration in the 21st century.* Boca Raton, FL: CRC Press. http://dx.doi.org/10.1201/b15343

Crouch, C., La Galès, P., Trigilia, C., & Voelzkow, H. (2004). *Changing governance of local economies: Response of European local production systems.* Oxford: Oxford University Press. http://dx.doi.org/10.1093/0199259402.001.0001

Dachner, N., & Tarasuk, V. (2002). Homeless "squeegee kids": Food insecurity and daily survival. *Social Science and Medicine, 54*(7), 1039–49. http://dx.doi.org/10.1016/S0277-9536(01)00079-X

Damanpour, F. (1991) "Organisational innovation: A meta-analysis of effects of determinants and moderators." *Academy of Management Journal, 34*(3), 555–90.

Damgaard, B. (2006). Lessons on meta-governance from a longitudinal policy network study. Paper presented at EGPA/ASPA conference, "A performing public sector: The second transatlantic dialogue," Leuven, Belgium, June 1–3.

Dill, W. (1958). Environment as an influence on managerial autonomy. *Administrative Science Quarterly, 2*(4), 409–43. http://dx.doi.org/10.2307/2390794

Doberstein, C. (2011). Institutional creation and death: Urban development agreements in Canada. *Journal of Urban Affairs, 33*(5), 529–48.

–. (2012). Applying European ideas on federalism and doing it better? The Government of Canada's homelessness policy experiment. *Canadian Public Policy, 38*(3), 395–410.

–. (2013). Metagovernance of urban governance networks in Canada: In pursuit of legitimacy and accountability. *Canadian Public Administration, 56*(4), 584–609. http://dx.doi.org/10.1111/capa.12041

–. (2015). Designing collaborative governance decision making in search of a "collaborative advantage." *Public Management Review, 18*(6), 819–41. http://dx.doi.org/10.1080/14719037.2015.1045019

Doberstein, C., & Millar, H. (2014). Balancing a house of cards: Throughput legitimacy in Canadian governance networks. *Canadian Journal of Political Science, 47*(02), 259–80. http://dx.doi.org/10.1017/S0008423914000420

Doberstein, C., & Nichols, N. (Eds.). (2016). *Exploring effective systems responses to homelessness.* Toronto: Canadian Observatory on Homelessness.

Doberstein, C., & Smith, A. (2015). "Housing first, but affordable housing last." In T. Healy & S. Trew (Eds.), *The Harper Record, 2008–2015* (pp. 265–80). Ottawa: Canadian Centre for Policy Alternatives.

Dowding, K. (1995). Model or metaphor? A critical review of the policy network approach. *Political Studies, 43*(1), 136–58. http://dx.doi.org/10.1111/j.1467-9248.1995.tb01705.x

Dryzek, J. (2007). Networks and democratic ideals: Equality, freedom, and communication. In E. Sørensen & J. Torfing (Eds.), *Theories of democratic network governance* (pp. 262–73). London: Palgrave.

–. (2010). *Foundations and frontiers of deliberative governance.* Oxford: Oxford University Press. http://dx.doi.org/10.1093/acprof:oso/9780199562947.001.0001

Dufour, P. (2004). L'adoption du projet de loi 112 au Québec: Le produit d'une mobilisation ou une simple question de conjoncture politique? *Politique et Sociétés, 23*(2–3), 159–82. http://dx.doi.org/10.7202/010888ar

Earl, J. (2008). An admirable call to improve, but not fundamentally change, our collective methodological practices. *Qualitative Sociology, 31*(4), 355–59. http://dx.doi.org/10.1007/s11133-008-9105-1

Eberle, M. (2001). Homelessness causes and effects: A profile, policy review and analysis of homelessness in British Columbia. Report prepared for the Government of British Columbia, April.

Edelenbos, J., & Klijn, E. (2006). Managing stakeholder involvement in decision making: A comparative analysis of six interactive processes in the Netherlands. *Journal of Public Administration: Research and Theory, 16*(3), 417–46. http://dx.doi.org/10.1093/jopart/mui049

Eggleton, A. (2009). *In from the margins: A call to action on poverty, housing and homelessness.* Ottawa: Standing Senate Committee on Social Affairs, Science, and Technology.

Elster, J. (1999). *Alchemies of the mind: Rationality and the emotions.* Cambridge: Cambridge University Press.

Esmark, A. (2007). Democratic accountability and network governance: Problems and potentials. In E. Sørensen & J. Torfing (Eds.), *Theories of democratic network governance* (pp. 274–96). London: Palgrave.

Evans, B.M., & Shields, J. (1998). Reinventing the third sector: Alternative service delivery, partnerships and the new public administration of the Canadian post-welfare state. Ryerson University Centre for Voluntary Sector Studies Working Paper Series.

Falleti, T., & Lynch, J. (2009). Context and causal mechanisms in political analysis. *Comparative Political Studies, 42*(9), 1143–66. http://dx.doi.org/10.1177/0010414009331724

Falvo, N. (2010). Homelessness, Toronto's Streets to Homes Program. In J.D. Hulchanski, P. Campsie, S. Chau, S. Hwang, & E. Paradis (Eds.), *Finding home: Policy options for addressing homelessness in Canada* (pp. 95–127). Toronto: Cities Centre, University of Toronto. www.homelesshub.ca/findinghome

Fontan, J.M., Hamel, P., Morin, R., & Shragge, E. (2009). Community organizations and local governance in a metropolitan region. *Urban Affairs Review, 44*(6), 832–57. http://dx.doi.org/10.1177/1078087408326901

Ford, R., & Zussman, D. (1997). *Alternative service delivery: Sharing governance in Canada.* Toronto: Institute of Public Administration of Canada.

Foster-Fishman, P.G., Nowell, B., & Yang, H. (2007). Putting the system back into systems change: A framework for understanding and changing organizational and community systems. *American Journal of Community Psychology, 39*(3–4), 197–215. http://dx.doi.org/10.1007/s10464-007-9109-0

Frideres, J. (2008). Aboriginal identity in the Canadian context. *Canadian Journal of Native Studies, 28*(2), 313–42.

Fung, A. (2008). Citizen participation in governance innovations. In S. Borins (Ed.), *Innovations in government: Research, recognition, and replication* (pp. 52–70). Washington, DC: Brookings Institution Press.

Fung, A., & Wright, E.O. (2003). *Deepening democracy: Innovations in empowered participatory governance.* London: Verso.

Gaetz, S. (2010). The struggle to end homelessness in Canada: How we created the crisis, and how we can end it. *Open Health Services and Policy Journal, 3*(21), 21–26.

Gaetz, S., Gulliver, T., & Richter, T. (2014). *The state of homelessness in Canada 2014.* Toronto: Canadian Homelessness Research Network.

George, A., & Bennett, A. (2005). *Case studies and theory development in the social sciences.* Cambridge, MA: MIT Press.

Gerring, J. (2008). The mechanismic worldview: Thinking inside the box. *British Journal of Political Science, 38*(1), 161–79. http://dx.doi.org/10.1017/S0007123408000082

Gertler, M., & Wolfe, D. (2004). Local social knowledge management: Community actors, institutions, and multi-level governance in regional foresight exercises. *Futures, 36*(1), 45–65. http://dx.doi.org/10.1016/S0016-3287(03)00139-3

Golden, A. (1999). Taking responsibility for homelessness: An action plan for Toronto. Mayor's Homelessness Action Task Force, Toronto.

Goldsmith, S., & Eggers, W. (2001). *Governing by network: The new shape of the public sector.* Washington, DC: Brookings Institution Press.

Government of Canada. (2016). *Budget 2016: Growing the middle class.* Ottawa: Ministry of Finance. http://www.budget.gc.ca/2016/docs/plan/budget2016-en.pdf

Graham, K.A., & Phillips, S.D. (1998). *Citizen engagement: Lessons in participation from local government.* Toronto: Institute of Public Administration of Canada.

Greater Vancouver Regional Steering Committee on Homelessness (RSCH). (2002). *Greater Vancouver homeless count report.* Vancouver: Metro Vancouver.

–. (2003). *Three ways to home: The Regional Homelessness Plan for Greater Vancouver.* Vancouver: Metro Vancouver. http://www.metrovancouver.org/services/regional-planning/homelessness/Pages/default.aspx

–. (2007). *Regional Steering Committee on Homelessness: Vision.* Vancouver: Metro Vancouver. http://www.metrovancouver.org/services/regional-planning/homelessness/Pages/default.aspx.

–. (2008). *Metro Vancouver homelessness count: Final report.* Vancouver: Metro Vancouver.

–. (2012a). Survey of service call review members. Metro Vancouver.

–. (2012b). *Metro Vancouver homeless count report.* Vancouver: Metro Vancouver. http://stophomelessness.ca/wp-content/uploads/2012/02/2011HomelessCount FinalReport28Feb2012-FinalVersion-Tuesday.pdf

–. (2014a). *Metro Vancouver homelessness count: Final report.* Vancouver: Metro Vancouver.

–. (2014b). Briefing note for the Metro Vancouver Housing Committee, September 12. Retrieved from administrative secretariat.

Greater Vancouver Shelter Strategy (GVSS). (2007a). Greater Vancouver Shelter Strategy strategic plan. October. http://www.gvss.ca

–. (2007b). Homeless voices: What we heard from Metropolitan Vancouver residents who have experienced homelessness. Report prepared by James Pratt, October 10. Retrieved from administrative secretariat.

–. (2008). Greater Vancouver Shelter Strategy annual evaluation, 2006–07. April 25. http://www.gvss.ca

–. (2010). GVSS 2010–2012, shelter service plan. September 30. http://www.gvss.ca/

–. (2012). Understanding Metro Vancouver's homeless shelter system. http://www.gvss.ca/

Groton, D. (2013). Are housing first programs effective? A research note. *Journal of Sociology and Social Welfare, 40*, 51–63.

Habermas, J. (1991). *The structural transformation of the public sphere: An inquiry into a category of bourgeois society.* Cambridge, MA: MIT Press.

Hackworth, J., & Moriah, A. (2006). Neoliberalism, contingency, and urban policy: The case of social housing in Ontario. *International Journal of Urban and Regional Research, 30*(3), 510–27. http://dx.doi.org/10.1111/j.1468-2427.2006. 00675.x

Hall, P.A. (1986). *Governing the economy: The politics of state intervention in Britain and France.* New York: Oxford University Press.

–. (1993). Policy paradigms, social learning, and the state: The case of economic policymaking in Britain. *Comparative Politics, 25*(3), 275–96. http://dx.doi. org/10.2307/422246

Hamel, P., & Jouve, B. (2006). *Un modèle québécois? Gouvernance et participation dans la gestion publique.* Montreal: Presses de l'Université de Montréal.

Hartley, J. (2005). Innovation in governance and public services: Past and present. *Public Money and Management, 25*(1), 27–34.

Hawkesworth, B. (2003). Examining collaborative relationships to alleviate homelessness. Master's thesis. University of Calgary.

Hay, C. (1995). Structure and agency. In D. Marsh & G. Stoker (Eds.), *Theory and methods in political science* (pp. 189–206). Basingstoke: Macmillan. http:// dx.doi.org/10.1007/978-1-349-24106-4_11

Head, B. (2008). Assessing network-based collaborations: Effectiveness for whom? *Public Management Review, 10*(6), 733–49. http://dx.doi.org/10.1080/147190 30802423087

Heritier, A., & Rhodes, M. (2011). *New modes of governance in Europe: Governing in the shadow of hierarchy.* New York: Palgrave Macmillan.

Holbeche, L. (2005). *The high performance organization: Creating dynamic stability and sustainable success.* London: Routledge.

Horak, M. (2012). Conclusion: Understanding multilevel governance in Canada's cities. In M. Horak and R. Young (Eds.), *Sites of governance: Multilevel governance and policy making in Canada's big cities* (pp. 339–70). Montreal and Kingston: McGill-Queen's University Press.

Horak, M., & Young, R. (Eds.). (2012). *Sites of governance: Multilevel governance and policy making in Canada's big cities.* Montreal and Kingston: McGill-Queen's University Press.

Howlett, M. (2002). Do networks matter? Linking policy network structure to policy outcomes: Evidence from four Canadian policy sectors, 1990–2000. *Canadian Journal of Political Science, 35*(2), 235–67. http://dx.doi.org/10.1017/S00084 23902778232

Hulchanski, J.D. (1995). The concept of housing affordability: Six contemporary uses of the housing expenditure-to-income ratio. *Housing Studies, 10*(4), 471–91. http://dx.doi.org/10.1080/02673039508720833

–. (2000). A new Canadian pastime? Counting homeless people: Addressing and preventing homelessness is a political problem, not a statistical or definitional problem. University of Toronto Centre for Urban and Community Studies, December.

–. (2002). *Housing policy for tomorrow's cities.* Ottawa: Canadian Policy Research Networks.

Hulchanski, J.D., & Shapcott, M. (2005). *Finding room: Policy options for a Canadian rental housing strategy.* Toronto: CSUS Press.

Human Resources and Social Development Canada. (2003). *Evaluation of the National Homelessness Initiative: Implementation and early outcomes of the HRDC-based components.* Ottawa: Strategic Policy Branch.

–. (2009). Evaluation of the Homelessness Partnering Strategy. Strategic Policy and Research Branch, Ottawa, July.

Hunter, E. (2008). What's good for the gays is good for the gander: Making homeless youth safer for lesbian, gay, bisexual and transgender youth. *Family Court Review, 46*(3), 543–57. http://dx.doi.org/10.1111/j.1744-1617.2008.00220.x

Huxham, C. (1993). Collaborative capability: An intra-organizational perspective on collaborative advantage. *Public Money and Management, 13*(3), 21–28. http://dx.doi.org/10.1080/09540969309387771

Hwang, S.W. (2001). Homelessness and health. *Canadian Medical Association Journal, 164*(2), 229–233.

Jessop, B. (1998). The rise of governance and the risks of failure: The case of economic development. *International Social Science Journal, 50*(155), 29–45.

–. (2003). Governance and meta-governance: On reflexivity, requisite variety and requisite irony. In H. Bang (Ed.), *Governance as social and political communication* (pp. 142–72). Manchester: Manchester University Press.

Justason Market Intelligence. (2014). Over half of Vancouverites identify ending homelessness as the top priority for Vancouver for the next three years. July 31. http://www.justasonmi.com/?p=4029

Keast, R., Brown, K., & Mandell, M. (2007). Getting the right mix: Unpacking integration meanings and strategies. *International Public Management Journal, 10*(1), 9–33. http://dx.doi.org/10.1080/10967490601185716

Keast, R., & Mandell, M. (2014). A composite theory of leadership and management: Process catalyst and strategic leveraging – Theory of deliberate action in collaborative networks. In R. Keast, M. Mandell, & R. Angranoff (Eds.), *Network theory in the public sector: Building new theoretical frameworks* (pp. 33–49). Abingdon, UK: Routledge.

Keast, R., Mandell, M., & Agranoff, R. (2014). *Network theory in the public sector: Building new theoretical frameworks.* Abingdon, UK: Routledge.

Kenis, P., & Schneider, V. (1991). Policy networks and policy analysis: Scrutinizing a new analytical toolbox. In B. Marin and R. Mayntz (Eds.), *Policy networks: Empirical evidence and theoretical considerations* (pp. 25–59). Boulder, CO: Westview Press.

Kickert, W., & Koppenjan, J. (1997). Public management and network management: An overview. In W. Kickert, E.H. Klijn, & J. Koppenjan (Eds.), *Managing complex networks: Strategies for the public sector* (pp. 35–61). London: Sage. http://dx.doi.org/10.4135/9781446217658.n3

Kittel, B. (2006). A crazy methodology? On the limits of macro-quantitative social science research. *International Sociology, 21*(5), 647–77. http://dx.doi.org/10.1177/0268580906067835

Klein, J.L., Tremblay, D.G., & Fontan, J.M. (2014). Social actors and hybrid governance in community economic development in Montreal. In N. Bradford &

A. Bramwell (Eds.), *Governing urban economies: Innovation and inclusion in Canadian city-regions* (pp. 37–57). Toronto: University of Toronto Press.

Klijn, E., & Koppenjan, J. (2000). Public management and policy networks: Foundations of a network approach to governance. *Public Management an International Journal of Research and Theory, 2*(2), 135–58.

–. (2004). *Managing uncertainty in networks: A network approach to problem solving and decision making*. London: Routledge.

–. (2012). Governance network theory: Past, present and future. *Policy and Politics, 40*(4), 587–606. http://dx.doi.org/10.1332/030557312X655431

Klijn, E., & Skelcher, C. (2007). Democracy and governance networks: Compatible or not? *Public Administration, 85*(3), 587–608. http://dx.doi.org/10.1111/j.1467 -9299.2007.00662.x

Kohler-Koch, B. (2010). Civil society and EU democracy: "Astroturf" representation? *Journal of European Public Policy, 17*(1), 100–16. http://dx.doi. org/10.1080/13501760903464986

Kooiman, J. (1993). *Modern governance: New government society interactions*. London: Sage.

Kubik, J. (2009). Ethnography of politics: Foundations, applications, prospects. In E. Schatz (Ed.), *Political ethnography: What immersion contributes to the study of politics* (pp. 25–52). Chicago: University of Chicago Press.

Laird, G. (2007). *Shelter: Homelessness in a growth economy – Canada's twenty-first century paradox*. A report for the Sheldon Chumir Foundation for Ethics in Leadership, Calgary.

LaMarche, Pat. (2014). "Housing First doesn't work: The homeless need community support." *Huffington Post,* The Blog, January 16. http://www.huffingtonpost. com/pat-lamarche/housing-first-doesnt-homelessness_b_4611639.html

Layton, J. (2000). *Homelessness: The making and unmaking of a crisis*. Toronto: Penguin Group.

–. (2008). *Homelessness: How to end the national crisis.* Toronto: Penguin Group.

Leach, W. (2006). Collaborative public management and democracy: Evidence from western watershed partnerships. *Public Administration Review, 66*(s1), 100–10.

Leo, C., & August, M. (2006). National policy and community initiative: Mismanaging homelessness in a slow growth city. *Canadian Journal of Urban Research, 15*(s1), 1–21.

–. (2009a). The multilevel governance of immigration and settlement: Making deep federalism work. *Canadian Journal of Political Science, 42*(2), 491–510. http:// dx.doi.org/10.1017/S0008423909090337

–. (2009b). Is the federal government dividing the Aboriginal community? Can it stop? A Winnipeg case study. Paper prepared for the annual meeting of the Canadian Political Science Association Ottawa, May.

Leone, R., & Ohemeng, F. (2011). *Approaching public administration: Core debates and emerging issues*. Toronto: Emond Montgomery Publications.

Lichbach, M. (2008). Modeling mechanisms of contention: MTT's positivist constructivism. *Qualitative Sociology, 31*(4), 345–54. http://dx.doi.org/10.1007/ s11133-008-9104-2

Lieberman, E. (2001). Causal inference in historical institutional analysis: A specification of periodization strategies. *Comparative Political Studies, 34*(9), 1011–35. http://dx.doi.org/10.1177/0010414001034009003

Lindquist, E.A. (1992). Public managers and policy communities: Learning to meet new challenges. *Canadian Public Administration, 35*(2), 127–59. http://dx.doi.org/10.1111/j.1754-7121.1992.tb00685.x

Little, D. (1991). *Varieties of social explanation: An introduction to the philosophy of social science*. Boulder, CO: Westview Press.

Lundvall, B. (1992). *National systems of innovation: Towards a theory of innovation and interactive learning*. London: Pinter Press.

MacPherson, D. (2001). A framework for action: A four-pillar approach to drug problems in Vancouver. City of Vancouver, April 24. http://council.vancouver.ca/010424/RR1.htm

Magnusson, W., & Kataoka, S. (2009). Settling the unsettled: Migrants, municipalities and multilevel governance in British Columbia. Paper prepared for the annual meeting of the Urban Affairs Association, Seattle, WA, April.

Mahoney, J. (2001). Beyond correlational analysis: Recent innovations in theory and method. *Sociological Forum, 16*(3), 575–93. http://dx.doi.org/10.1023/A:1011912816997

Mansbridge, J. (1983). *Beyond adversary democracy*. Chicago: University of Chicago Press.

Mansbridge, J., Bohman, J., Chambers, S., Estlund, D., Føllesdal, A., Fung, A., ..., & Martí, J. (2010). The place of self-interest and the role of power in deliberative democracy. *Journal of Political Philosophy, 18*(1), 64–100. http://dx.doi.org/10.1111/j.1467-9760.2009.00344.x

Marin, B., & Maytnz, R. (1991). *Policy networks: Empirical evidence and theoretical considerations*. Boulder, CO: Westview Press.

Martin, P., & Fontana, J. (1990). Finding room: Housing solutions for the future. Report of the National Liberal Caucus Task Force on Housing, May 14.

May, P. (1992). Policy learning and failure. *Journal of Public Policy, 12*(4), 331–54. http://dx.doi.org/10.1017/S0143814X00005602

McAdam, D., Tarrow, S., & Tilly, C. (2001). *Dynamics of contention*. Cambridge: Cambridge University Press. http://dx.doi.org/10.1017/CBO9780511805431

–. (2008). Methods for measuring mechanisms of contention. *Qualitative Sociology, 31*(4): 307–31.

McGuire, M., & Agranoff, R. (2011). The limitations of public management networks. *Public Administration, 89*(2), 265–84. http://dx.doi.org/10.1111/j.1467-9299.2011.01917.x

Meier, K.J., & O'Toole, L.J. (2005). Managerial networking: Issues of management and research design. *Administration and Society, 37*(5), 523–41. http://dx.doi.org/10.1177/0095399705277142

Mendell, M., & Neamtan, N. (2010). The social economy in Quebec: Towards a new political economy. In L. Mook, J. Quarter, & S. Ryan (Eds.), *Researching the Social Economy* (pp. 63–83). Toronto: University of Toronto Press.

Mill, J.S. ([1859] 1956). *On liberty*. Ed. C.V. Shields. Indianapolis: Bobbs-Merril.

Mintrom, M. (1997). Policy entrepreneurs and the diffusion of innovation. *American Journal of Political Science, 41*(3), 738–70. http://dx.doi.org/10.2307/2111674

Mintrom, M., & Vergari, S. (1998). Policy networks and innovation diffusion: The case of state education reforms. *Journal of Politics, 60*(1), 126–48. http://dx.doi.org/10.2307/2648004

Montreal Gazette. (2014). Anti-homelessness group urges Ottawa to turn over funds. *Montreal Gazette,* July 23. http://montrealgazette.com/news/local-news/anti-homelessness-group-urges-ottawa-to-turn-over-funds

Mutz, D.C. (2002). Cross-cutting social networks: Testing democratic theory in practice. *American Political Science Review, 96*(01), 111–26. http://dx.doi.org/10.1017/S0003055402004264

Noël, A. (2002). *Law against poverty: Quebec's new approach to combatting poverty and social exclusion.* Ottawa: Canadian Policy Research Networks.

Núñez, R. (2013). Rapidly rehousing homeless families: New York City, a case study. Institute for Children, Poverty and Homelessness. http://www.icphusa.org/filelibrary/ICPH_brief_RapidlyRehousingHomelessFamilies.pdf

Ontario Ministry of Health and Long-Term Care. (2008). Local Health Integration Network effectiveness review. In *Final Report,* September 30. Toronto: Ministry of Health and Long-Term Care.

Ontario Non-Profit Housing Association. (2007). Timeline: History of social housing in Ontario. http://www.onpha.on.ca

O'Reilly Fleming, T. (1993). *Down and out in Canada: Homeless Canadians.* Toronto: Canadian Scholars' Press.

Papadopoulos, Y. (2007). Problems of democratic accountability in network and multilevel governance. *European Law Journal, 13*(4), 469–86. http://dx.doi.org/10.1111/j.1468-0386.2007.00379.x

Paquet, G. (1999). *Governance through social learning.* Ottawa: University of Ottawa Press.

Paradis, E.K. (2009). A little room of hope: Feminist participatory action research with "homeless" women. PhD diss., University of Toronto.

Parliament of Canada (2013). Question Period from the financial statement of the minister of finance. https://openparliament.ca/bills/41-1/C-400/?tab=mentions&singlepage=1

Passifume, B. (2015). Calgary homeless population remains tops in Alberta, says new count. *Calgary Sun,* February 8. http://www.calgarysun.com/2015/02/08/calgary-homeless-population-remains-tops-in-alberta-says-new-count

Peters, B.G. (2007). Virtuous and vicious circles in democratic network governance. In E. Sørensen & J. Torfing (Eds.), *Theories of democratic network governance* (pp. 61–76). London: Palgrave Macmillan.

Peters, B.G., & Pierre, J. (1998). Governance without government? Rethinking public administration. *Journal of Public Administration: Research and Theory, 8*(2), 223–43. http://dx.doi.org/10.1093/oxfordjournals.jpart.a024379

Peters, E.J. (2011). Emerging themes in academic research in urban Aboriginal identities in Canada, 1996–2010. *Aboriginal Policy Studies, 1*(1), 78–105.

Peters, E. & Andersen, C. (Eds.). (2013). *Indigenous in the city: Contemporary identities and cultural innovation.* Vancouver: UBC Press.

Phillips, S., & Levasseur, K. (2004). The snakes and ladders of accountability: Contradictions between contracting and collaboration for Canada's voluntary sector. *Canadian Public Administration, 47*(4), 451–74. http://dx.doi. org/10.1111/j.1754-7121.2004.tb01188.x

Pierre, J. (Ed.). (1998). *Partnerships in urban governance: European and American experience.* London: Macmillan Press. http://dx.doi.org/10.1007/978-1-349-14408-2

Pierre, J., & Peters, B.G. (2005). *Governing complex societies.* Houndmills: Palgrave Macmillan. http://dx.doi.org/10.1057/9780230512641

Pierson, P. (2004). *Politics in time: History, institutions, and social analysis.* Princeton, NJ: Princeton University Press.

Pratt, J. (2001). Evaluation of the 2000–2001 year. Prepared by James Pratt for the Lower Mainland Cold-Wet Weather Strategy, October 23. Retrieved from administrative secretariat.

Presthus, R. (1975). *Public administration.* New York: Ronald Press.

Pross, P. (1975). Pressure groups: Adaptive instruments of political communication. In P. Pross (Ed.), *Pressure group behaviour in canadian politics* (pp. 1–26). Scarborough: McGraw-Hill Ryerson.

Provan, K., & Kenis, P. (2008). Modes of network governance: Structure, management, and effectiveness. *Journal of Public Administration: Research and Theory, 18*(2), 229–52. http://dx.doi.org/10.1093/jopart/mum015

Provan, K., & Milward, H. (1995). A preliminary theory of interorganizational network effectiveness: A comparative study of four community mental health systems. *Administrative Science Quarterly, 40*(1), 1–33. http://dx.doi.org/10.2307/2393698

Rethemeyer, K., & Hatmaker, D. (2008). Network management reconsidered: An inquiry into management of network structures in public sector service. *Journal of Public Administration: Research and Theory, 18*(4), 617–46. http://dx.doi.org/10.1093/jopart/mum027

Rhodes, R.A.W., & Marsh, D. (1992). New directions in the study of policy networks. *European Journal of Political Research, 21*(1–2), 181–205.

Rice, D. (2014). Governing through networks: A systemic approach. In R. Keast, M. Mandell, & R. Agranoff (Eds.), *Network theory in the public sector: Building new theoretical frameworks* (pp. 103–17). Abingdon, UK: Routledge.

Rosato, S. (2003). The flawed logic of democratic peace theory. *American Political Science Review, 97*(04), 585–602. http://dx.doi.org/10.1017/S0003055403000893

Ryan, K., & Kelley, T. (2012). *Almost home: Helping kids move from homelessness to hope.* Hoboken, NJ: John Wiley and Sons.

Sabatier, P.A. (1987). Knowledge, policy-oriented learning, and policy change an advocacy coalition framework. *Science Communication, 8*(4), 649–92. http://dx.doi.org/10.1177/0164025987008004005

Sabatier, P., & Jenkins-Smith, H. (Eds.). (1993). *Policy change and learning: An advocacy coalition approach.* Boulder, CO: Westview Press.

Safe Communities and Opportunities Resource Centre. (2014). Introduction to SORCe. Presentation by Calgary Homeless Foundation Summit, March.

Salamon, L.M. (Ed.). (2002). *The tools of government: A guide to the new governance.* New York: Oxford University Press.

Sandström, A., & Carlsson, L. (2008). The performance of policy networks: The relation between network structure and network performance. *Policy Studies Journal, 36*(4), 497–524. http://dx.doi.org/10.1111/j.1541-0072.2008.00281.x

Savoie, D.J. (1999). *Governing from the centre: The concentration of power in Canadian politics.* Toronto: University of Toronto Press.

–. (2008). *Court government and the collapse of accountability in Canada and the United Kingdom.* Cambridge: Cambridge University Press.

Scharpf, F. (1997). *Games real actors play: Actor-centered institutionalism in policy research.* Boulder, CO: Westview Press.

–. (1999). *Governing in Europe: Effective and democratic?* Oxford: Oxford University Press. http://dx.doi.org/10.1093/acprof:oso/9780198295457.001.0001

Schiff, J.W., & Schiff, R.A. (2014). Housing first: Paradigm or program? *Journal of Social Distress and the Homeless, 23*(2), 80–104.

Scott, S. (2012). *The beginning of the end: The story of the Calgary Homeless Foundation and one community's drive to end homelessness.* Calgary: Calgary Homeless Foundation.

Shapcott, M. (2001). Made in Ontario crisis. Technical Paper No. 12 for the Ontario Alternative Budget 2001, Canadian Centre for Policy Alternatives, May.

–. (2005). Social (subsidized) housing cures homelessness. Centre for Urban and Community Studies, Toronto.

–. (2007a). Ten things you should know about housing and homelessness. Policy primer, Toronto, Wellesley Institute. http://www.homelesshub.ca/sites/default/files/3jmkt15f.pdf

–. (2007b). *Framework for the blueprint to end homelessness in Toronto.* Toronto: Wellesley Institute.

–. (2014). Federal budget 2014 fails to deliver housing investments to meet national needs. Wellesley Institute, February 12. http://www.wellesleyinstitute.com/housing/federal-budget-2014-fails-to-deliver-housing-investments-to-meet-national-needs/

Skelcher, C., & Sullivan, H. (2008). Theory-driven approaches to analysing collaborative performance. *Public Management Review, 10*(6), 751–71. http://dx.doi.org/10.1080/14719030802423103

Skocpol, T. (1979). *States and social revolutions: A comparative analysis of France, Russia, and China.* Cambridge: Cambridge University Press. http://dx.doi.org/10.1017/CBO9780511815805

Skogstad, G. (2003). Who governs? Who should govern?: Political authority and legitimacy in Canada in the twenty-first century. *Canadian Journal of Political Science, 36*(5), 955–74. http://dx.doi.org/10.1017/S0008423903778925

Smith, R. (2004). *Policy development and implementation in complex Files: Lessons from the National Homelessness Initiative.* Ottawa: Canada School of Public Service, Government of Canada.

Social Services and Housing Administration. (2012). Hostel services: Homeless shelter locations. Data extracted from Open Data Toronto, www1.toronto.ca/

Sørensen, E., & Torfing, J. (2003). Network politics, political capital and democracy. *International Journal of Public Administration, 26*(6), 609–34. http://dx.doi.org/10.1081/PAD-120019238

–. (2007a). Governance network research: Towards a second generation. In E. Sørensen & J. Torfing (Eds.), *Theories of democratic network governance* (pp. 1–20). London: Palgrave Macmillan. http://dx.doi.org/10.1016/B978-012374262-9.50003-3

–. (2007b). *Theories of democratic network governance.* London: Palgrave Macmillan.

–. (2007c). Theoretical approaches to governance network failure." In E. Sørensen & J. Torfing (Eds.), *Theories of democratic network governance* (pp. 95–110). London: Palgrave Macmillan. http://dx.doi.org/10.1016/B978-012374262-9.50003-3

Sproule-Jones, M. (2000). Horizontal management: Implementing programs across interdependent organizations. *Canadian Public Administration, 43*(1), 93–109. http://dx.doi.org/10.1111/j.1754-7121.2000.tb01562.x

Spurr, B. (2013). City blocks view into homelessness centre. *NOW Magazine.* February 8. https://nowtoronto.com/news/city-blocks-view-into-homelessness-centre/

Stanhope, V., & Dunn, K. (2011). The curious case of housing first: The limits of evidence based policy. *International Journal of Law and Psychiatry, 34*(4), 275–82.

Strumpf, K. (2002). Does government decentralization increase policy innovation? *Journal of Public Economic Theory, 4*(2), 207–41. http://dx.doi.org/10.1111/1467-9779.00096

Thatcher, M. (1998). The development of policy network analyses: From modest origins to overarching frameworks. *Journal of Theoretical Politics, 10*(4), 389–416. http://dx.doi.org/10.1177/0951692898010004002

Thompson, G., Frances, J., Levačić, R., & Mitchell, J. (Eds.). (1991). *Markets, hierarchies, and networks: The coordination of social life.* London: Sage.

Tilly, C. (2003). Social boundary mechanisms. *Philosophy of the Social Sciences, 43*(2), 211–37.

Torfing, J. (2012). *Interactive governance: Advancing the paradigm.* New York: Oxford University Press. http://dx.doi.org/10.1093/acprof:oso/9780199596751.001.0001

Toronto Central LHIN. (2012). Toronto Central LHIN: Key facts. http://www.torontocentrallhin.on.ca/

Toronto Disaster Relief Committee. (1998). State of emergency declaration: An urgent call for emergency humanitarian relief and prevention measures. http://tdrc.net/resources/public/Report-98-TDRC.htm.

Toronto Star. (2013). "Rob Ford and the disappearing homelessness task force." *Toronto Star,* October 20.

Triadafilopoulos, T. (1999). Politics, speech, and the art of persuasion: Toward an Aristotelian conception of the public sphere. *Journal of Politics, 61*(3), 741–57. http://dx.doi.org/10.2307/2647826

Turrini, A., Cristofoli, D., Frosini, F., & Nasi, G. (2010). Networking literature about determinants of network effectiveness. *Public Administration, 88*(2), 528–50. http://dx.doi.org/10.1111/j.1467-9299.2009.01791.x

Valverde, M. (2012). *Everyday law on the street: City governance in an age of diversity.* Chicago: University of Chicago Press. http://dx.doi.org/10.7208/chicago/9780226921914.001.0001

Van Waarden, F. (1992). Dimensions and types of policy networks. *European Journal of Political Research, 21*(1–2), 29–52. http://dx.doi.org/10.1111/j.1475-6765.1992. tb00287.x

Vancouver Sun. (2008). Homelessness, poverty top issues in Vancouver. *Vancouver Sun,* September 12. http://www.canada.com/story.html?id=a216ddd5-f8ed-4315 -9eee-e3518294ee65.

–. (2014). Affordable housing the biggest issue facing Vancouver: poll. *Vancouver Sun,* March 5. http://www.vancouversun.com/business/Affordable+housing+ biggest+issue+facing+Vancouver+poll/9589143/story.html.

Vangen, S., & Huxham, C. (2010). Introducing the theory of collaborative advantage. In S. Osborne (Ed.), *The new public governance? Emerging perspectives on the theory and practice of public governance* (pp. 163–84). London: Routledge.

Voets, J. (2014). Developing network management theory through management channels and roles. In R. Keast, M. Mandell, & R. Angranoff (Eds.), *Network theory in the public sector: Building new theoretical frameworks* (pp 119–134). Abingdon, UK: Routledge.

Ward, J. (2008) Dealing effectively with Aboriginal homelessness in Toronto. Report for the Toronto Aboriginal Social Services Association, April.

Watson, H.G. (2015). Toronto budget approves shelter beds for LGBT youth. *Daily Xtra,* March 16. http://www.dailyxtra.com/toronto/news-and-ideas/news/ toronto-budget-approves-shelter-beds-lgbt-homeless-youth-100622

Wedel, J., Shore, C., Feldman, G., & Lathrop, S. (2005). Towards an anthropology of public policy. *Annals of the American Academy of Political and Social Science, 600*(1), 30–51. http://dx.doi.org/10.1177/0002716205276734

Weiss, L. (1998). *The myth of the powerless state: Governing the economy in a global era.* Cambridge: Polity Press.

Wildavsky, A. (1974). *The politics of the budgetary process.* (2nd ed.). Boston, MA: Little, Brown.

Young, I.M. (2000). *Inclusion and democracy.* New York: Oxford University Press.

Young, R., & Leuprecht, C. (2006). *Municipal-federal-provincial relations in Canada.* Montreal and Kingston: McGill-Queens University Press.

Index